DUMBARTON OAKS
MEDIEVAL LIBRARY

Daniel Donoghue, General Editor

THE OLD ENGLISH CHRONICLE

VOLUME I

DOML 91

The Old English Chronicle

VOLUME I

THE A-TEXT TO 1001

Edited and Translated by

JANET BATELY
with SUSAN IRVINE and
KATHERINE O'BRIEN O'KEEFFE

RELATED POEMS

Edited and Translated by

KATHERINE O'BRIEN O'KEEFFE
and JOSEPH C. HARRIS

DUMBARTON OAKS
MEDIEVAL LIBRARY

HARVARD UNIVERSITY PRESS
CAMBRIDGE, MASSACHUSETTS
LONDON, ENGLAND
2025

Printed in the United States of America

First Printing

EU GPSR Authorised Representative
LOGOS EUROPE, 9 rue Nicolas Poussin, 17000, La Rochelle, France
E-mail: Contact@logoseurope.eu

Library of Congress Cataloging-in-Publication Data available from the Library of Congress at https://lccn.loc.gov/2025012416

ISBN 978-0-674-29087-7 (cloth : alk. paper)

Contents

Introduction

The Old English Chronicles

When in the year 731 the Northumbrian scholar, Venerable Bede, composed an account of the English Church of his time, the language he chose was Latin and the genre *historia* (history), a form characterized by narrative sweep.[1] An alternative form, *chronica* (chronicle), is a genre on a much smaller scale, organized as a sequence of entries each devoted to a specific year.[2] At the conclusion of his *Ecclesiastical History,* Bede shifted to the conventions of chronicle for his *Recapitulatio* (Recapitulation), a kind of index at the end of the main text, in which each brief entry begins with the annal year: for example, "Anno DCCV Aldfrid rex Nordanhymbrorum defunctus est" (In the year 705, Aldfrith, king of the Northumbrians, died).[3] *Anno* is abbreviated AN in Latin and Old English texts, and the annals in the Old English Chronicle, manuscript A, open with that sign.

By contrast with Bede's *Ecclesiastical History,* the "Old English Chronicles" survive as a group of seven texts of annals structured in chronicle format, similar to the *Ecclesiastical History*'s *Recapitulatio,* beginning with an annal number followed by information for that year. The importance of these seven groups of texts, composed in Old English and collectively known under the name "The Anglo-Saxon

Chronicle, Manuscripts A–G," is strikingly disproportionate to their small size. Indeed, in spite of the constraints of the genre to which these texts belong, they have rightly been described as providing a historical backbone for the period between the arrival of the first Germanic invaders in Britain in the fifth century and events in the early decades of the twelfth century. The Chronicle texts also provide precious information about the development of their language, Old English, into Middle English some decades after the Norman Conquest.[4] At the same time, the wealth of references to towns and cities that they contain makes them a first point of reference for English place-name studies.[5]

The title "Anglo-Saxon Chronicle" has its own distinct history. It was first used by J. A. Giles in 1847 for his rendering into English of what had previously been called the *Chronicon Saxonicum,* or *The Saxon Chronicle,* in preparation for which he drew heavily on a groundbreaking translation by Anna Gurney (1819) published under that name.[6] However, the concept of the several manuscript versions constituting a single chronicle, whether "Saxon" or "Anglo-Saxon," was already being challenged. It was indeed a "collection of Chronicles, rather than one uniform work, as the received appellation seems to imply," wrote James Ingram of the former in 1823.[7] While following John Earle in editing "two of the Saxon chronicles parallel," Charles Plummer, in 1899, went further to argue that although it is "commonly stated that *the Anglo-Saxon Chronicle* is contained in seven MSS., . . . it would be truer to say that these MSS. contain four Anglo-Saxon Chronicles."[8] Indeed, of the seven texts, all but one fall into pairs that are very closely connected textually and frequently agree with each other against the rest, pairings that endure for the rest of their lifetime. However, again to quote Plummer, all seven "grow out of a common stock."[9] Right up to the end of an entry variously headed AN 892 or 893, all the versions have lying behind them the same basic collection of annals and an almost identical layout. After that, section by section, and at different periods, individual copies branching out have gone their own way, providing an excellent illustration of the flexible nature of annals as a genre, its strengths as well as its weaknesses. Although attempts have been made to reconstruct, where possible, the original texts behind the various components and give them appropriate names—one of the ambitions of David N. Dumville and Simon Keynes's *Collaborative Edition*—Ingram was right: there never has been a single text, now lost, at the end of the line to carry an exclusive title, whether it be that of a "Saxon" or an "Anglo-Saxon" Chronicle. The text in this edition, covering the years up to 1001 and hitherto called "The Anglo-Saxon Chronicle, Manuscript A," is accordingly given the new name that recognizes its language: "The Old English Chronicle, the A-Text to 1001."

The A-Text: Cambridge, Corpus Christi College MS 173, Fols. 1–56

The Manuscript

Cambridge, Corpus Christi College MS 173 is a composite manuscript, made up of five items of varying dates and subject matter, of which three are wholly or mainly in Old English.[10] Of its history prior to the Reformation practically nothing is known, except that by the late eleventh century it was at Christ Church, Canterbury, where it continued to be used and added to. However, in the mid-sixteenth century it was acquired from Nicholas Wotton (d. 1567), the first dean of Canterbury after the Dissolution of the Monasteries, by the then-archbishop of Canterbury, Matthew Parker. It was Parker (d. 1575), a renowned bibliophile, who bequeathed the manuscript to Corpus Christi College, Cambridge, and after whom it is often named.[11] Parker's chaplain and Latin secretary, John Joscelyn (d. 1603), both annotated it and transcribed parts into the manuscripts of B and D.[12]

In CCCC 173, the copy of the annals is preceded by a brief Old English text, the Genealogical and Regnal List, often referred to as the Genealogical Preface to the A-text, comprising a mixture of family trees and regnal lists that link Cerdic (d. 534), one of the first Germanic invaders supposedly landing in Britain in the middle of the fifth century, to the ninth-century West Saxon king Æthelwulf (d. 858).[13] The text ends with a reference to the subsequent accessions of three of the latter's sons, the last of whom, Alfred (d. 899), is the king during whose reign the idea of compiling a record of the history of the West Saxons up to the year 892 would seem first to have taken shape. It is now generally accepted that there is no evidence, linguistic or otherwise, to suggest that the king himself had a hand in any part of the production of the sets of annals making up the extended Common Stock. The third Old English text in CCCC 173, written in a mid-tenth century hand, is a collection of the laws of Alfred and his ancestor, Ine, with a preface in the voice of King Alfred himself.[14]

The A-Text: Annals 1 to 1001 CE

Although for most of its modern editorial history grouped with six other texts under the title "The Anglo-Saxon Chronicle," the A-text is in a number of ways unique. Sharing only some of its contents with any of the others (apart from its direct copy, London, British Library, Cotton MS Otho B. xi, the G-text),[15] it is itself composed of a series of entries made at different times by different people over a period of roughly one hundred years. While none of the other texts is preserved in a copy older than the second half of the tenth century, the part of CCCC 173 that contains the A-text, in contrast, is written in a series of hands ranging from the late ninth or early tenth century to the early eleventh century.[16] Covering just over a thousand years of history, its annals fall into groups according to the period during which they were entered in the manuscript. Following an initial entry referring to an event in 60 BCE, the main entries in the opening section, dated AN 1 to AN 892, were made by a scribe working either in the last decade of the ninth century or the beginning of the tenth.[17] This is the part of the text shared with manuscripts A through G that Plummer labeled the Common Stock.

The Common Stock: BCE 60 to AN *892*

There is considerable dispute over which of the annals—890, 891, or 892—constitutes the final entry for the Common Stock. This edition takes the annal for 892 as the final entry of the Common Stock on the grounds that it is the last of the annals shared by all Old English versions, the A-text through the E-text.[18] How the Common Stock came to take the form it did, and where and when its compilers obtained their material, has long been a matter for conjecture. It has been suggested, for instance, that the framework ultimately adopted by the seven Chronicle texts was based on that of a set of Easter tables—an arrangement by which each year (rendered with or without a prefixed AN) begins a new line.[19] However, although it is possible that an annotated page of the numerical calculations used to determine future dates of that movable feast might on occasion have provided an item of historical interest to one of the compilers, what internal evidence there is points to more than one source capable of contributing to the Common Stock's framework and its contents. For example, the opening entries, up to and including AN 449 and the announcement of the arrival of the first Germanic invaders of Britain, contain material drawn from a range of Latin texts, including the Vulgate New Testament, chronicles, and histories (Bede's *Ecclesiastical History* among them). The individual items making up the framework of the Common Stock were all easily available from chronicles, together with the *Recapitulatio* (hereafter *Recap.*), or list of datable events, that ends the *Ecclesiastical History.* It is owing to Bede's *Recap.* that the annals proper are preceded by an unheaded prefatory paragraph based on its entry for 60 BCE, while the adoption, by both Common Stock and its continuations, of the abbreviation AN followed by year number in the left-hand margin is again a feature of Bede's list, as is the use of *and* to join two or more otherwise unconnected statements in the same annal. However, at what stage this framework was adopted, with every year given an entry whether or not it had an annal attached, there is no way of determining.

The materials found in the entries from AN 449 to AN 892 vary considerably.[20] How, when, and in what form the great majority of the material they contain reached the Common Stock can only be guessed at. That said, a handful of translations of the final entries in Bede's *Recap.,* ending with AN 731, show the chroniclers working with the *Ecclesiastical History.* The insertion of a number of genealogies suggests that the chroniclers were also working with genealogical lists.[21] In this section, moreover, there are tantalizing hints as to what might have been added from untapped early southern Old English sources. The announcement of the arrival of the mythological characters Hengest and Horsa in AN 449, for instance, is followed by a virtually unbroken and uniform block of entries, from AN 455 to AN 593, consisting almost entirely of a series of brief reports of attacks on the local Britons by Cerdic and his successors. That these reports are not new creations by the compiler of the section but an extraction from now-lost older sources is suggested by the use, in some of the annals, of language that belongs to a very different literary genre from that of its surroundings. The defeated, we are told, flee the English "as though from fire" (AN 473), Ceawlin returns "enraged . . . to his own people" (AN 584), while the noun *wælfill* (slaughter, AN 592), is constructed in a manner typical in Old English verse for describing heavy loss of life in battle.

Similarly set apart from its proper surroundings is the lengthy account in AN 755 (of events in 757) of a successful attack on a king (Cynewulf) by a rival (Cyneheard). This entry, known as "Cynewulf and Cyneheard," has often been anthologized for its thematization of the warrior ethos and its compact narrative presentation. Having deposed King Sigeberht for misdeeds, Cynewulf reigns for thirty-one years, until Cyneheard, a pretender to the throne as Sigeberht's brother, catches him unawares visiting a woman at a royal estate. Although the king defends himself valiantly, he is ultimately killed. When his small troop of men arrives too late to save him, they refuse Cyneheard's offer of "money and life" and choose to die fighting rather than survive their lord. Swiftly thereafter, a larger force of Cynewulf's men traps Cyneheard's men inside the gates of the fortification where the king lies dead. Cynewulf's men offer safe passage to some of their own kinsmen who are inside before taking vengeance, but this offer, too, is refused, and Cyneheard and his men are all killed with the exception of a single survivor. The use of narrative in AN 755 is exceptional, if not unique, as is the removal of the account from its proper location at AN 784, where the text simply notes the death of King Cynewulf and that of eighty-four men with him. Distinct as well from other Chronicle entries is the narrative style of "Cynewulf and Cyneheard," characterized by careful balance in the elements of the plot, rhetorical patterning, subordination, and direct as well as indirect speech. The entry's theme of loyalty until death suggests that it might have been a retelling of an old tale.

The Final Annals of King Alfred's Reign: AN 893 to AN 896

The material in this section, by contrast, allows a great deal more latitude to the annalist. Already by AN 787 a forward-looking reference is heralding a new development to come, the arrival in England of waves of hostile Danes. This narrative signaling presages a general change in the approach to the annal structure as it was employed from AN 455, both a narrowing and a deepening of the focus, and an increasing of the length of almost every annal from AN 832 to AN 892. Annals now use a range of subordinate clauses, of adjectives, and of abstract nouns, look back or forward, and comment freely. The only constraint still imposed by the annal structure is the need to observe the annal boundaries.

At this stage in the development of the Old English Chronicles, the Peterborough Chronicle (E) has now split away from the rest. In the other manuscripts, the entries for 893 to 896 constitute what is known as "The First Continuation." At this point a new author has taken over to produce an impressive group of four substantial annals dealing with the last wars of Alfred's reign. They record the king's handling of the grave threat posed by *se micla here* (the great army) coming from the Continent in 892 (actually two separate groups moving west from Boulogne after a famine to resettle in England). These annals adapt what was originally a single narrative with a carefully constructed and integrated account of the final defeat of Alfred's Danish enemies. The annals in this group no longer open with *Her* (Here), but with temporal phrases connecting the events across the separate annals: 893, *On þys geare* (In this year); 894, *Ond þa sona æfter* (And then immediately after that); 895, *On þy ilcan gere* (In the same year); 896, *Đa þæs on sumera on ðysum gere* (Then in the summer of this year). The annals from 893 to the beginning of 896 also exhibit a comparatively wide range of syntactical constructions, including greater use of subordination and a high number of main clauses, rhetorical patterning with doublets and triplets, and the use of adjectives and abstract nouns. Also characteristic of these annals is marked use of attributed motives and explanations for particular actions.[22] As Cecily Clark observes, "Whereas the earliest annals recorded facts, excluding condition, concession, comparison and causality, these late Alfredian annals go some way towards interpreting the facts they record."[23]

Annals from 897 to 1001

After a brief entry (AN 897) cobbled together from two differently phrased clauses, both introduced by *Her,* the text proper of this section begins. Using the annal framework of its predecessors, this part of the text falls into four distinct sections, entered in the manuscript during the early, middle, and second half of the tenth century and the early eleventh century, respectively. Only the first of these is of any appreciable size. Covering the events after the death of King Alfred (d. 899), the entries for 897 to 914 constitute "The Second Continuation," whose subject matter includes a rebellion against King Edward the Elder by his cousin, the ætheling Æthelwold, and Edward's early campaigns against the Danes, including information on the strategy of defensive works employed by the king. Up to the end of annal 914, the A-text continues to share material with B, C, and D. A third "Continuation" (entries for 915 to 920) covers the rest of Edward's reign, including his campaigns against the Danes. However, where B and C use a text known as the Mercian Register for this period, A stands alone. The generally brief entries of the Mercian Register (annals for 902 to 924) cover the achievements of Æthelflæd, Lady of the Mercians, in protecting Mercia through the building of defensive works and through successful military actions.[24] In subsequent sections of the A-text after 920, the annals are mainly short, reverting to a basic annalistic style and once again sometimes sharing material with one or more of texts

B, C, and D. Exceptional here are annals 937, 942, 973, and 975, which are in alliterative verse, and the lengthy final (prose) annal 1001.

The inclusion of verse entries in several of the Chronicle texts is a surprising addition within the annals genre.[25] But the dismay of the historian is the delight of the student of Old English literature. Of the four poems preserved in A, *The Battle of Brunanburh* is the longest, a praise poem celebrating the victory of King Æthelstan and his half brother Edmund in a battle at Brunanburh, a location otherwise unknown. The king and the ætheling routed the forces of Olaf, viking king of Dublin, and of Constantine, king of the Scots, as well as the forces of the Strathclyde Welsh. The poem takes pleasure in the humiliating flight of the defeated forces, imagining the prospects of the beasts of battle—the raven, the eagle, and the wolf—left behind to enjoy the slaughter.[26] The other three poems are generally regarded as lesser efforts. Those commemorating the coronation of Edgar and his death show a striking interest in calendrical circumlocution.[27]

The dozen scrappy entries from 1002 to 1066 are primarily in a twelfth-century hand. It is thus annal 1001 that brings to an end recordkeeping in the manuscript until after the Norman Conquest, when the A-text was taken over for the purpose of annotation in Latin by Canterbury scribes, thus bringing to a close its series of annals in Old English put together before the Conquest.[28]

The Translation

The A-text has been translated into English previously by Norman Garmonsway (1953) and Michael Swanton (1996).[29]

This translation has benefited throughout from the scholarship of translators, historians, and commentators on the Old English Chronicles and acknowledges its many debts in the notes. Because of the range of styles adopted at widely different times by various contributors to the A-text, each of its segments presents its own challenge to the modern translator. Much depends on the extent to which its annals have moved away from the basic pattern of a sequence of short statements, unadorned with adjectives or adverbs, and joined by "and." However, overall, there is the vexed question of the extent to which it is desirable, or indeed proper, to make changes to the syntax and sentence structure of an annal in order to produce a rendering in smooth, idiomatic Modern English. The following translation adheres closely to the Old English text, making only relatively minor changes to syntax when the structure of Modern English requires it—for example, in cases of extended syndetic parataxis. The lexicon of the Old English Chronicles presents different problems. These can arise with names of peoples, ethnic groups, or shifting political entities; with positions or titles (especially when there is interference between Old English and Old Norse words); or, notoriously, with words for fighting forces and fortifications.

Names of Peoples, Ethnic Groups, or Political Entities

There are several groups of peoples that the A-text names repeatedly, but the names that are used for them are often confusing in their Modern English reflexes, particularly Old English terms for Celtic peoples. The Chronicle refers repeatedly to the native inhabitants of Britain (Romano-Britons) before the migrations of Germanic peoples in the fifth and sixth centuries as *Brettas* (Britons). These are people that Venerable Bede refers to as *Brettones* in his *Ecclesiastical History.*[30] Complications set in when the Old English Chronicles also refer to the same Romano-British people as *Walas* or *Wealas* (as, for example, in AN 465, 477), a word with a complex history.[31] In the annals where the context is Romano-Britain and the early Germanic invasions, the word is translated here as "Britons." But *Walas/Wealas* can also refer to peoples living within the borders of what are now Wales and Cornwall. And *Walas* can be a base word for names of other Celtic peoples, for example, *Galwalas* (AN 650, Gauls) or *Norþwalas* (AN 828, here "Welsh"), or *Bretwalas* (AN 682, "Britons"). When the reference is ambiguous or uncertain, a note to the text provides background. Another vexed term is *Scottas,* whose Modern English reflex is "Scots." However, as in Bede's *Ecclesiastical History,* where the Latin word *Scotti* refers to the Irish peoples, or Ireland, or Scotland, OE *Scottas* can refer to the Irish (AN 891) or the Gaelic inhabitants of Scotland (AN 937, line 32a, *Sceotta*). This edition translates the word according to context.

Another Old English usage that presents difficulties for reader and translator is the use of the names of peoples to refer to territory. For example, in AN 896: *drehton þa hergas on Eastenglum ond on Norðhymbrum Westseaxna lond* (the armies in East Anglia and Northumbria greatly harassed the land of the West Saxons). The dative plurals in *Eastenglum* and *Norðhymbrum* refer literally to East Anglians and Northumbrians, but the referent is the territories, East Anglia and Northumbria. By contrast, in the same clause the object of the viking incursion is spelled out as the "*land* of the West Saxons." The translation silently clarifies the referents throughout. To assist the reader's identification of place-names, the translation gives the Modern English names of all places where the referent is known (for example, *Ligeraceaster* is translated "Leicester"). However, there are many instances where there is no Modern English reflex of a place-name or its location is not known. In these cases, the Old English place-name is given in italics in the translation (for example, *Peonnum*).

Old English titles can pose difficulties for translators either because they may have a familiar register from Old English heroic poetry not applicable in prose, or because they show interference from Old Norse loanwords, or because their previously traditional Modern English translations no longer work smoothly. *Æþeling* and *þegn* are words that may feel familiar from Old English heroic poetry: for example, in *Beowulf, æþeling* can mean "noble," or "prince," or simply "man," and the meaning of *þegn* in *Beowulf* ranges from "attendant" to "warrior." However, these words have particular meanings in the social world represented in the Chronicle. In the ninth century and later, *æþeling* is used to refer to the son or brother of a king.[32] Although *þegn* is etymologically related to *þenian* (to serve), *þegn* refers to a man of the elite. He would be landed, likely holding considerable property, be locally influential, required to perform military service, and serve as a local judge. His wergeld (the set price for compensation) was a multiple of that for a *ceorl* (a common man). The thegns played a critical role in the king's ability to conduct warfare.[33] *Horsþegn* (in AN 896) for a thegn who supplied the king with horses, a highly responsible position, is an example of a word whose traditional translation, "marshal," does not readily assist the modern reader. To avoid interference from the well-known referents in heroic poetry, the translation keeps such words in Old English, adapting for spelling.[34] The title *ealdormann* similarly creates problems because of its various references. Early on, *ealdormann* was the Old English term used to translate Latin titles for high-ranking men, such as *princeps* or *dux*. In the ninth century, it was used for members of the nobility, and in the case of Æthelred, Lord of the Mercians, his title *ealdormann* indicated that his status and power were subordinate only to those of King Alfred. By the tenth century, *ealdormann* indicated that the holder of the title was a local ruler and representative of a king of the English, as, for example, Byrhtnoth, leading the men of Essex at the Battle of Maldon.

Two titles borrowed from Norse have meanings that are best conserved by keeping them as their Old English reflex. In AN 904, the ætheling Æthelwold recruits support from the "Danes" in the north. In recounting Edward the Elder's victory, the entry records the deaths of a *Hold* Ysopa and a *Hold* Oscytel. *Hold* is a Norse title applied to nobles in the Danelaw whose wergeld was double that of a thegn.[35] Similarly, the title *jarl* (which would eventually coalesce with OE *eorl*) is a Scandinavian term for nobleman. In the early Chronicle, the Danish title *jarl* is often rendered by OE *eorl* (nobleman). In the later Chronicle entries dealing with the second viking wars and following, *jarl* was a title for an under-king or governor under Cnut's rule, there essentially synonymous with *ealdormann*.[36] These words have been defined in the Notes to the Translations at the first instance of their use.

Terms for Warfare, Fighting Forces, Fortifications

Several terms for warfare in the Old English Chronicles present difficulties for translators. After the Norman Conquest, English was replaced by French as the language of the new rulers. Although the term "fight" (OE *gefeoht*) has survived, it has had to compete with loanwords from that source, such as "battle" (Old French *bataille*), "war" (Norman French *were*), and "combat" (Old French *combatre*), while the descendants of *winnan* and *gewinn,* which in Old English also meant "fight" or "struggle," have survived only as words denoting victory. Other words in this category, such as *sige* (victory) and the compound *sigeleas* (victory-less), have vanished from English.

The noun *here,* an Old English word found widely in the annals of the 800s and early 900s, has also vanished from the language and lacks any single close equivalent in Modern English. In the surviving corpus of Old English, this word is found in contexts for which the *Dictionary of Old English* (DOE) suggests Modern English "army, body of armed men, armed forces (in various contexts including any or all of infantry, cavalry or naval forces)."[37] In Chronicle texts, *here* most frequently refers specifically to the various groups of invaders from Denmark mentioned in the entries from the 830s up to the end of the reign of Edward the Elder. A difficulty in translating is that *here* is often used irrespective of the size of the force referred to, although on occasion the chronicler will refer to *se micla here* (the great army) to indicate a significantly large force. It has been estimated that *here* often refers to small bands, in the dozens and hundreds, rather than thousands, while some *hergas* are more like armies of occupation, enemy forces that have taken control of a region and whose hostile acts are often plunder-seeking hit-and-run raids carried out by parties of marauders, and who end up settling down to till appropriated English land.[38] This word is the hostile member of the pair *here* and *fierd,* the latter a body of men on call for duty in the West Saxon militia, in modern terms a levy, and its members, the levies. In this translation, *here* (whatever the actual size of the force in question) is normally translated "army," and *fierd* is translated "levy."[39]

As for places of security and defense, Modern English "forts," "fortresses," "fortifications," "fortified towns," "strongholds," the Chronicle has at first only two terms: *fæsten,* a place made fast to resist attack, and *geweorc,* a word related to the Modern English noun, a "work." These Old English terms are used here mainly for constructions made by vikings and quickly thrown together during the wars of Alfred and Edward, though *geweorc* is also found for the structure that Alfred builds to protect himself on Athelney and for its half-finished equivalent in eastern Kent, occupied only by rustics, that the vikings seize in AN 892. However, there are two further words in this category, both extensions of the words for town and city, *burg* and (though only exceptionally) *ceaster.* The creation of a network of additional defenses for existing towns in the form of strategically located strongholds confusingly also given the name *burg* (often given the distinguishing alternative OE spelling *burh* by historians), and manned by *burgware,* is a subject given prominence in the annals of both Alfred and his son Edward.

Issues of Chronology

For the years 756 to 845, the annal numbers in all surviving texts of the Old English Chronicles are chronologically dislocated and offer dates for events that are two or on occasion three years too early. The correct chronology must have been in an original version of the Chronicle, since the Annals of Saint Neots (a Latin chronicle that uses the Old English Chronicle) does not have the dislocation.[40] By contrast, the versions of the Chronicle used by Asser and Æthelweard in their Latin works both have the dislocations for these years.[41] Corrections to errors in dating are dealt with in the Notes to the Translations and Index of Personal Names.

Two different sources of difficulty for the modern reader of the Chronicle arise from the text's practice of dating according to feast days and from its use of different possible methods of setting the beginning of the year. Broadly speaking, in Bede's *Ecclesiastical History,* the new year (called the year of grace) began on Christmas Day (Feast of the Nativity). We see this calculation in the annal for 763 (properly 765), which gives *midwinter* (meaning Christmas) as the point from which to reckon Jænberht's consecration as archbishop of Canterbury. January 1 (Feast of the Circumcision) and March 25 (Feast of the Annunciation) were other possible beginnings for the year of grace. In the secular dating system, called the indiction year, the beginning of the year could be September 1 or 24. Examples of using the indiction year occur in the annals for 827 and 900 (see notes for these years). These different possible methods of dating at times impact the statement of the year in question. This edition translates all saints' days into modern calendar dates. The dates of Easter (a moveable feast) and those dates dependent on Easter (Rogation Days, Ascension Thursday, Pentecost) are also given as modern calendar dates and indicated in the notes.[42]

Euphemisms

One of the most common references in the Chronicle is to death, and although the words *acwelan, forweorþan, sweltan,* and *asweltan,* all of which have the primary meaning "to die," are found half a dozen times, more frequent are euphemisms, describing dying as movement. So apart from a number of expressions in verse such as “chose another light” (see AN 975, line 2b), the majority use the language of departure. Of these the A-text uses forms based on the verbs *faran* and *feran* (to go), the choice varying from one section to another. So *forþferde* (“went forth,” rendered here “passed away”) is the most common, but with *gefor* (“went,” rendered by “departed this life”), used alongside *forþferde* in annals 855 to 918, the only exceptions to *forþferde* otherwise occurring in annals 571, 731, and the section 855 to 918, where *gefor* occurs sixteen times, beside a single instance of *feorh gesealde* (gave up his life). Other points of interest with respect to the vocabulary of the text and its translation are discussed in the Notes to the Translations.

The Death of Alfred *and* The Death of Edward

Background

The Death of Alfred and *The Death of Edward* are highly political poems cast in the form of obituaries for royal figures. The C-text’s annal for 1036, presenting the mutilation and killing of Ætheling Alfred in a bitter dispute over succession to the English throne, has the whiff of martyrdom about it. And the C-text’s annal for 1065 takes the death of the childless Edward the Confessor as an opportunity to use the tropes of kingship and lordship to promote Harold Godwinson as Edward’s chosen and deserving heir. Thematically connected as obituaries of the last two sons of Æthelred the Unready, these poems also share political backgrounds entangled in the fortunes of Earl Godwine and his family, beginning early in the reign of Cnut. England had already suffered decades of raids since the early 990s when Swein Forkbeard successfully invaded in 1013. In defeat, King Æthelred subsequently joined his wife Emma and their young sons Edward and Alfred in Normandy, but in 1014, after Swein died and his son Cnut returned to Denmark, Æthelred returned to the throne of England. In 1015, however, Cnut invaded again. When Edmund Ironside died in November 1016 (his father, King Æthelred, having died in April of that year), Cnut became king of England. As part of his consolidation of power, Cnut married Emma, the Norman widow of Æthelred, and fathered a son by her, Harthacnut. Cnut had another son by Æthelgifu of Northampton, Harold Harefoot. The sons of Æthelred, Edward, and Alfred, remained in Normandy during the reign of Cnut. When Cnut died in 1035 and the succession was disputed, Emma supported their son Harthacnut (who was in Denmark), and it would appear that Earl Godwine (made earl of Wessex by Cnut in 1022 or 1023) supported him as well. But by 1036 Harold Harefoot was gaining support, and Godwine switched sides. At this point, Emma apparently decided to back a claim by one of her sons by Æthelred, either Edward or Alfred. The *Encomium Emmae reginae,* a work commissioned by Emma, describes an elaborate plot in which Harold Harefoot schemed to kill the æthelings by luring them to England with a letter purportedly from Emma.[43] In any event, Alfred set out to his mother at Winchester, traveling from Normandy to Flanders and then across to England. However, he and his retinue were intercepted by Godwine, who turned them over to Harold's men. The annal for 1036 in the C-text blames Godwine bitterly for the murder of Alfred, and the poem suggests that there were efforts to promote veneration of the murdered ætheling.[44] By contrast, the D-text of the poem carefully avoids blaming Godwine, and the E-text avoids the issue entirely.

Harold Harefoot became king in 1037 but died in 1040. At that point, Harthacnut acceded, and Emma returned to England from Flanders, where she had sought refuge with Count Baldwin. But Harthacnut proved unpopular, and so Edward was invited to return to England from Normandy in 1041 on the understanding that he would succeed Harthacnut. Upon Harthacnut's untimely death in 1042, Edward (later known as "the Confessor") became king and ruled until his death in 1066.

In all of this, Earl Godwine played an outsized role. His fortunes had been considerably advanced under Cnut from the early 1020s. Godwine had navigated the crisis of succession sufficiently well and with sufficient power that when Edward became king he had little choice but to show him favor, despite Godwine's role in the murder of his brother Alfred.[45] The king made Godwine's sons Swein and Harold earls, and he married Godwine's daughter Edith.[46] The Godwines continued to build their power and wealth through the 1040s, but in 1051 they revolted against Edward and fled to Bruges. Edward then appropriated their earldoms and put Edith in a convent. But in 1052 the wind changed again, and Edward was forced to restore the Godwines to their titles and properties and take Edith back as queen. This fraught background makes the poem's earnest praise of Harold's loyalty more special pleading than testimony.

Verse Forms

While joined in their commemorations of Æthelred the Unready's youngest sons, these two poems of the C-text could not be more different in their verse forms. Though composed late in the Old English period, *The Death of Edward* is a self-consciously traditional Old English poem that calls on the tropes of lordship and the language of heroic verse to mourn Edward's death but also to shore up Harold II's claim to the throne of England.[47] Edward is praised as king (lines 1, 13, 15, 23), lord (line 1), and ruler (lines 6, 8). His descent from Æthelred (and thus from the Cerdicing line) is noted at line 10, to which is connected his nobility (lines 13, 24). And the poem celebrates the return of rule by an English king in its comments on twenty-eight years of Danish rule. Its praise of Harold II as Edward's successor carefully avoids mention of Harold's own descent. Rather, his qualifications are nobility and loyalty to Edward. In making these claims, the poem uses both traditional language and carefully traditional verse. It echoes numerous lines of earlier Old English poetry, and metrically it is highly regular. It means to look like a praise poem of a king along the models of earlier verse.

The poem on the death of Alfred is so strikingly different from the form of *The Death of Edward* and from earlier Chronicle poems that some have considered the piece no poem at all.[48] Its verse is strongly rhythmical and makes prominent use of rhyme. Alliteration is lacking in eight lines, and when it does occur, is often incorrectly placed. *The Death of Alfred* lacks the lexicon of English kingship and lordship so ably used in *The Death of Edward* with good reason: Alfred had spent his youth and young manhood in Normandy and had no sooner landed in England than he was captured and murdered. The composition of *The Death of Alfred* looks elsewhere for its models, specifically to the tropes of hagiography found in Old English homiletic prose and to the sound patterns in Ælfric's rhythmical prose.[49] Within this tradition the poem deploys its *sum*-catalog (lines 3–5) of the outrages done to the men of Alfred's retinue, all described as innocents. Alfred's death is thus presented within the tropes of martyrdom through which both the form of the poem and its language take their meaning.

The Battle of Maldon

On August 10, 991, a battle was fought between a levy of Englishmen led by Byrhtnoth, *ealdormann* of Essex, and an army of invading Northmen encamped at a place now generally identified as Northey Island in the estuary of the river Blackwater, two miles downstream from the village of Maldon.[50] The battle, in which Byrhtnoth was killed, was one among many defeats leading to the ascent of a Dane, Cnut (Canute, Knútr), to the English throne in 1016. The Old English poem *The Battle of Maldon* was composed probably within a few years of the battle by an anonymous poet who was perhaps native to Essex or surrounding areas, to judge by certain linguistic features of the text. The poem celebrates the valor, in the face of certain defeat, of Byrhtnoth and of those of his men who refused to yield even after the death of their leader.

Maldon is one of the richest and most interesting poems in the corpus of Old English literature, despite its incomplete state. The only copy is an eighteenth-century transcription of a now-lost medieval manuscript, and it is missing an unknown number of lines from the beginning and the end. The poet uses traditional conventions and figures in a sophisticated way, although some formal features are uncharacteristic of classical Old English poems like *Beowulf* and seem to correlate to changes in the Old English language and its poetic conventions as they evolved prior to this relatively late date of composition.[51] *Maldon* has a claim to being the most "historical" extended poem in the Old English corpus. It narrates a real battle, and Byrhtnoth, at least, is a well-attested historical figure. The poet makes no effort to gloss over or glorify this English defeat by exaggerating the accomplishments of the warriors who stayed and fought to the end or insisting that the vikings suffered such enormous casualties that their victory was a Pyrrhic one. The details of the physical features of the area in which the battle took place are supported reasonably well by archeology and geographical research, although the topography of rivers and islands at the mouth of rivers can change quite substantially over time. Although the names of the English fighters in *Maldon* are not all attested in external records, some of them may be associated with known families in the area. The poem's factual accuracy can be glimpsed by indirect evidence: the traitor who broke the English battle line by fleeing on Byrhtnoth's horse was named Godric, and Godric was also the name of one of the heroes who continued to fight when defeat and death were imminent. A poet who did not feel compelled to honor the "facts" of the battle would hardly make a villain and a hero bear the same name. The majority of scholars who have worked on the poem agree that *Maldon* was composed by a poet who knew the area and who had access to textual records or oral accounts about the battle, or both. The story's essential events are plausible, although other historical records of the battle do not support every detail.[52]

Complicating our historical understanding is the fact that the social organization of early medieval England is not well understood. One immediate example is the question of how Byrhtnoth's army was recruited and trained and whether the English soldiers were the "select *fyrd*" (an elite group) or recruited from the able-bodied men of the surrounding region, or both. On this issue, historians differ, and the poem is not explicit. Similarly, one of the crucial junctures of the poem is Byrhtnoth's decision to allow the vikings to cross the tidal estuary that separated the two armies so the armies could engage each other directly. The poet glosses this decision as a mistake, but scholars have pointed out that the vikings had easy access to their boats and could simply have sailed away and ravaged some other area of the country. This possibility would affect the reader's judgment of Byrhtnoth's decision, but the poet says nothing of it. Attempting to interpret the poem as an armchair general is obviously problematic from our historical distance.

This brief discussion of the historicity of the poem must at least touch on the question of oral history and its implications in this context. In the premodern world, and indeed until very recently, all history was oral until someone chose to set down a written record. Some English warriors survived the battle and told their family, friends, and acquaintances what they experienced and what they heard from their peers. These accounts as well as those of other witnesses were then retold to new audiences until sagas of Byrhtnoth and the Battle of Maldon emerged with some variation around a core set of facts.

Analyzing the poem as a literary artifact is on firmer ground than trying to resolve its historical ambiguities. The poem falls into two parts: the first two hundred lines or so narrate the battle up to the death of Byrhtnoth, while the remainder celebrates the warriors who stay to avenge their dead lord. Throughout the poem the vikings are anonymous, lethal adversaries. The two portions differ stylistically from each other.[53] The earlier portion specifies details that pertain to a particular moment of history: this time and this place. The English troops must be told where to hold their position, for instance, and when the vikings cannot break through on the causeway, they negotiate with Byrhtnoth about allowing them to cross the tidal estuary unimpeded. After he is mortally wounded, he pauses to pray for the salvation of his soul before dying. The cowards flee from the ranks in an unforgiveable betrayal of their lord, which then precipitates the collapse of the bulk of the English army.

The remainder of the poem concerns the heroic speeches and the death in battle of the warriors who honor their commitment to Byrhtnoth and stay to avenge him at the cost of their lives. At this point, the language and narrative of the poem become more abstract and traditional. The specific details of the earlier narrative give way to something else; it is as if the warriors who stayed to avenge Byrhtnoth are leaving the realm of history and entering the world of heroic epic. Their exhortations affirm it is a matter of honor to stay and fight, even though there is no practical reason for their sacrifice. This commitment to honor is paralleled strikingly in Tacitus's *Germania* but, while not unparalleled elsewhere, is rarer than some commentators imagine. For warriors to fight bravely and defend their lord while he is alive is a commonplace, as is fighting for vengeance. But to fight with no hope of victory or survival involves a high level of commitment indeed.

The scholarly reception of *Maldon* has elicited a wide range of responses. Critics such as W. P. Ker, writing shortly before the First World War, accepted the ideal of glory in a good war without question or moral hesitation, and there are other late nineteenth- and early twentieth-century critics whose enthusiasm is embarrassing from today's perspective.[54] Other commentators discern irony or raise the question of whether Christian doctrine complicates the poem's elevation of heroic death. And yet, however the poem is interpreted today, those warriors whose names are singled out continue to enjoy a measure of *dom* (glory, honor). The poem is about an English defeat to a cruel adversary, and the C-text of the Old English Chronicle claims the defeat was a prelude to national humiliation, since the English king finally chose to pay the tribute that the vikings demanded. The poem does not celebrate war. It celebrates courage in war, and the despair and cruelty of an absolute defeat are the background for the expression of an idealism that has moved poets and readers for generations, even in a world that has grown very different.

A Note on Personal Names

The spellings of personal names in the various translations in this volume are based on the orthographic usage of *The Wiley Blackwell Encyclopedia of Anglo-Saxon England,* ed. Michael Lapidge, John Blair, Simon Keynes, and Donald Scragg, 2nd ed. (Chichester, West Sussex, 2014), hereafter *Wiley Blackwell Encyclopedia.* Following established practice, exceptions include a handful of names with close equivalents in modern usage, such as Alfred, Augustine, Edward, James, Peter, or which are otherwise familiar, as Vortigern.

An enormous debt of gratitude goes to Jo Jennings, who played a crucial role in shepherding Janet Bately's draft of *The Old English Chronicle* to completion. The project could not have been finished without Jo's role in entering her mother-in-law's final edits in a computer file. Thanks also go to Joseph Shack and Blake Lopez, who as Dumbarton Oaks interns provided important readings of early drafts, and to Rob Fulk and Tom Hill for their contributions to the sections on *The Battle of Maldon.* Finally, thanks to Nicole Eddy for assembling and copyediting everything with her usual professionalism and good humor.

Notes

1 Bertram Colgrave and R. A. B. Mynors, eds. and trans., *Bede's Ecclesiastical History of the English People,* Oxford Medieval Texts (Oxford, 1969; repr., Oxford, 1991), hereafter *EH.* On the writing of histories in England, see Renée R. Trilling, "The Writing of History in the Early Middle Ages: The Anglo-Saxon Chronicle in Context," in *The Cambridge History of Early Medieval English Literature,* ed. Clare A. Lees (Cambridge, 2012), 232–56.

2 Antonia Gransden, "The Chronicles of Medieval England and Scotland," in *Legends, Traditions and History in Medieval England* (London, 1992), 199–238, at 199–201. On the narrative possibilities of formulaic language in annal entries, see Jacqueline Stodnick, "Sentence to Story: Reading the Anglo-Saxon Chronicle as Formulary," in *Reading the Anglo-Saxon Chron-*

icle: Language, Literature, History, ed. Alice Jorgensen (Turnhout, 2010), 91–119.

3 *EH* 5.24, pp. 566–67.

4 A date in the case of the late West Saxon spellings in the Peterborough Chronicle would be "around 1121." See Susan Irvine, ed., *MS. E,* vol. 7 of *The Anglo-Saxon Chronicle: A Collaborative Edition,* ed. David N. Dumville and Simon Keynes (Cambridge, 2004), ciii–clxvi.

5 For place-names, see the online Survey of English Place-Names: https://epns.nottingham.ac.uk/search.

6 See Edmund Gibson, ed., *Chronicon Saxonicum, seu, Annales rerum in Anglia* (Oxford, 1692); James Ingram, trans., *The Saxon Chronicle, with an English Translation and Notes* (London, 1823); J. A. Giles, ed., *The Venerable Bede's Ecclesiastical History of England: Also the Anglo-Saxon Chronicle* (London, 1847). The first English translation was by Anna Gurney, *A Literal Translation of the Saxon Chronicle* (London, 1819).

7 Ingram, *Saxon Chronicle,* 1n2.

8 Charles Plummer, ed., *Two of the Saxon Chronicles Parallel* (Oxford, 1892–1899), vol. 2, p. xxiii.

9 Plummer, *Two of the Saxon Chronicles,* vol. 2, p. xxiii.

10 Helmut Gneuss and Michael Lapidge, *Anglo-Saxon Manuscripts: A Bibliographical Handbook of Manuscripts and Manuscript Fragments Written or Owned in England up to 1100* (Toronto, 2014), no. 52; N. R. Ker, *A Catalogue of Manuscripts Containing Anglo-Saxon* (Oxford, 1957; repr., Oxford, 1990), no. 39. See Parker Library on the Web (https://parker.stanford.edu/parker/) for detailed contents and bibliography, and reproduction of the entire manuscript.

11 For example, Robin Flower and A. H. Smith, eds., *Parker Chronicle and Laws: A Facsimile* (London, 1941).

12 See further Janet Bately, ed., *MS. A,* vol. 3 of Dumville and Keynes, *Collaborative Edition* (Cambridge, 1986), xliv.

13 For this item, also known as the West Saxon Genealogical Regnal List and, though circulating independently from it, often seen as a preface to the Chronicle, see David N. Dumville, "The West Saxon Genealogical Regnal List: Manuscripts and Texts," *Anglia* 104 (1986): 1–32.

14 See Stefan Jurasinski and Lisi Oliver, eds. and trans., *The Laws of Alfred: The Domboc and the Making of Anglo-Saxon Law* (Cambridge, 2021).

15 Angelika Lutz, ed., *Die Version G der angelsächsischen Chronik: Rekonstruktion und Edition* (Munich, 1981).

16 Bately, *MS. A,* xxi–xlvi.

17 Bately, *MS. A,* xxi. This edition and translation replaces the Roman numerals in each annal heading with Arabic numerals.

18 For a paleographical argument in favor of an endpoint at 891, see Malcolm Parkes, "The Parker Manuscript of the 'Chronicle,' Laws, and Sedulius," *Anglo-Saxon England* 5 (1976): 149–71, at 155–56; for linguistic and stylistic evidence in favor of 892, see Janet Bately, "The Compilation of the 'Anglo-Saxon Chronicle' Once More," *Leeds Studies in English* 16 (1985): 7–26. For a detailed discussion of the arguments over the terminal date of the Common Stock, see Simon Keynes and Michael Lapidge, eds. and trans., *Alfred the Great: Asser's Life of King Alfred and Other Contemporary Sources,* Penguin Classics (Harmondsworth, Middlesex, 1983), 277–81.

19 The argument about Easter tables was advanced by Reginald Lane Poole, *Chronicles and Annals* (Oxford, 1926), 41–43, and repeated by Antonia Gransden, *Historical Writing in England,* vol. 1, *c. 550–c. 1307* (London, 1974), 30.

20 This discussion considers details from the A-text only. For the readings of the other texts, see Bately, *MS. A,* lxxiii–lxxix.

21 On the genealogical and regnal lists, see David N. Dumville, "The West Saxon Genealogical Regnal List and the Chronology of Early Wessex," *Peritia* 4 (1985): 21–66, and Dumville, "The West Saxon Genealogical Regnal List: Manuscripts and Texts."

22 On the details of narrative style, see Cecily Clark, "The Narrative Mode of *The Anglo-Saxon Chronicle* Before the Conquest," in *England Before the Conquest: Studies in Primary Sources Presented to Dorothy Whitelock,* ed. Peter Clemoes and Kathleen Hughes (Cambridge, 1971), 215–35, especially 221–24.

23 Clark, "Narrative Mode," 223.

24 Katherine O'Brien O'Keeffe, ed., *MS. C,* vol. 5 of Dumville and Keynes, *Collaborative Edition* (Cambridge, 2001), 74–76.

25 There are five poems in "classical" Old English verse and a sixth, *The Death of Alfred,* in prose and verse preserved in different texts of the Old English Chronicles. Four poems are preserved in the A-text, those for 937

and 942 (also appearing in B, C, and D) and for 973 and 975 (also appearing in B and C). These are absent from the E-text.

26 Alistair Campbell, ed., *The Battle of Brunanburh* (London, 1938); John C. Pope, ed., *Eight Old English Poems,* 3rd ed., prepared by R. D. Fulk (New York, 2001), 5–8.

27 For the aesthetic and ideological goals of these poems, see Scott Thompson Smith, "The Edgar Poems and the Poetics of Failure in the *Anglo-Saxon Chronicle,*" *Anglo-Saxon England* 39 (2010): 105–37.

28 For details of the additions, corrections, and continuations, see Bately, *MS. A;* for interventions in a range of post-Conquest hands, see especially pp. xl–xlii, and for early modern hands, pp. xliv–xlvi.

29 Norman Garmonsway, ed. and trans., *The Anglo-Saxon Chronicle,* Everyman's Library (London, 1953); Michael Swanton, ed. and trans., *The Anglo-Saxon Chronicle* (London, 1996). Much but not all of the A-text is translated as well in *English Historical Documents,* ed. David C. Douglas, 2nd ed., vol. 1, *c. 500–1042,* ed. Dorothy Whitelock (London, 1979), 145–238.

30 *EH* 1.1, p. 16.

31 Margaret Lindsay Faull, "The Semantic Development of Old English *Wealh,*" *Leeds Studies in English* 8 (1975): 20–44, at 24–25.

32 On the application of *æþeling* as a title, see David N. Dumville, "The Ætheling: A Study in Anglo-Saxon Constitutional History," *Anglo-Saxon England* 8 (1979): 1–33.

33 For a concise account, see Simon Keynes, "Thegn," in *The Wiley Blackwell Encyclopedia of Anglo-Saxon England,* ed. Michael Lapidge, John Blair, Simon Keynes, and Donald Scragg, 2nd ed. (Chichester, West Sussex, 2014), 459–61.

34 The exception is *þegn,* since its Modern English spelling, "thegn," is sufficiently distinct.

35 F. M. Stenton, *Anglo-Saxon England,* 3rd ed. (Oxford, 1971), 509. See also DOE, under *hold* noun^2, "an aristocratic landowner ranking between *þegn* and *ealdormann/eorl* and corresponding to the English *hēahgerēfa* (cf. ON *höldr*)."

36 See DOE, under *eorl,* sense 3.

37 See also DOE, under *here,* sense 1.e: "referring to the invading Danish army in England (esp. in chronicles treating conflicts between the English

and Scandinavians, where the English army is regularly referred to as a *fyrd,* cf. *fyrd* sense 3.a)."

38 Referred to by the related term *hergaþ* (act of plundering, looting, raiding).

39 On assembling the *fyrd,* see John Baker and Stuart Brookes, "Explaining Anglo-Saxon Military Efficiency: The Landscape of Mobilization," *Anglo-Saxon England* 44 (2015): 221–58.

40 David N. Dumville and Michael Lapidge, eds., *The Annals of St Neots, with Vita prima sancti Neoti,* vol. 17 of Dumville and Keynes, *Collaborative Edition* (Cambridge, 1984), xxxii.

41 William Henry Stevenson, ed., *Asser's Life of King Alfred: Together with the Annals of Saint Neots Erroneously Ascribed to Asser,* new impression with article by Dorothy Whitelock (Oxford, 1959; originally published, Oxford, 1904); Alistair Campbell, ed., *The Chronicle of Æthelweard* (London, 1962).

42 For navigating such dates, see C. R. Cheney, ed., *A Handbook of Dates for Students of British History,* new ed., rev. Michael Jones (Cambridge, 2000).

43 Alistair Campbell, ed. and trans., *Encomium Emmae reginae,* with a supplementary introduction by Simon Keynes, Camden Classic Reprints 4 (Cambridge, 1998; originally published, London, 1949), 40–43.

44 See also Campbell, *Encomium Emmae,* 46–47.

45 Simon Keynes and Rosalind Love, "Earl Godwine's Ship," *Anglo-Saxon England* 38 (2010): 185–223, at 191–92.

46 For an argument that the Godwine family wealth and power grew rapidly under Edward the Confessor, see Robin Fleming, "Domesday Estates of the King and the Godwines: A Study in Late Saxon Politics," *Speculum* 58, no. 4 (1983): 987–1007.

47 On the form of the poem, see Katherine O'Brien O'Keeffe, "Deaths and Transformations: Thinking Through the 'End' of Old English Verse," in *New Directions in Oral Theory,* ed. Mark C. Amodio (Tempe, AZ, 2005), 149–78, at 167–71 and appendix.

48 Julie Townsend, "The Metre of the *Chronicle*-Verse," *Studia Neophilologica* 68 (1996): 143–76, at 143, declines to consider the meter of *The Death of Alfred* due to its strong use of rhyme. On rhyme and "unreliable witnesses" to metrical developments, see R. D. Fulk, *A History of Old English Meter* (Philadelphia, 1992), 258.

49 See O'Brien O'Keeffe, "Deaths and Transformations," 156–65.

50 The editors gratefully acknowledge Thomas D. Hill for drafting this portion of the Introduction dedicated to *The Battle of Maldon,* and R. D. Fulk for extensive editing.

51 On the use of rhyme and sound effects, see, for example, Mark Atherton, "Rhyme and Reason in *The Battle of Maldon,*" in *Tradition and Innovation in Old English Metre,* ed. Rachel A. Burns and Rafael J. Pascual (Leeds, 2022), 103–20; see also Richard Dance, "'Þær wearð hream ahafen': A Note on Old English Spelling and the Sound of *The Battle of Maldon,*" in *The Power of Words: Anglo-Saxon Studies Presented to Donald G. Scragg on His Seventieth Birthday,* ed. Hugh Magennis and Jonathan Wilcox (Morgantown, WV, 2006), 278–317. On innovative syntactic and metrical characteristics, see Megan E. Hartman, "Style and Politics in *The Battle of Brunanburh* and *The Battle of Maldon,*" in *Studies in the History of the English Language VI: Evidence and Method in Histories of English,* ed. Michael Adams, Laurel J. Brinton, and R. D. Fulk (Berlin, 2015), 201–18.

52 See the discussion concerning historical accounts in Donald G. Scragg's edition of *The Battle of Maldon* (Manchester, UK, 1981), 8–14. See also the entry for the year 991 in O'Brien O'Keeffe, *MS. C,* 86. Additionally, see E. O. Blake, ed., *Liber Eliensis,* Camden Third Series 92 (London, 1962). See also the new edition by Mark S. Griffith, *The Battle of Maldon: A New Critical Edition,* Exeter Medieval Texts and Studies (Liverpool, 2024).

53 Edward B. Irving, Jr., "The Heroic Style in *The Battle of Maldon,*" *Studies in Philology* 58 (1961): 458–60.

54 W. P. Ker, *The Dark Ages* (New York, 1904), 81–86.

THE OLD ENGLISH CHRONICLE, THE A-TEXT TO 1001

Genealogical and Regnal List

Þy geare þe wæs agan fram Cristes acennesse CCCC wintra ond XCIV wintra, þa Cerdic ond Cynric his sunu cuom up æt Cerdicesoran mid V scipum. Ond se Cerdic wæs Elesing, Elesa Esling, Esla Gewising, Giwis Wiging, Wig Freawining, Freawine Friþugaring, Friþugar Bronding, Brond Bældæging, Bældæg Wodening. Ond þæs ymb VI gear þæs þe hie up cuomon geeodon Westseaxna rice, ond þæt wærun þa ærestan cyningas þe Westseaxna lond on Wealum geeodon.

2 Ond he hæfde þæt rice XVI gear, ond þa he gefor, þa feng his sunu Cynric to þam rice ond heold XVII winter. Þa he gefor, þa feng Ceol to þam rice ond heold VI gear. Þa he gefor, þa feng Ceolwulf to his broþur, ond he ricsode XVII gear, ond hiera cyn gæþ to Cerdice. Þa feng Cynegils Ceolwulfes broþur sunu to rice ond ricsode XXXI wintra, ond he onfeng ærest fulwihte Wesseaxna cyninga, ond þa feng Cenwalh to ond heold XXXI wintra, ond se Cenwalh wæs Cynegilses sunu; ond þa heold Seaxburg his cuen an gear þæt rice æfter him. Þa feng Æscwine to rice, þæs cyn gæþ to Cerdice, ond heold II gear. Þa feng Centwine to Wesseaxna rice Cynegilsing ond ricsode VII gear. Þa feng Ceadwalla to þam rice, þæs

Genealogical and Regnal List

In this year, which was four hundred and ninety-four years since the birth of Christ, Cerdic, and Cynric, his son, arrived at *Cerdicesora* with five ships. And this Cerdic was Elesa's son, Elesa Esla's son, Esla Gewis's son, Gewis Wig's son, Wig Freawine's son, Freawine Friþugar's son, Friþugar Brond's son, Brond Bældæg's son, Bældæg Woden's son. And six years after they arrived, they conquered the kingdom of the West Saxons, and they were the first kings that conquered the land of the West Saxons from the Britons.

And he ruled that kingdom sixteen years, and when he 2
died, his son Cynric succeeded to the kingdom and held it seventeen years. When he died, then Ceol succeeded to the kingdom and ruled six years. When he died, then Ceolwulf succeeded his brother, and he ruled seventeen years, and their lineage goes back to Cerdic. Then Cynegils, Ceolwulf's nephew, succeeded to the kingdom and ruled thirty-one years, and he was first of the West Saxon kings to receive baptism, and then Cenwalh succeeded and ruled thirty-one years, and this Cenwalh was Cynegils's son; and then Seaxburg, his queen, held the kingdom one year after him. Then Æscwine, whose lineage goes back to Cerdic, succeeded to the kingdom and ruled two years. Then Centwine, Cynegils's son, succeeded to the kingdom of the West Saxons and ruled seven years. Then Ceadwalla, whose lineage goes back

cyn geþ to Cerdice, ond heold iii gear. Ða feng Ine to Westseaxna rice, þæs cyn gæþ to Ceardice, ond heold xxxvii wintra. Þa feng Æthelheard to, þæs cyn gæþ to Ceardice, ond heold xiv winter. Þa feng Cuþred to, þæs cyn gæþ to Cerdice, ond heold xvii gear. Þa feng Sigebryht to, þæs cyn gæþ to Cerdice, ond heold an gear. Þa feng Cynewulf to rice, þæs cyn gæþ to Ceardice, ond heold xxxi wintra. Þa feng Beorhtric to rice, þæs cyn gæþ to Cerdice, ond heold xvi gear. Þa feng Ecgbryht to þam rice ond heold xxxvii wintra ond vii monaþ. Ond þa feng Æþelwulf his sunu to ond heold nigonteoðe healf gear. Se Æþelwulf wæs Ecgbryhting, Ecgbryht Ealhmunding, Ealhmund Eafing, Eafa Eopping, Eoppa Ingilding, Ingild Cenreding, ond Ine Ċenreding, ond Cuþburg Cenreding, ond Cuenburg Cenreding, Cenred Ceolwalding, Ceolwald Cuþwulfing, Cuþwulf Cuþwining, Cuþwine Ceaulining, Ceawlin Cynricing, Cynric Cerdicing.

3 Ond þa feng Æþelbald his sunu to rice ond heold v gear. Þa feng Æþelbryht his broþur to ond heold v gear. Þa feng Æþered hiera broþur to rice ond heold v gear. Þa feng Ælfred hiera broþur to rice, ond þa was agan his ielde xxiii wintra, ond ccc ond xcvi wintra þæs þe his cyn ærest Westseaxna lond on Wealum geeodon.

to Cerdic, succeeded to the kingdom and ruled three years. Then Ine, whose lineage goes back to Cerdic, succeeded to the kingdom of the West Saxons and ruled thirty-seven years. Then Æthelheard, whose lineage goes back to Cerdic, succeeded and ruled fourteen years. Then Cuthred, whose lineage goes back to Cerdic, succeeded and ruled seventeen years. Then Sigeberht, whose lineage goes back to Cerdic, succeeded and ruled one year. Then Cynewulf, whose lineage goes back to Cerdic, succeeded to the kingdom and ruled thirty-one years. Then Beorhtric, whose lineage goes back to Cerdic, succeeded to the kingdom and ruled sixteen years. Then Ecgberht succeeded to the kingdom and ruled thirty-seven years and seven months. And then Æthelwulf, his son, succeeded and ruled eighteen and a half years. This Æthelwulf was the son of Ecgberht, Ecgberht son of Ealhmund, Ealhmund son of Eafa, Eafa son of Eoppa, Eoppa son of Ingeld, Ingeld son of Cenred, and Ine son of Cenred, and Cuthburg daughter of Cenred, and Cwenburg daughter of Cenred, Cenred son of Ceolwald, Ceolwald son of Cuthwulf, Cuthwulf son of Cuthwine, Cuthwine son of Ceawlin, Ceawlin son of Cynric, Cynric son of Cerdic.

And then Æthelbald, his son, succeeded to the kingdom 3
and ruled five years. Then Æthelberht, his brother, succeeded and ruled five years. Then Æþelred, their brother, succeeded and ruled five years. Then Alfred, their brother, succeeded to the kingdom, and his age was twenty-three, and it was three hundred and ninety-six years since his ancestors first conquered the land of the West Saxons from the Britons.

Annals

[60 BCE] Aer Cristes geflæscnesse LX wintra, Gaius Iulius se casere ærest Romana Bretenlond gesohte ond Brettas mid gefeohte cnysede ond hie oferswiþde ond swa þeah ne meahte þær rice gewinnan.

AN 1 Octauianus ricsode LVI wintra, ond on þam LII geare his rices Crist wæs acenned.

AN 2 Þa tungelwitgan of eastdæle cuomon to þon þæt hie Crist weorþedon, ond þa cild on Bethlem ofslægene wærun for Cristes ehtnesse from Herode.

AN 3 Her swealt Herodus from him selfum ofsticod, ond Archilaus his sunu feng to rice.

———

AN 6 From frymþe middangeardes oþ þis gear wæron agan v þusendu wintra ond CC wintra.

———

AN 12 Philippus ond Herodes todældun Lysiam, ond Iudeam feowericum todældun.

———

AN 16 Her feng Tiberius to rice.

———

Annals

[60 BCE] Sixty years before Christ's incarnation, the emperor Gaius Julius was the first of the Romans to come to the land of Britain and struck the Britons down in battle and overcame them but was nevertheless not able to gain power there.

AN 1 Octavian ruled for fifty-six years, and in the fifty-second year of his reign Christ was born.

AN 2 The astrologers came from the East in order to worship Christ, and the children in Bethlehem were killed because of Herod's persecution of Christ.

AN 3 In this year Herod died, having stabbed himself, and his son Archelaus succeeded to the kingdom.

——

AN 6 From the beginning of the world up to this year five thousand and two hundred years had passed.

——

AN 12 Philip and Herod divided up Lycia and separated Judaea into tetrarchies.

——

AN 16 In this year Tiberius succeeded to the kingdom.

——

AN 26 Her onfeng Pilatus gyminge ofer Iudeas.

—

AN 30 Her wæs Crist gefulluhtud, ond Petrus ond Andreas gehwierfede ond Iacobus ond Iohannes ond Philippus ond þa XII apostolas.

—

AN 33 Her wæs Crist ahangen, from fruman middangeardes ymb V þusendo wintra ond CC ond XXVI wintra.

AN 34 Her wæs Paulus gehwierfed ond sanctus Stephanus oftorfod.

AN 35 Her se eadiga Petrus se apostol gesæt biscepsetl in Antiochia þære ceastre.

—

AN 39 Her onfeng Gaius rice.

—

AN 44 Her se eadiga Petrus se apostol gesæt biscepsetl on Rome.

AN 45 Her Herodes aswalt, se þe Iacobum ofslog ane geare ær his agnum deaþe.

AN 46 Her Claudius, oþer Romana cyninga, Bretene lond gesohte ond þone mæstan dæl þæs ealondes

AN 26 In this year Pilate obtained authority over the Jews.

AN 30 In this year Christ was baptized, and Peter and Andrew were converted along with James and John and Philip and the twelve apostles.

AN 33 In this year Christ was crucified, five thousand two hundred and twenty-six years from the beginning of the world.

AN 34 In this year Paul was converted and Saint Stephen stoned to death.

AN 35 In this year the blessed apostle Peter established the episcopal see of the city of Antioch.

AN 39 In this year Gaius came to power.

AN 44 In this year the blessed apostle Peter established the see of Rome.

AN 45 In this year Herod died—the one who killed James one year before his own death.

AN 46 In this year Claudius, the second of the kings of the Romans to do so, came to the land of Britain and took the bulk of the island under his control, on his gewald onfeng ond eac swelce Orcadus þa ealond Romana cynedome underþeodde.

———

AN 62 Her Iacobus, *frater Domini,* þrowode.

AN 63 Her Marcus se godspellere forþferde.

———

AN 69 Her Petrus ond Paulus þrowodon.

AN 70 Her Uespassianus onfeng rice.

AN 71 Her Titus, Uespessianus sunu, in Hierusalem ofslog Iudea CXI þusenda.

———

AN 81 Her Titus feng to rice, se þe sæde þæt he þone dæg forlure þe he noht to gode on ne gedyde.

———

AN 83 Her Domittianus, Tites broþur, feng to rice.

AN 84 Her Iohannes se godspellere in Pathma þam ealonde wrat þa boc *Apocalipsis.*

———

AN 90 Her Simon Petrus wæs ahangen, ond Iohannes se godspellere hine gereste in Effesio.

———

and likewise subjected the Orkney Islands to the sovereignty of the Romans.

———

AN 62 In this year James, brother of the Lord, suffered martyrdom.

AN 63 In this year Mark the evangelist passed away.

———

AN 69 In this year Peter and Paul suffered martyrdom.

AN 70 In this year Vespasian came to power.

AN 71 In this year Vespasian's son Titus killed one hundred and eleven thousand Jews in Jerusalem.

———

AN 81 In this year Titus came to power: It was he who said that he lost the day on which he did nothing good.

———

AN 83 In this year Domitian, Titus's brother, came to power.

AN 84 In this year on the island of Patmos, John the evangelist wrote the book called *Apocalypse*.

———

AN 90 In this year Simon Peter was crucified, and John the evangelist went to his rest in Ephesus.

———

AN 92 Her Clemens papa forþferde.

AN 110 Her Ignatus biscep þrowude.

AN 167 Her Eleuther on Rome onfeng biscepdom ond þone wuldorfæstlice xv winter geheold. To þam Lucius, Bretene kyning, sende stafas, bæd þæt he wære cristen gedon, ond he þurhteah þæt he bæd.

AN 189 Her Seuerus onfeng rice ond ricsode xvii winter. Se Bretenlond mid dice begyrdde from sæ oþ sæ.

AN 381 Her Maximianus se casere feng to rice. He wæs on Bretenlonde geboren ond þonne for in Gallia.

AN 409 Her Gotan abræcon Romeburg, ond næfre siþþan Romane ne ricsodon on Bretone.

AN 418 Her Romane gesomnodon al þa goldhord þe on Bretene wæron, ond sume on eorþan ahyddon

AN 92 In this year Pope Clement passed away.

AN 110 In this year Bishop Ignatius suffered martyrdom.

AN 167 In this year Eleutherius received the episcopal see of Rome and held it with glory for fifteen years. To him Lucius, king of the Britons, sent a letter, asking to be made a Christian, and he granted what he asked.

AN 189 In this year Severus came to power and ruled for seventeen years. It was he who enclosed the land of Britain with a dike from sea to sea.

AN 381 In this year the emperor Maximianus came to power. He was born in the land of Britain but later went to Gaul.

AN 409 In this year the Goths took the city of Rome by storm, and the Romans never afterward ruled in Britain.

AN 418 In this year the Romans gathered together all the hoards of gold that there were in Britain, and some they hid in the ground so that no one was þæt hie nænig mon siþþan findan ne meahte, ond sume mid him on Gallia læddon.

AN 430 Her Paladius se biscep wæs onsended to Scottum þæt he hiera geleafan trymede from Cælestino þam papan.

AN 449 Her Mauricius ond Ualentines onfengon rice ond ricsodon VII winter. On hiera dagum Hengest ond Horsa, from Wyrtgeorne geleaþade, Bretta kyninge, gesohton Bretene on þam staþe þe is genemned Ypwinesfleot, ærest Brettum to fultume, ac hie eft on hie fuhton.

AN 455 Her Hengest ond Horsa fuhton wiþ Wyrtgeorne þam cyninge in þære stowe þe is gecueden Agælesþrep, ond his broþur Horsan man ofslog, ond æfter þam Hengest feng to rice ond Æsc his sunu.

AN 457 Her Hengest ond Æsc fuhton wiþ Brettas in þære stowe þe is gecueden Crecganford ond þær ofslogon IV M wera, ond þa Brettas þa forleton Centlond ond mid micle ege flugon to Lundenbyrg.

---

able afterward to find them, and some they took with them to Gaul.

AN 430 In this year Bishop Palladius was sent by Pope Celestine to the Irish so that he could strengthen their faith.

AN 449 In this year Mauricius and Valentinus succeeded to the kingdom and ruled for seven years. In their days Hengest and Horsa, at the invitation of Vortigern, king of the Britons, arrived in Britain at the shore that is called Ebbsfleet, at first in aid of the Britons, though they later fought against them.

AN 455 In this year Hengest and Horsa fought against King Vortigern in the place that is called *Agælesthrep,* and Horsa, Hengest's brother, was killed, and after that Hengest came to power, along with Æsc his son.

AN 457 In this year Hengest and Æsc fought against the Britons at the place that is called *Crecganford* and killed four thousand men there, and the Britons then abandoned the land of Kent and in great terror fled to London.

AN 465 Her Hengest ond Æsc gefuhton wiþ Walas neah Wippedesfleote ond þær XII wilisce aldormenn ofslogon. Ond hiera þegn an þær wearþ ofslægen þam wæs noma Wipped.

—

AN 473 Her Hengest ond Æsc gefuhton wiþ Walas ond genamon unarimedlico herereaf. Ond þa Walas flugon þa Englan swa fyr.

—

AN 477 Her cuom Ælle on Bretenlond ond his III suna, Cymen ond Wlencing ond Cissa, mid III scipum on þa stowe þe is nemned Cymenesora, ond þær ofslogon monige Wealas ond sume on fleame bedrifon on þone wudu þe is genemned Andredesleage.

—

AN 485 Her Ælle gefeaht wiþ Walas neah Mearcrædesburnan stæðe.

—

AN 488 Her Æsc feng to rice ond was XXIV wintra Cantwara cyning.

—

AN 465 In this year Hengest and Æsc fought against the Britons near *Wippedesfleot* and there killed twelve local leaders. And one thegn of their own, whose name was Wipped, was also killed there.

———

AN 473 In this year Hengest and Æsc fought against the Britons and took an incalculable amount of booty. And the Britons fled from the English as though from fire.

———

AN 477 In this year Ælle and his three sons, Cymen, Wlencing, and Cissa, came with three ships to the land of Britain, to the place that is called *Cymenesora* and there killed many Britons and drove others in flight to the wood that is called *Andredesleag.*

———

AN 485 In this year Ælle fought against the Britons near the bank of *Mearcrædesburna.*

———

AN 488 In this year Æsc came to power and was king of the people of Kent for twenty-four years.

———

AN 491 Her Ælle ond Cissa ymbsæton Andredescester ond ofslogon alle þa þe þærinne eardedon: Ne wearþ þær forþon an Bret to lafe.

———

AN 495 Her cuomon twegen aldormen on Bretene, Cerdic ond Cynric his sunu, mid v scipum in þone stede þe is gecueden Cerdicesora ond þy ilcan dæge gefuhtun wiþ Walum.

———

AN 501 Her cuom Port on Bretene ond his II suna, Bieda ond Mægla, mid II scipum on þære stowe þe is gecueden Portesmuþa ond ofslogon anne giongne Brettiscmonnan, swiþe æþelne monnan.

———

AN 508 Her Cerdic ond Cynric ofslogon ænne Brettisccyning, þam was nama Natanleod, ond v þusendu wera mid him. Æfter was þæt lond nemned Natanleaga oþ Cerdicesford.

———

AN 514 Her cuomon Westseaxe in Bretene mid III scipum in þa stowe þe is gecueden Cerdicesora. Ond Stuf ond Wihtgar fuhtun wiþ Brettas ond hie gefliemdon.

———

AN 491 In this year Ælle and Cissa besieged *Andredes-ceaster* and killed everyone who lived there: Not a single Briton was left.

——

AN 495 In this year two chieftains, Cerdic and his son Cynric, came to Britain with five ships, to the site that is called *Cerdicesora* and that same day fought against the Britons.

——

AN 501 In this year Port and his two sons, Bieda and Mægla, came with two ships to Britain, to the place that is called Portsmouth and there killed a certain young British man, a person of very high rank.

——

AN 508 In this year Cerdic and Cynric killed a certain British king whose name was Natanleod and five thousand men with him. Afterward that land was named Netley as far as Charford.

——

AN 514 In this year the West Saxons came to Britain with three ships to the place that is called *Cerdicesora.* And Stuf and Wihtgar fought against the Britons and put them to flight.

——

AN 519 Her Cerdic ond Cynric rice onfengun, ond þy ilcan geare hie fuhton wiþ Brettas þær mon nu nemneþ Cerdicesford.

———

AN 527 Her Cerdic ond Cynric fuhton wiþ Brettas in þære stowe þe is gecueden Cerdicesleaga.

———

AN 530 Her Cerdic ond Cynric genamon Wihte ealond ond ofslogon fea men on Wihtgarabyrg.

———

AN 534 Her Cerdic forþferde, ond Cynric, his sunu, ricsode forþ XXVI wintra, ond hie saldon hiera tuæm nefum, Stufe ond Wihtgare, Wiehte ealond.

———

AN 538 Her sunne aþiestrode XIV dagum ær *kalendas Martii* from ærmergenne oþ undern.

———

AN 540 Her sunne aþiestrode on XII *kalendas Iulius,* ond steorran hie oðiewdon fulneah healfe tid ofer undern.

———

AN 519 In this year Cerdic and Cynric took power, and that same year they fought against the Britons in the place that is now called Charford.

—

AN 527 In this year Cerdic and Cynric fought against the Britons in the place that is called *Cerdicesleag.*

—

AN 530 In this year Cerdic and Cynric seized the Isle of Wight and killed a few men in *Wihtgaraburg.*

—

AN 534 In this year Cerdic passed away, and Cynric, his son, continued to reign for twenty-six years, and they gave their two kinsmen, Stuf and Wihtgar, the Isle of Wight.

—

AN 538 In this year the sun grew dark on the sixteenth of February from daybreak until nine in the morning.

—

AN 540 In this year the sun grew dark on the twentieth of June, and the stars were visible for nearly half an hour after nine in the morning.

—

AN 544 Her Wihtgar forþferde, ond hiene mon bebyrgde on Wihtgarabyrg.

———

AN 547 Her Ida feng to rice, þonon Norþanhymbra cynecyn onwoc. Ida wæs Eopping, Eoppa wæs Esing, Esa Inguing, Ingui Angenwiting, Angenwit Aloching, Aloc Beonocing, Beonoc Branding, Brand Bældæging, Bældæg Wodening, Woden Friþowulfing, Friþowulf Finning, Finn Godwulfing, Godwulf Geating.

———

AN 552 Her Cynric gefeaht wiþ Brettas in þære stowe þe is genemned æt Searobyrg ond þa Bretwalas gefliemde. Cerdic wæs Cynrices fæder, Cerdic Elesing, Elesa Esling, Esla Gewising, Gewis Wiging, Wig Freawining, Freawine Friþogaring, Friþugar Branding, Brand Bældæging, Bældæg Wodening.

———

AN 556 Her Cynric ond Ceawlin fuhton wiþ Brettas æt Beranbyrg.

———

AN 560 Her Ceawlin feng to rice on Westseaxum, ond Ælle feng to Norþanhymbra rice ond heold xxx wintra. Ælle wæs Yffing, Yffe Uscfreaing,

AN 544 In this year Wihtgar passed away and was buried in *Wihtgaraburg*.

AN 547 In this year Ida, from whom the royal family of the Northumbrians sprang, came to power. Ida was Eoppa's son, Eoppa Esa's son, Esa Ingui's son, Ingui Angenwit's son, Angenwit Aloc's son, Aloc Beonoc's son, Beonoc Brand's son, Brand Bældæg's son, Bældæg Woden's son, Woden Frithuwulf's son, Frithuwulf Finn's son, Finn Godwulf's son, Godwulf Geat's son.

AN 552 In this year Cynric fought against the Britons in the place called Salisbury and put the Britons to flight. Cerdic was Cynric's father, Cerdic Elesa's son, Elesa Esla's son, Esla Gewis's son, Gewis Wig's son, Wig Freawine's son, Freawine Frithugar's son, Frithugar Brand's son, Brand Bældæg's son, Bældæg Woden's son.

AN 556 In this year Cynric and Ceawlin fought against the Britons at Barbury.

AN 560 In this year Ceawlin took power among the West Saxons, and Ælle succeeded to the kingdom of the Northumbrians and held it for thirty years. Ælle was Yffe's son, Yffe Uscfrea's son, Uscfrea

Uscfrea Wilgising, Wilgis Westerfalcning, Westerfalcna Sæfugling, Sæfugl Sæbalding, Sæbald Sigegeating, Sigegeat Swæfdæging, Swæfdæg Sigegearing, Sigegear Wægdæing, Wægdæg Wodening, Woden Friþowulfing.

—

AN 565 Her Columba mæssepreost of Scottum com in Brettas to lærenne Peohtas ond in Hi þam ealonde mynster worhte.

—

AN 568 Her Ceaulin ond Cuþa gefuhton wiþ Æþelbryht ond hine in Cent gefliemdon ond tuegen aldormen on Wibbandune ofslogon, Oslaf ond Cnebban.

—

AN 571 Her Cuþwulf feaht wiþ Bretwalas æt Bedcanforda ond IV tunas genom, Lygeanburg ond Ægelesburg, Benningtun ond Egonesham, ond þy ilcan geare he gefor.

—

AN 577 Her Cuþwine ond Ceawlin fuhton wiþ Brettas, ond hie III kyningas ofslogon, Coinmail ond Condidan ond Farinmail, in þære stowe þe is gecueden Deorham, ond genamon III ceastro, Gleawanceaster ond Cirenceaster ond Baþanceaster.

—

Wilgis's son, Wilgis Westerfalcna's son, Westerfalcna Sæfugl's son, Sæfugl Sæbald's son, Sæbald Sigegeat's son, Sigegeat Swæfdæg's son, Swæfdæg Sigegear's son, Sigegear Wægdæg's son, Wægdæg Woden's son, Woden Frithuwulf's son.

AN 565 In this year the priest Columba came to the Britons from the people of Ireland to instruct the Picts, and he built a monastery on the island of Iona.

AN 568 In this year Ceawlin and Cutha fought against Æthelberht and drove him into Kent and killed two noblemen, Oslaf and Cnebba, at *Wibbandun*.

AN 571 In this year Cuthwulf fought against the Britons at *Bedcanford* and captured four settlements, Limbury, Aylesbury, Benson, and Eynsham, and the same year he departed this life.

AN 577 In this year Cuthwine and Ceawlin fought against the Britons, and they killed three kings, Coinmail, Condidan, and Farinmail, in the place that is called Dyrham, and seized three cities, Gloucester, Cirencester, and Bath.

AN 584 Her Ceawlin ond Cuþa fuhton wiþ Brettas in þam stede þe mon nemneþ Feþanleag, ond Cuþan mon ofslog, ond Ceaulin monige tunas genom ond unarimedlice herereaf, ond ierre he hwearf þonan to his agnum.

—

AN 588 Her Ælle cyning forþferde, ond Æþelric ricsode æfter him v gear.

—

AN 591 Her Ceol ricsode v gear.

AN 592 Her micel wælfill wæs æt Woddesbeorge, ond Ceawlin wæs ut adrifen.

AN 593 Her Ceawlin ond Cuichelm ond Crida forwurdon, ond Æþelfriþ feng to rice.

—

AN 596 Her Gregorius papa sende to Bretene Augustinum mid wel monegum munecum þa Godes word Engla þeode godspellian.

AN 597 Her ongon Ceolwulf ricsian on Wessseaxum, ond simle he feaht ond won, oþþe wiþ Angelcyn, oþþe wiþ Walas, oþþe wiþ Peohtas, oþþe wiþ Scottas. Se wæs Cuþaing, Cuþa Cynricing, Cynric Cerdicing, Cerdic Elesing, Elesa Esling, Esla Gewising, Giwis Wiging, Wig Freawining,

AN 584 In this year Ceawlin and Cutha fought against the Britons in the place that is called *Fethanleag*, and Cutha was killed, and Ceawlin seized many settlements and an incalculable amount of booty, and he returned home, enraged, to his own people.

AN 588 In this year King Ælle passed away, and after him Æthelric ruled for five years.

AN 591 In this year Ceol ruled for five years.

AN 592 In this year there was great slaughter at Woden's Barrow, and Ceawlin was driven out.

AN 593 In this year Ceawlin, Cwichelm, and Crida perished, and Æthelfrith came to power.

AN 596 In this year Pope Gregory sent Augustine to Britain with a large number of monks, to preach the word of God to the English people.

AN 597 In this year Ceolwulf began to rule among the West Saxons, and he constantly fought and battled, either against the Angles, or against the Britons, or against the Picts, or against the Scots. He was Cutha's son, Cutha Cynric's son, Cynric Cerdic's son, Cerdic Elesa's son, Elesa Esla's son, Esla Gewis's son, Gewis Wig's son, Wig Freawine's

Freawine Friþugaring, Friþugar Bronding, Brond Bældæging, Bældæg Wodening.

—

AN 601 Her sende Gregorius papa Agustino ærcebiscepe pallium in Bretene ond wel monige godcunde lareowas him to fultome, ond Paulinus biscep gehwerfde Edwine, Norþhymbra cyning, to fulwihte.

—

AN 603 Her wæs gefeoht æt Egesanstane.

AN 604 Her Eastseaxe onfengon geleafan ond fulwihtes bæð under Sæbyrhte cyninge.

—

AN 606 Her forþferde Gregorius ymb x gear þæs þe he us fulwiht sende. Ond his fæder wæs haten Gordianus.

AN 607 Her Ceolwulf gefeaht wiþ Suþseaxe.

—

AN 611 Her Cynegils feng to rice on Wesseaxum ond heold XXXI wintra. Cynegils wæs Ceoling, Ceol Cuþaing, Cuþa Cynricing.

—

son, Freawine Frithugar's son, Frithugar Brand's son, Brand Bældæg's son, Bældæg Woden's son.

——

AN 601 In this year Pope Gregory sent the pallium to Britain to Archbishop Augustine, along with a large number of spiritual instructors to assist him, and Bishop Paulinus turned Edwin, king of the Northumbrians, to baptism.

——

AN 603 In this year there was a battle at Degsa's Stone.

AN 604 In this year the East Saxons received the Christian faith and the bath of baptism under their king, Sæberht.

——

AN 606 In this year Pope Gregory passed away ten years after he sent us baptism. His father was called Gordianus.

AN 607 In this year Ceolwulf fought against the South Saxons.

——

AN 611 In this year Cynegils succeeded to the kingdom of the West Saxons and ruled for thirty-one years. Cynegils was son of Ceol, Ceol son of Cutha, Cutha son of Cynric.

——

AN 614 Her Cynegils ond Cuichelm gefuhton on Beandune ond ofslogon II þusendo Wala ond XLVI.

———

AN 616 Her Æþelbryht, Contwara cyning, forþferde, ond Eadbald his sunu feng to rice. Ond þy ilcan geare wæs agan fram frymþe middangeardes fif þusendu wintra ond DCCC.

———

AN 625 Her Paulinus, fram Iusto þam ercebiscepe, wæs gehadod Norþhymbrum to biscepe.

AN 626 Her Eanflæd, Edwines dohtor cyninges, wæs gefulwad in þone halgan æfen Pentecosten. Ond Penda hæfde XXX wintra rice, ond he hæfde L wintra þa þa he to rice feng. Penda wæs Pybbing, Pybba Cryding, Cryda Cynewolding, Cynewold Cnebbing, Cnebba Iceling, Icel Eomæring, Eomær Angelþeowing, Angelþeow Offing, Offa Wærmunding, Wærmund Wihtlæging, Wihtlæg Wodening.

AN 627 Her Edwine kyning wæs gefulwad mid his þeode on Eastron.

AN 628 Her Cynegils ond Cuichelm gefuhtun wiþ Pendan æt Cirenceastre ond geþingodan þa.

———

AN 614 In this year Cynegils and Cwichelm fought at *Beandun* and killed two thousand and forty-six Britons.

AN 616 In this year Æthelberht, king of the people of Kent, passed away, and his son Eadbald came to power. And that same year five thousand and eight hundred years had gone by from the beginning of the world.

AN 625 In this year Paulinus was consecrated bishop of the Northumbrians by Archbishop Justus.

AN 626 In this year Eanflæd, daughter of King Edwin, was baptized on the holy eve of Pentecost. And Penda held power for thirty years, having first succeeded to the kingdom when he was fifty years old. Penda was Pybba's son, Pybba Creoda's son, Creoda Cynewald's son, Cynewald Cnebba's son, Cnebba Icel's son, Icel Eomær's son, Eomær Angeltheow's son, Angeltheow Offa's son, Offa Wærmund's son, Wærmund Wihtlæg's son, Wihtlæg Woden's son.

AN 627 In this year King Edwin was baptized at Easter along with his people.

AN 628 In this year Cynegils and Cwichelm fought against Penda at Cirencester and then came to terms.

AN 632 Her was Eorpwald gefulwad.

AN 633 Her Edwine wæs ofslægen, ond Paulinus huerf eft to Cantwarum ond gesæt þæt biscepsetl on Hrofesceastre.

AN 634 Her Birinus biscep bodude Westseaxum fulwuht.

AN 635 Her Cynegils wæs gefulwad from Birino þæm biscepe in Dorkeceastre, ond Oswold his onfeng.

AN 636 Her Cuichelm wæs gefulwad in Dorcesceastre ond þy ilcan geare forþferde. Ond Felix biscep bodade Eastenglum Cristes geleafan.

———

AN 639 Her Birinus fulwade Cuþræd on Dorcesceastre ond onfeng hine him to suna.

AN 640 Her Eadbald, Cantwara cyning, forþferde, ond he ricsode xxv wintra.

———

AN 642 Her Oswald, Norþanhymbra cyning, ofslægen wæs.

AN 643 Her Cenwalh feng to Wesseaxna rice ond heold xxxi wintra. Ond se Cenwalh het atimbran þa ciricean on Wintanceastre.

AN 632 In this year Eorpwald was baptized.

AN 633 In this year Edwin was killed, and Paulinus returned to the people of Kent and occupied the episcopal see of Rochester.

AN 634 In this year Bishop Birinus preached baptism to the West Saxons.

AN 635 In this year Cynegils was baptized by Bishop Birinus in Dorchester, and Oswald sponsored him.

AN 636 In this year Cwichelm was baptized in Dorchester and passed away that same year. And Bishop Felix preached the Christian faith to the East Angles.

———

AN 639 In this year Birinus baptized Cuthred in Dorchester and received him as his godson.

AN 640 In this year Eadbald, king of the Kentish people, passed away, having ruled for twenty-five years.

———

AN 642 In this year Oswald, king of the Northumbrians, was killed.

AN 643 In this year Cenwalh succeeded to the kingdom of the West Saxons and reigned for thirty-one years. And this same Cenwalh ordered the building of the church in Winchester.

AN 644 Her Paulinus forþferde se was ærcebiscep on Eoforwicceastre ond eft on Hrofesceastre.

AN 645 Her Cenwalh adrifen wæs from Pendan cyninge.

AN 646 Her Cenwalh wæs gefulwad.

———

AN 648 Her Cenwalh gesalde Cuþrede his mæge III þusendo londes be Æscesdune. Se Cuþred wæs Cuichelming, Cuichelm Cynegilsing.

———

AN 650 Her Ægelbryht of Galwalum, æfter Birine þam Romaniscan biscepe, onfeng Wesseaxna biscepdome.

AN 651 Her Oswine kyning wæs ofslægen, ond Aidan biscep forþferde.

AN 652 Her Cenwalh gefeaht æt Bradanforda be Afne.

AN 653 Her Middelengle onfengon under Peadan aldormen ryhtne geleafan.

AN 654 Her Onna cyning wearþ ofslægen. Ond Botulf ongon mynster timbran æt Icanho.

AN 655 Her Penda forwearþ, ond Mierce wurdon Cristne. Þa was agan from fruman middangeardes V M wintra ond DCCC ond L wintra, ond Peada feng to Mercna rice Pending.

———

AN 644 In this year Paulinus, who was archbishop at York and later at Rochester, passed away.

AN 645 In this year Cenwalh was driven out by King Penda.

AN 646 In this year Cenwalh was baptized.

———

AN 648 In this year Cenwalh gave his kinsman Cuthred three thousand hides of land around Ashdown. This Cuthred was Cwichelm's son, Cwichelm Cynegils's son.

———

AN 650 In this year Agilbert of Gaul received the episcopal see of the West Saxons after Birinus, the Roman bishop.

AN 651 In this year King Oswine was killed, and Bishop Aidan passed away.

AN 652 In this year Cenwalh fought at Bradford on Avon.

AN 653 In this year the Middle Angles received the true faith under Ealdorman Peada.

AN 654 In this year King Anna was killed. And Botwulf began to build a monastery at *Icanho*.

AN 655 In this year Penda perished, and the Mercians became Christian. By that time five thousand eight hundred and fifty years had passed since the beginning of the world, and Peada, Penda's son, succeeded to the kingdom of the Mercians.

———

AN 657 Her forþferde Peada, ond Wulfhere Pending feng to Miercna rice.

AN 658 Her Cenwalh gefeaht æt Peonnum wiþ Walas ond hie gefliemde oþ Pedridan. Þis wæs gefohten siþþan he of Eastenglum com. He wæs þær III gear on wrece—hæfde hine Penda adrifenne ond rices benumenne, forþon he his swostor anforlet.

———

AN 660 Her Ægelbryht biscep gewat from Cenwale, ond Wine heold þone biscepdom III gear. Ond se Ægelbryht onfeng Persa biscepdomes on Galwalum bi Signe.

AN 661 Her Cenwalh gefeaht in Eastron on Posentesbyrg ond gehergeade Wulfhere Pending oþ Æscesdune; ond Cuþred Cuichelming, ond Coenbryht cyning on anum geare forþferdun. Ond on Wiht gehergade Wulfhere Pending ond gesalde Wihtwaran Æþelwalde, Suþseaxna cyninge, forþon Wulfhere hine onfeng æt fulwihte. Ond Eoppa mæssepreost, be Wilferþes worde, ond Wulfhere cyning brohte Wihtwarum fulwiht ærest.

———

AN 657 In this year Peada passed away, and Wulfhere, Penda's son, succeeded to the kingdom of the Mercians.

AN 658 In this year Cenwalh fought against the Britons at *Peonnum* and drove them as far as the River Parret. This battle was fought after he came back from East Anglia. He had been three years in exile there—Penda had driven him out and deprived him of power, for having abandoned his sister.

AN 660 In this year Bishop Agilbert departed from Cenwalh, and Wine held the episcopal see for three years. And that Agilbert had received the episcopal see of Paris, on the Seine, in the land of the Gauls.

AN 661 In this year Cenwalh fought at Easter at *Posentesburg* and Wulfhere, Penda's son, went raiding as far as Ashdown; and Cuthred, Cwichelm's son, and King Coenberht passed away in one and the same year. And Wulfhere, Penda's son, went raiding on the Isle of Wight and gave the inhabitants of the island to Æthelwald, king of the South Saxons, because Wulfhere had stood sponsor for him at baptism. And the priest Eoppa (acting on the instructions of Wilfrid) and King Wulfhere first brought baptism to the inhabitants of the Isle of Wight.

AN 664 Her sunne aþiestrode, ond Arcenbryht, Cantwara cyng, forþferde, ond Colman mid his geferum for to his cyððe. Þy ilcan geare wæs micel mancuealm, ond Ceadda ond Wilferþ wæron gehadode, ond þy ilcan geare Deusdedit forþferde.

AN 668 Her Þeodorus mon hadode to ercebiscepe.

AN 669 Her Ecgbryht cyning salde Basse mæsseprioste Reculf mynster on to timbranne.

AN 670 Her forþferde Osweo, Norþanhymbra cyning, ond Ecgferþ ricsode æfter him. Ond Hloþhere feng to biscepdome ofer Wesseaxan, Ægelbryhtes biscepes nefa, ond heold VII gear. Þeodor biscep hine gehalgode. Ond se Oswio wæs Æþelferþing, Æþelferþ Æþelricing, Æþelric Iding, Ida Eopping.

AN 671 Her wæs þæt micle fugla wæl.

AN 672 Her forþferde Cenwalh, ond Seaxburg an gear ricsode his cuen æfter him.

AN 673 Her Ecgbryht, Cantwara cyning, forþferde. Ond þy geare wæs senoð æt Heorotforda, ond sancte Æþeldryht ongon þæt mynster æt Elige.

AN 664 In this year the sun grew dark, and Earconberht, king of the people of Kent, passed away, and Colman, with his companions, went home to his fellow countrymen. This same year there was a serious outbreak of deadly disease, and Chad and Wilfrid were consecrated as bishops, and this same year Deusdedit passed away.

AN 668 In this year Theodore was consecrated archbishop.

AN 669 In this year King Ecgberht gave Reculver to the priest Bass, in which to build a monastery.

AN 670 In this year Oswiu, king of the Northumbrians, passed away, and Ecgfrith reigned after him. And Hlothhere, a nephew of Bishop Agilbert, succeeded to the episcopal see of the West Saxons and held it for seven years. Bishop Theodore consecrated him. And this Oswiu was Æthelfrith's son, Æthelfrith Æthelric's son, Æthelric Ida's son, Ida Eoppa's son.

AN 671 In this year there was the great carnage of birds.

AN 672 In this year Cenwalh passed away, and Seaxburg, his queen, ruled for one year after him.

AN 673 In this year Ecgberht, king of the people of Kent, passed away. And this year there was a synod at Hertford, and Saint Æthelthryth founded the monastery at Ely.

AN 674 Her feng Æscwine to rice on Wesseaxum; se wes Cenfusing, Cenfus Cenferþing, Cenferþ Cuþgilsing, Cuþgils Ceolwulfing, Ceolwulf Cynricing, Cynric Cerdicing.

AN 675 Her Wulfhere Pending ond Æscwine gefuhton æt Biedanheafde, ond þy ilcan geare Wulfhere forþferde, ond Æþelræd feng to rice.

AN 676 Her Æscwine forþferde, ond Hedde feng to biscepdome, ond Centwine feng to rice. Ond Centwine was Cynegilsing, Cynegils Ceolwulfing, ond Æþered, Miercna cyning, oferhergeade Centlond.

AN 678 Her oþiewde *cometa* se steorra, ond Wilfriþ biscop wæs adrifen of his biscepdome from Ecgferþe cyninge.

AN 679 Her Ælfwine wæs ofslægen, ond sancte Æþelþryþ forþferde.

AN 680 Her gesæt Þeodorius ærcebiscop senoþ on Hæþfelda, forþon he wolde þone Cristes geleafan geryhtan. Ond þy ilcan geare forþferde Hild abbodesse on Streonesheale.

AN 674 In this year Æscwine came to power among the West Saxons; he was Cenfus's son, Cenfus Cenferth's son, Cenferth Cuthgils's son, Cuthgils Ceolwulf's son, Ceolwulf Cynric's son, Cynric Cerdic's son.

AN 675 In this year Wulfhere, son of Penda, and Æscwine fought at *Biedanheafde,* and that same year Wulfhere passed away, and Æthelred came to power.

AN 676 In this year Æscwine passed away, and Hedde became bishop, and Centwine succeeded to the kingdom. And Centwine was Cynegils's son, Cynegils Ceolwulf's son. And Æthelred, king of the Mercians, ravaged Kent.

———

AN 678 In this year the star known as *comet* appeared, and Bishop Wilfrid was driven from his see by King Ecgfrith.

AN 679 In this year Ælfwine was killed, and Saint Æthelthryth passed away.

AN 680 In this year Archbishop Theodore presided over a synod at Hatfield, since he wished to set right observance of the Christian faith. And this same year Hild, abbess of Whitby, passed away.

———

AN 682 On þissum geare Centwine gefliemde Bretwalas oþ sæ.

———

AN 685 Her Ceadwalla ongan æfter rice winnan. Se Ceadwalla was Coenbryhting. Coenbryht Cadding, Cadda Cuþaing, Cuþa Ceawlining, Ceawlin Cynricing, Cynric Cerdicing. Ond Mul was Ceadwallan broþur, ond þone mon eft on Cent forbærnde. Ond þy ilcan geare Ecgferþ cyning mon ofslog. Se Ecgferþ was Osweoing, Osweo Æþelferþing, Æþelferþ Æþelricing, Æþelric Iding, Ida Eopping. Ond Hloþhere þy ilcan geare forþferde.

AN 686 Her Ceadwalla ond Mul Cent ond Wieht forhergedon.

AN 687 Her Mul wearþ on Cent forbærned ond oþre XII men mid him, ond þy geare Ceadwalla eft Cent forhergeade.

AN 688 Her Ine feng to Wesseaxna rice ond heold XXXVII wintra. Ond he getimbrade þæt menster æt Glæstingabyrig. Ond þy ilcan geare Ceadwalla for to Rome ond fulwihte onfeng from þam papan, ond se papa hine heht Petrus, ond ymb VII niht he forþferde. Þonne was se Ine Cenreding, Cenred Ceolwalding; Ceolwald was Cynegilses

AN 682 In this year Centwine put the Britons to flight all the way to the sea.

AN 685 In this year Cædwalla began to contend for power. This Cædwalla was Coenberht's son, Coenberht Cadda's son, Cadda Cutha's son, Cutha Ceawlin's son, Ceawlin Cynric's son, Cynric Cerdic's son. And Ceadwalla's brother was called Mul, and he was later burned to death in Kent. And the same year King Ecgfrith was killed. This Ecgfrith was Oswiu's son, Oswiu Æthelfrith's son, Æthelfrith Æthelric's son, Æthelric Ida's son, Ida Eoppa's son. And this same year Hlothhere passed away.

AN 686 In this year Cædwall and Mul ravaged Kent and the Isle of Wight.

AN 687 In this year Mul was burned to death in Kent, and twelve other men with him, and that year Cædwalla once again ravaged Kent.

AN 688 In this year Ine succeeded to the kingdom of the West Saxons and held it for thirty-seven years. And he built the monastery at Glastonbury. And the same year Cædwalla traveled to Rome and received baptism from the pope, who named him Peter, and seven days later he passed away. Now this Ine was Cenred's son, Cenred Ceolwald's son; Ceolwald was the brother of Cynegils, broþur, ond þa wæron Cuþwines suna Ceaulininges, Ceaulin Cynricing, Cynric Cerdicing.

—

AN 690 Her Þeodorius ærcebiscep forþferde, ond feng Beorhtwald to þam biscepdome. Ær wærun Romanisce biscepas, siþþan wærun Englisce.

—

AN 694 Her Cantware geþingodan wiþ Ine ond him gesaldon XXX M, forþon þe hie ær Mul forbærndon. Ond Wihtred feng to Cantwara rice ond heold XXXIII wintra. Se Wihtred was Ecgbryhting, Ecgbryht Arcenbryhting, Erconbryht Eadbalding, Eadbald Æþelbryhting.

—

AN 703 Her Hedde biscep forþferde, ond he heold þone biscepdom XXVII wintra on Wintaceastre.

AN 704 Her Æþelred Pending, Miercna cyning, onfeng munuchade ond þæt rice heold XXIX wintra. Þa feng Coenred to.

AN 705 Her Aldferþ, Norþanhymbra cyning, forþferde, ond Seaxwulf biscep.

—

and they were sons of Cuthwine Ceawlin's son, Ceawlin Cynric's son, Cynric Cerdic's son.

AN 690 In this year Archbishop Theodore passed away, and Beorhtwald succeeded to the archiepiscopal see. Previously the archbishops had been Roman; afterward they were English.

AN 694 In this year the people of Kent came to terms with Ine and gave him thirty thousand *sceattas* because they had burned Mul to death. And Wihtred succeeded to the kingdom of the people of Kent and held it for thirty-three years. This Wihtred was Ecgberht's son, Ecgberht Earconberht's son, Earconberht Eadbald's son, Eadbald Æthelberht's son.

AN 703 In this year Bishop Hedde passed away and he had held the episcopal see in Winchester for twenty-seven years.

AN 704 In this year Æthelred, Penda's son, king of the Mercians, took monastic orders, and he had held that kingdom for twenty-nine years. Then Coenred succeeded.

AN 705 In this year Aldfrith, king of the Northumbrians, and Bishop Seaxwulf passed away.

AN 709 Her Aldhelm biscep forþferde, se wæs be westan wuda biscep. Ond wæs todæled in foreweardum Danieles dagum in tua biscepscira Westseaxna lond. Ond ær hit wæs an: oþer heold Daniel, oþer Aldhelm. Æfter Aldhelme feng Forþhere to. Ond Ceolred feng to Miercna rice, ond Coenred for to Rome ond Offa mid him.

AN 710 Her Beorhtfriþ ealdormon feaht wiþ Peohtas, ond Ine ond Nun, his mæg, gefuhton wiþ Gerente, Wala cyninge.

———

AN 714 Her forþferde Guþlac se halga.

AN 715 Her Ine ond Ceolred fuhton æt Woddesbeorge.

AN 716 Her Osred, Norþanhymbra cyning, wearþ ofslægen, se hæfde VII winter rice æfter Aldferþe. Þa feng Coenred to rice ond heold II gear, þa Osric ond heold XI gear. Ond on þam ilcan geare Ceolred Miercna cyning forþferde, ond his lic resteþ on Licetfelda ond Æþelrædes Pendinges on Bearddanigge. Ond þa feng Æþelbald to rice on Mercium ond heold XLI wintra. Æþelbald wæs Alweoing, Alweo Eawing, Eawa Pybing, þæs

AN 709 In this year Bishop Aldhelm, who was bishop of the region to the west of Selwood, passed away. It was in Daniel's earliest days that the land of the West Saxons had been divided into two dioceses. Earlier it had been one: Daniel held one, Aldhelm the other. After Aldhelm, Forthhere succeeded as bishop. And Ceolred became king of the Mercians, and Coenred went to Rome, and Offa with him.

AN 710 In this year Ealdorman Beorhtferth fought against the Picts; and Ine and his kinsman Nun fought against Geraint, king of the Britons of Devon and Cornwall.

AN 714 In this year the holy Guthlac passed away.

AN 715 In this year Ine and Ceolred fought at Woden's Barrow.

AN 716 In this year Osred, king of the Northumbrians, who had held power for seven years after Aldfrith, was killed. Then Coenred succeeded to the kingdom and held it for two years; then Osric, and he held it for eleven years. And in the same year Ceolred, king of the Mercians, passed away, and his body rests in Lichfield, and the body of Æthelred, Penda's son, rests in Bardney. After that Æthelbald succeeded to the kingdom of the Mercians and held it for forty-one years. Æthelbald was Alweo's son, and Alweo Eawa's cyn is beforan awriten. Ond Ecgbryht se arwierþa wer on Hii þam ealonde þa munecas on ryht gecierde þæt hie Eastron on ryht heoldon ond þa ciriclecan scare.

—

AN 718 Her Ingild forþferde, Ines broþur. Ond hiera swostur wærun Cuenburg ond Cuþburh. Ond sio Cuþburg þæt liif æt Winburnan arærde. Ond hio wæs forgifen Norþanhymbra cyninge Aldferþe, ond hie be him lifgendum hie gedældun.

—

AN 721 Her Daniel ferde to Rome, ond þy ilcan geare Ine ofslog Cynewulf.

AN 722 Her Æþelburg cuen towearp Tantun, ond Ine ær timbrede. Ond Aldbryht wræccea gewat on Suþrige ond on Suþseaxe, ond Ine gefeaht wiþ Suþseaxum.

—

AN 725 Her Wihtræd, Cantwara cyning, forþferde, þæs cyn is beforan, ond Ine feaht wiþ Suþseaxan ond þær ofslog Aldbryht.

—

son, Eawa son of Pybba, whose lineage is recorded above. And that venerable man, Ecgberht, converted the monks on the island of Iona to observe Easter correctly and to adopt the clerical tonsure.

AN 718 In this year Ingeld, brother of Ine, passed away. Their sisters were Cwenburg and Cuthburg. It was Cuthburg who established the monastic life at Wimborne. She had been given as wife to Aldfrith, king of the Northumbrians, but they separated during their lifetime.

AN 721 In this year Daniel went to Rome, and this same year Ine killed Cynewulf.

AN 722 In this year Queen Æthelburg destroyed Taunton, which Ine had built. And the exile Ealdberht moved to the territories of the people of Surrey and the South Saxons, and Ine fought against the South Saxons.

AN 725 In this year Wihtred, king of the inhabitants of Kent, whose ancestry is recorded above, passed away, and Ine fought against the South Saxons, killing Ealdberht there.

AN 728 Her Ine ferde to Rome ond þær his feorh gesealde, ond feng Æþelheard to Wesseaxna rice ond heold XIV gear. Ond þy geare gefuhton Æþelheard ond Oswald se æþeling. Ond se Oswald was Æþelbalding, Æþelbald Cynebalding, Cynebald Cuþwining, Cuþwine Ceaulining.

AN 729 Her *cometa* se steorra hiene oþiewde, ond sanctus Ecgbryht forþferde.

AN 730 Her Oswald se æþeling forþferde.

AN 731 Her was ofslægen Osric, Norþanhymbra cyning, ond feng Ceolwulf to þam rice ond heold VIII gear, ond se Ceolwulf wæs Cuþaing, Cuþa Cuþwining, Cuþwine Leodwalding, Leodwald Ecgwalding, Ecgwald Aldhelming, Aldhelm Ocging, Ocga Iding, Ida Eopping. Ond Beorhtwald ærcebiscep gefor, ond þy ilcan geare Tatwine wæs gehalgod to ærcebiscepe.

—

AN 733 Her Æþelbald geeode Sumurtun, ond sunne aþiestrode.

AN 734 Her wæs se mona swelce he wære mid blode begoten, ond ferdon forþ Tatwine ond Bieda.

—

AN 728 In this year Ine went to Rome and died there, and Æthelheard succeeded to the kingdom of the West Saxons and held it for fourteen years. And that year there was fighting between Æthelheard and the ætheling Oswald. And this Oswald was Æthelbald's son, Æthelbald Cynebald's son, Cynebald Cuthwine's son, Cuthwine Ceawlin's son.

AN 729 In this year the star known as *comet* showed itself; and Saint Ecgberht passed away.

AN 730 In this year the ætheling Oswald passed away.

AN 731 In this year Osric, king of the Northumbrians, was killed, and Ceolwulf succeeded to that kingdom and held it for eight years, and this Ceolwulf was Cutha's son, Cutha Cuthwine's son, Cuthwine Leodwald's son, Leodwald Ecgwald's son, Ecgwald Aldhelm's son, Aldhelm Ocga's son, Ocga Ida's son, Ida Eoppa's son. And Archbishop Beorhtwald departed this life, and this same year Tatwine was consecrated archbishop.

AN 733 In this year Æthelbald took Somerton, and the sun grew dark.

AN 734 In this year the moon was as if it were drenched with blood, and Tatwine and Bede passed away.

AN 736 Her Noþhelm ærcebiscep onfeng pallium from Romana biscepe.

AN 737 Her Forþhere biscep ond Friþogiþ cuen ferdun to Rome.

AN 738 Her Eadbryht Eating, Eata Leodwalding feng to Norþanhymbra rice ond heold XXI wintra. Ond his broþor wæs Ecgbryht Eating ærcebiscep, ond hie restaþ begen on Eoforwicceastre on anum portice.

———

AN 741 Her Æþelheard cyning forþferde, ond feng Cuþræd to Wesseaxna rice ond heold XVI wintra ond heardlice gewon wiþ Æþelbald cyning. Ond Cuþbryht wæs to ærcebiscepe gehalgod ond Dun biscep to Hrofesceastre.

———

AN 743 Her Æþelbald ond Cuþræd fuhton wiþ Walas.

AN 744 Her Danihel gesæt on Wintanceastre, ond Hunferþ feng to biscepdome.

AN 745 Her Danihel forþferde. Þa was XLIII wintra agan siþþan he onfeng biscepdome.

AN 736 In this year Archbishop Nothhelm received the pallium from the bishop of the Romans.

AN 737 In this year Bishop Forthhere and Queen Frithogith journeyed to Rome.

AN 738 In this year Eadberht, son of Eata and grandson of Leodwald, succeeded to the kingdom of the Northumbrians and held it for twenty-one years. His brother was Archbishop Ecgberht, Eata's son, and they both rest in the city of York, in the same side chapel.

AN 741 In this year King Æthelheard passed away, and Cuthred succeeded to the kingdom of the West Saxons and held it for sixteen years and fought vigorously against King Æthelbald. And Cuthberht was consecrated archbishop and Dunn bishop for Rochester.

AN 743 In this year Æthelbald and Cuthred fought against the Britons.

AN 744 In this year Daniel retired from office in Winchester, and Hunferth succeeded to the episcopal see.

AN 745 In this year Daniel passed away. Forty-three years had then gone by since he succeeded to the episcopal see.

AN 746 Her mon slog Selred cyning.

—

AN 748 Her wæs ofslægen Cynric, Wesseaxna æþeling, ond Eadbryht, Cantwara cyning, forþferde.

—

AN 750 Her Cuþred cyning gefeaht wiþ Æþelhun þone ofermedan aldormonn.

—

AN 752 Her Cuþred gefeaht þy xii geare his rices æt Beorgforda wiþ Æþelbald.

AN 753 Her Cuþred feaht wiþ Walas.

AN 754 Her Cuþred forþferde, ond Cyneheard onfeng biscepdome æfter Hunferþe on Wintanceastre. Ond Cantwaraburg forbærn þy geare, ond Sigebryht feng to Wesseaxna rice ond heold an gear.

AN 755 Her Cynewulf benam Sigebryht his rices ond Westseaxna wiotan for unryhtum dædum buton Hamtunscire, ond he hæfde þa oþ he ofslog þone aldormon þe him lengest wunode. Ond hiene þa Cynewulf on Andred adræfde, ond he þær wunade oþ þæt hiene an swan ofstang æt Pryfetesflodan, ond he wræc þone aldormon

AN 746 In this year King Selered was killed.

—

AN 748 In this year Cynric, ætheling of the West Saxons, was killed, and Eadberht, king of the people of Kent, passed away.

—

AN 750 In this year King Cuthred fought against Æthelhun, the arrogant ealdorman.

—

AN 752 Here, in the twelfth year of his rule, Cuthred fought against Æthelbald at *Beorgford.*

AN 753 In this year Cuthred fought against the Britons.

AN 754 In this year Cuthred passed away, and Cyneheard succeeded to the episcopal see of Winchester after Hunferth. And that year Canterbury burned down, and Sigeberht succeeded to the kingdom of the West Saxons and held it for one year.

AN 755 In this year, because of his unlawful deeds, Cynewulf and the councilors of the West Saxons deprived Sigeberht of his kingdom, with the exception of Hampshire, and he had that until he killed the ealdorman that had stood by him longest. And then Cynewulf drove him away into the Weald, and he remained there until a swineherd stabbed him to death at the stream at Privett: He was avenging the ealdorman Cumbra. And this

Cumbran. Ond se Cynewulf oft miclum gefeohtum feaht wiþ Bretwalum, ond ymb xxxi wintra þæs þe he rice hæfde, he wolde adræfan anne æþeling se was Cyneheard haten; ond se Cyneheard wæs þæs Sigebryhtes broþur. Ond þa geascode he þone cyning lytle werode on wifcyþþe on Merantune ond hine þær berad ond þone bur utan beeode, ær hine þa men onfunden þe mid þam kyninge wærun. Ond þa ongeat se cyning þæt, ond he on þa duru eode ond þa unheanlice hine werede, oþ he on þone æþeling locude, ond þa ut ræsde on hine ond hine miclum gewundode. Ond hie alle on þone cyning wærun feohtende oþ þæt hie hine ofslægenne hæfdon. Ond þa on þæs wifes gebærum onfundon þæs cyninges þegnas þa unstilnesse ond þa þider urnon, swa hwelc swa þonne gearo wearþ ond radost. Ond hiera se æþeling gehwelcum feoh ond feorh gebead, ond hiera nænig hit geþicgean nolde, ac hie simle feohtende wæran oþ hie alle lægon butan anum Bryttiscum gisle, ond se swiþe gewundad wæs.

2 Þa on morgenne gehierdun þæt þæs cyninges þegnas þe him beæftan wærun, þæt se cyning ofslægen wæs, þa ridon hie þider, ond his aldormon Osric, ond Wiferþ his þegn, ond þa men þe he beæftan him læfde ær. Ond þone æþeling on þære byrig metton þær se cyning ofslægen læg—ond þa gatu him to belocen hæfdon—ond þa

Cynewulf often engaged in great fights against the Britons, and thirty-one years after he took power, he sought to drive out an ætheling who was called Cyneheard. Now this Cyneheard was the brother of the abovementioned Sigebryht. And when Cyneheard discovered the king, with a small retinue, at Merton in the company of a woman, he besieged him there, and surrounded the lady's chamber on the outside before the men that were with the king found out he was there. When the king realized this, he went to the door and defended himself valiantly until he came face to face with the ætheling, and then he rushed him and severely wounded him. Cyneheard's men all kept on attacking the king until they had killed him. When the king's thegns became aware of the disturbance from the woman's outcry, whoever was ready and quickest ran there. And the ætheling offered each of them money and life, and not one of them was willing to accept this, but instead kept on fighting until they all lay dead apart from a single British hostage, and he was badly wounded.

When, in the morning, those of the king's 2
thegns that had remained behind him heard that the king was killed, they too rode there—his ealdorman Osric and Wigfrith his thegn and the men he had previously left behind. And when they found the ætheling in the fortification where the king lay killed, with the gates locked against them, then they went up to it. And the

þærto eodon. Ond þa gebead he him hiera agenne dom feos ond londes gif hie him þæs rices uþon, ond him cyþdon þæt hiera mægas him mid wæron, þa þe him from noldon. Ond þa cuædon hie þæt him nænig mæg leofra nære þonne hiera hlaford, ond hie næfre his banan folgian noldon.

3 Ond þa budon hie hiera mægum þæt hie gesunde from eodon. Ond hie cuædon þæt tæt ilce hiera geferum geboden wære þe ær mid þam cyninge wærun. Þa cuædon hie þæt hie hie þæs ne onmunden "þon ma þe eowre geferan þe mid þam cyninge ofslægene wærun." Ond hie þa ymb þa gatu feohtende wæron oþ þæt hie þærinne fulgon ond þone æþeling ofslogon ond þa men þe him mid wærun, alle butan anum, se wæs þæs aldormonnes godsunu, ond he his feorh generede, ond þeah he wæs oft gewundad.

4 Ond se Cynewulf ricsode XXXI wintra, ond his lic liþ æt Wintanceastre ond þæs æþelinges æt Ascanmynster, ond hiera ryhtfæderencyn gæþ to Cerdice. Ond þy ilcan geare mon ofslog Æþelbald, Miercna cyning, on Seccandune, ond his lic liþ on Hreopadune. Ond Beornræd feng to rice ond lytle hwile heold ond ungefealice. Ond þy ilcan geare Offa feng to rice ond heold XXXIX wintra, ond his sunu Ecgferþ heold XLI daga ond

ætheling then offered them their own choice of money and land if they would grant him the kingdom, and they told them that their kinsmen were with them who did not wish to leave them. The king's men then replied that no kinsman was dearer to them than their lord, and they would never follow his slayer.

And then they offered their kinsmen the 3
chance to go away unharmed. And the ætheling's men replied that the same had been offered to their own companions who had previously been with the king. And they said they did not consider this for themselves "any more than your companions who were killed with the king." Then they kept on fighting around the gates until the king's men forced their way in and killed the ætheling and the men that were with him, all except one, who was the ealdorman's godson, and he saved his life, although he had been wounded many times.

And this Cynewulf ruled for thirty-one years, 4
and his body lies at Winchester, and the ætheling's at Axminster; and their direct paternal kin goes back to Cerdic. And that same year Æthelbald, king of the Mercians, was killed at Seckington, and his body lies in Repton. And Beornred succeeded to the kingdom and held it for a short time and unhappily. And that same year Offa succeeded to the kingdom and held it for thirty-nine years, and his son Ecgfrith held it for one hundred and forty-one days. This Offa

c daga. Se Offa wæs Þincgferþing, Þincgferþ Eanwulfing, Eanwulf Osmoding, Osmod Eawing, Eawa Pybing, Pybba Creoding, Creoda Cynewalding, Cynewald Cnebing, Cnebba Iceling, Icel Eomæring, Eomær Angelþowing, Angelþeow Offing, Offa Wærmunding, Wærmund Wihtlæging, Wihtlæg Wodening.

AN 758 Her Cuþbryht arcebiscep forþferde.

AN 759 Her Bregowine wæs to ercebiscepe gehadod to sancte Michaeles tide.

AN 760 Her Æþelbryht, Cantwara cyning, forþferde.

AN 761 Her wæs se micla winter.

AN 763 Her Ianbryht wæs gehadod to ærcebiscepe on þone feowertegan dæg ofer midne winter.

AN 764 Her Iaenbryht ærcebiscep onfeng pallium.

AN 772 Her Milred biscep forþferde.

AN 773 Her oþiewde read Cristes mæl on hefenum æfter sunnan setlgonge. Ond þy geare gefuhton Mierce was Thingferth's son, Thingferth Eanwulf's son, Eanwulf Osmod's son, Osmod Eawa's son, Eawa Pybba's son, Pybba Creoda's son, Creoda Cynewald's son, Cynewald Cnebba's son, Cnebba Icel's son, Icel Eomær's son, Eomær Angeltheow's son, Angeltheow Offa's son, Offa Wærmund's son, Wærmund Wihtlæg's son, Wihtlæg Woden's son.

———

AN 758 In this year Archbishop Cuthberht passed away.

AN 759 In this year, at Michaelmas, Bregowine was consecrated archbishop.

AN 760 In this year Æthelberht, king of the people of Kent, passed away.

AN 761 In this year was the great winter.

———

AN 763 In this year Jænberht was consecrated archbishop on the fortieth day after midwinter.

AN 764 In this year Archbishop Jænberht received the pallium.

———

AN 772 In this year Bishop Milred passed away.

AN 773 In this year a red sign of the cross appeared in the heavens after the setting of the sun. And that year the Mercians and the people of Kent fought ond Cantware æt Ottanforda, ond wunderleca nædran wæron gesewene on Suþseaxna londe.

AN 777 Her Cynewulf ond Offa gefuhton ymb Benesingtun, ond Offa nam þone tuun.

AN 780 Her Aldseaxe ond Francan gefuhtun.

AN 784 Her Cyneheard ofslog Cynewulf cyning, ond he þær wearþ ofslægen ond LXXXIV monna mid him. Ond þa onfeng Beorhtric Wesseaxna rices, ond he ricsode XVI gear, ond his lic liþ æt Werham, ond his ryhtfædrencyn gæþ to Cerdice.

AN 785 Her wæs geflitfullic senoþ æt Cealchyþe, ond Iaenbryht ærcebiscep forlet sumne dæl his biscepdomes, ond from Offan kyninge Hygebryht wæs gecoren ond Ecgferþ to cyninge gehalgod.

AN 787 Her nom Beorhtric cyning Offan dohtor Eadburge. Ond on his dagum comon ærest III scipu, ond þa se gerefa þærto rad ond hie wolde drifan at Otford, and extraordinary snakes were seen in the land of the South Saxons.

AN 777 In this year Cynewulf and Offa fought around Bensington, and Offa seized that settlement.

AN 780 In this year the Old Saxons and the Franks fought one another.

AN 784 In this year Cyneheard killed King Cynewulf, and he was himself killed on that occasion, and eighty-four men with him. And Beorhtric succeeded to the kingdom of the West Saxons, and he reigned for sixteen years, and his body lies at Wareham, and his direct paternal line goes back to Cerdic.

AN 785 In this year there was a contentious synod at Chelsea, and Archbishop Jænberht relinquished some part of his episcopal see, and Hygeberht was selected by King Offa, and Ecgfrith consecrated as king.

AN 787 In this year Beorhtric took King Offa's daughter Eadburg as his wife. And in his time there came three ships, and when the reeve rode up to inspect them, and, not knowing what they were, to þæs cyninges tune, þy he nyste hwæt hie wæron, ond hiene mon ofslog. Þæt wæron þa ærestan scipu Deniscra monna þe Angelcynnes lond gesohton.

AN 790 Her Iaenbryht ærcebiscep forþferde, ond þy ilcan geare wæs gecoren Æþelheard abbud to ærcebiscepe.

AN 792 Her Offa Miercna cyning het Æþelbryhte *rex* þæt heafod ofaslean.

AN 794 Her Adrianus papa ond Offa cyning forþferdon, ond Æþelred Norþanhymbra cyning wæs ofslægen from his agenre þeode, ond Ceolwulf biscep ond Eadbald biscep of þæm londe aforon, ond Ecgferþ feng to Miercna rice ond þy ilcan geare forþferde. Ond Eadbryht onfeng rice on Cent, þam was oþer noma nemned Præn.

AN 796 Her Coenwulf, Miercna cyning, oferhergeade Cantware oþ Mersc, ond gefengun Praen hiera cyning ond gebundenne hine on Mierce læddon.

sought to compel them to go to the king's residence, he was killed. Those were the first ships containing Danish men to seek the land of the English.

AN 790 In this year Archbishop Jænberht passed away, and the same year Abbot Æthelheard was elected as archbishop.

AN 792 In this year Offa, king of the Mercians, ordered King Æthelberht's head to be struck off.

AN 794 In this year Pope Hadrian and King Offa passed away, and Æthelred, king of the Northumbrians, was killed by his own people, and Bishop Ceolwulf and Bishop Eadbald departed from the land, and Ecgfrith succeeded to the kingdom of the Mercians and passed away the same year. And Eadberht, whose other name was Præn, succeeded to the kingdom in Kent.

AN 796 In this year Coenwulf, king of the Mercians, laid waste the land of the people of Kent as far as Romney Marsh, and captured Præn, their king, and led him bound into Mercia.

AN 797 Her Romane Leone þæm papan his tungon forcurfon ond his eagan astungon ond hine of his setle afliemdon, ond þa sona eft, Gode fultomiendum, he meahte geseon ond sprecan ond eft was papa swa he ær wæs.

AN 799 Her Æþelheard ærcebiscep ond Cynebryht, Wesseaxna biscep, foron to Rome.

AN 800 Her Beorhtric cyning forþferde ond Worr aldormon. Ond Ecgbryht feng to Wesseaxna rice. Ond þy ilcan dæge rad Æþelmund aldorman of Hwiccium ofer æt Cynemæresforda; þa mette hine Weoxstan aldorman mid Wilsætum. Þær wearþ micel gefeoht, ond þær begen ofslægene þa aldormen, ond Wilsætan namon sige.

AN 802 Her wæs gehadod Beornmod biscep to Hrofesceastre.

AN 803 Her Æþelheard ærcebiscep forþferde, ond Wulfred wæs to ærcebiscepe gehadod, ond Forþred abbud forþferde.

AN 804 Her Wulfred ærcebiscep pallium onfeng.

AN 797 In this year the Romans cut off the tongue of Pope Leo and stabbed him in the eyes and expelled him from his see; and then immediately afterward, with God's help, he could both see and speak, and was pope again as he was before.

—

AN 799 In this year Archbishop Æthelheard and Cynebryht, bishop of the West Saxons, traveled to Rome.

AN 800 In this year King Beorhtric and Ealdorman Worr passed away. And Ecgberht succeeded to the kingdom of the West Saxons. And on the same day Ealdorman Æthelmund rode from the Hwicce over to Kempsford, where Ealdorman Weoxstan met him with the men of Wiltshire. There ensued a major battle, and both ealdormen were killed there, and the men of Wiltshire took the victory.

—

AN 802 In this year Beornmod was consecrated bishop of Rochester.

AN 803 In this year Archbishop Æthelheard passed away, and Wulfred was consecrated archbishop, and Abbot Forthred passed away.

AN 804 In this year Archbishop Wulfred received the pallium.

AN 805 Her Cuþred cyning forþferde on Cantwarum, ond Ceolburg abbudesse, ond Heabryht aldormon.

AN 812 Her Carl cyning forþferde, ond he ricsode XLV wintra, ond Wulfred arcebiscep ond Wigbryht, Wesseaxna biscep, foron begen to Rome.

AN 813 Her Wulfred ærcebiscep mid bledsunge þæs papan Leon hwearf eft to his agnum biscepdome, ond þy geare gehergade Ecgbryht cyning on Westwalas from easteweardum oþ westewearde.

AN 814 Her Leo, se æþela papa ond se halga, forþferde, ond æfter him Stephanus feng to rice.

AN 816 Her Stephanus papa forþferde, ond æfter him was Paschalis to papan gehadod, ond þy ilcan geare forborn Ongolcynnes scolu.

AN 819 Her Cenwulf, Miercna cyning, forþferde, ond Ceolwulf feng to rice, ond Eadbryht aldormon forþferde.

AN 821 Her wearþ Ceolwulf his rices besciered.

AN 805 In this year King Cuthred passed away among the people of Kent, and so did Abbess Ceolburg and Ealdorman Heahberht.

———

AN 812 In this year King Charlemagne passed away, having reigned for forty-five years, and Archbishop Wulfred and Wigberht, bishop of the West Saxons, both journeyed to Rome.

AN 813 In this year Archbishop Wulfred returned to his own see with the blessing of Pope Leo, and that year King Ecgberht went raiding in Cornwall from east to west.

AN 814 In this year the noble and holy Pope Leo passed away, and Stephen succeeded him.

———

AN 816 In this year Pope Stephen passed away, and after him Paschal was consecrated pope, and the same year the English Quarter in Rome burned down.

———

AN 819 In this year Coenwulf, king of the Mercians, passed away, and Ceolwulf succeeded to the kingdom, and Ealdorman Eadberht passed away.

———

AN 821 In this year Ceolwulf was deprived of his kingdom.

AN 822 Her tuegen aldormen wurdon ofslægene, Burghelm ond Muca. Ond senoþ wæs æt Clofeshoo.

AN 823 Her wæs Wala gefeoht ond Defna æt Gafulforda, ond þy ilcan geare gefeaht Ecgbryht cyning ond Beornwulf cyning on Ellendune. Ond Ecgbryht sige nam, ond þær wæs micel wæl geslægen. Þa sende he Æþelwulf his sunu of þære fierde, ond Ealhstan, his biscep, ond Wulfheard, his aldormon, to Cent micle werede, ond hie Baldred þone cyning norþ ofer Temese adrifon. Ond Cantware him to cirdon, ond Suþrige, ond Suþseaxe, ond Eastseaxe, þy hie from his mægum ær mid unryhte anidde wærun. Ond þy ilcan geare Eastengla cyning ond seo þeod gesohte Ecgbryht cyning him to friþe ond to mundboran for Miercna ege, ond þy geare slogon Eastengle Beornwulf, Miercna cyning.

AN 825 Her Ludecan, Miercna cyning, ond his v aldormen mon ofslog mid him, ond Wiiglaf feng to rice.

AN 827 Her mona aþistrode on middes wintres mæsseniht, ond þy ilcan geare geeode Ecgbryht cyning Miercna rice ond al þæt be suþan Humbre

AN 822 In this year two ealdormen, Burghelm and Muca, were killed. And there was a synod at *Clofesho.*

AN 823 In this year there was a battle at Galford between the Britons and men of Devon, and the same year King Ecgberht and King Beornwulf fought at Wroughton. And Ecgberht took the victory, and there was a great slaughter there. He then sent his son, Æthelwulf, and Ealhstan, his bishop, and Wulfheard, his ealdorman, away from the levies with a large body of men to Kent, and these drove King Baldred north over the Thames. And the people of Kent went over to him, along with the people of Surrey, the South Saxons, and the East Saxons, since earlier they had been unjustly forced away from his kinsmen. And the same year, for fear of the Mercians, the king and the people of the East Angles sought King Ecgberht for security and protection, and in this same year the East Angles killed Beornwulf, the king of the Mercians.

———

AN 825 In this year Ludeca, king of the Mercians, was killed, and his five ealdormen with him, and Wiglaf took power.

———

AN 827 In this year the moon grew dark on Christmas Eve, and the same year King Ecgberht conquered the kingdom of the Mercians and all that was wæs, ond he wæs se eahteþa cyning se þe Bretwalda wæs. Ærest Ælle, Suþseaxna cyning, se þus micel rice hæfde. Se æftera wæs Ceawlin, Wesseaxna cyning. Se þridda wæs Æþelbryht, Cantwara cyning. Se feorþa wæs Rædwald, Eastengla cyning. Fifta was Eadwine, Norþanhymbra cyning. Siexta wæs Oswald, se æfter him ricsode. Seofoþa wæs Oswio, Oswaldes broþur. Eahtoþa wæs Ecgbryht, Wesseaxna cyning. Ond se Ecgbryht lædde fierd to Dore wiþ Norþanhymbre, ond hie him þær eaþmedo budon ond geþuærnesse, ond hie on þam tohwurfon.

AN 828 Her eft Wiglaf onfeng Miercna rices, ond Æþelwald biscep forþferde. Ond þy ilcan geare lædde Ecgbryht cyning fierd on Norþwalas, ond he hie to eaþmodre hersumnesse gedyde.

AN 829 Her Wulfred ærcebiscep forþferde.

AN 830 Her Ceolnoþ wæs gecoren to biscepe ond gehadod, ond Feologild abbud forþferde.

AN 831 Her Ceolnoþ ærcebiscep onfeng pallium.

AN 832 Her hæþne men oferhergeadon Sceapige.

AN 833 Her gefeaht Ecgbryht wiþ xxxv sciphlæsta æt Carrum, ond þær wearþ micel wæl geslægen, south of the Humber, and he was the eighth king to be Bretwalda. The first who had so great a power was Ælle, king of the South Saxons. The second was Ceawlin, king of the West Saxons. The third was Æthelberht, king of the people of Kent. The fourth was Rædwald, king of the East Angles. Fifth was Edwin, king of the Northumbrians. Sixth was Oswald, who ruled after him. Seventh was Oswiu, Oswald's brother. Eighth was Ecgberht, king of the West Saxons. And this Ecgberht led his levies to Dore to confront the Northumbrians, where they offered him submission and peace, and on that they parted.

AN 828 In this year Wiglaf again seized the kingdom of the Mercians, and Bishop Æthelwald passed away. And the same year King Ecgberht led his troops against the Welsh, and he brought them to humble submission.

AN 829 In this year Archbishop Wulfred passed away.

AN 830 In this year Ceolnoth was chosen as bishop and consecrated, and Abbot Feologild passed away.

AN 831 In this year Archbishop Ceolnoth received the pallium.

AN 832 In this year heathen men went raiding across Sheppey.

AN 833 In this year King Ecgberht fought against thirty-five ship's companies of vikings at Carhampton, and great slaughter was inflicted there, and the ond þa Denescan ahton wælstowe gewald. Ond Hereferþ ond Wigþen, tuegen biscepas, forþferdon, ond Dudda ond Osmod, tuegen aldormen, forþferdon.

AN 835 Her cuom micel sciphere on Westwalas, ond hie to anum gecierdon ond wiþ Ecgbryht, Westseaxna cyning, winnende wæron. Þa he þæt hierde ond mid fierde ferde ond him wiþ feaht æt Hengestdune, ond þær gefliemde ge þa Walas ge þa Deniscan.

AN 836 Her Ecgbryht cyning forþferde. Ond hine hæfde ær Offa Miercna cyning ond Beorhtric Wesseaxna cyning afliemed III gear of Angelcynnes lande on Fronclond, ær he cyning wære. Ond þy fultomode Beorhtric Offan, þy he hæfde his dohtor him to cuene. Ond se Ecgbryht ricsode XXXVII wintra, VII monaþ, ond feng Æþelwulf Ecgbrehting to Wesseaxna rice, ond he salde his suna Æþelstane Cantwara rice ond Eastseaxna ond Suþrigea ond Suþseaxna.

AN 837 Her Wulfheard aldormon gefeaht æt Hamtune wiþ XXXIII sciphlæsta ond þær micel wæl geslog ond sige nom, ond þy geare forþferde Wulfheard. Ond þy ilcan geare gefeaht Æþelhelm *dux* wiþ Deniscne here on Port mid Dornsætum ond

Danes had control of the place of slaughter. And two bishops, Hereferth and Wigthegn, and two ealdormen, Dudda and Osmod, passed away.

AN 835 In this year a large viking fleet arrived in Cornwall, and they joined together in a single force and proceeded to fight against Ecgberht, king of the West Saxons. When he heard about this, he went with his levies and fought them at Hingston Down, and there put to flight both the people of Cornwall and the Danes.

AN 836 In this year Ecgberht passed away. Before he became king, Offa, king of the Mercians, and Beorhtric, king of the West Saxons, had expelled him from the land of the English into Francia for three years. Beorhtric had helped Offa, because he had his daughter as his queen. Now this Ecgberht had reigned for thirty-seven years and seven months, and Ecgberht's son Æthelwulf succeeded to the kingdom of the West Saxons, handing over to his son Æthelstan the kingdom of the people of Kent and of the East Saxons, the people of Surrey, and the South Saxons.

AN 837 In this year Ealdorman Wulfheard fought at Southampton against thirty-three ship's companies and inflicted great slaughter there and took the victory; and that year Wulfheard passed away. And that same year Ealdorman Æthelhelm, with the men of Dorset, fought against a Danish force gode hwile þone here gefliemde. Ond þa Deniscan ahton wælstowe gewald ond þone aldormon ofslogon.

AN 838 Her Herebryht aldormon wæs ofslægen from hæþnum monnum ond monige mid him on Merscwarum, ond þy ilcan geare eft on Lindesse ond on Eastenglum ond on Cantwarum wurdon monige men ofslægene from þam herige.

AN 839 Her wæs micel wælsliht on Lundenne ond on Cwantawic ond on Hrofesceastre.

AN 840 Her Æþelwulf cyning gefeaht æt Carrum wiþ xxxv sciphlæsta, ond þa Deniscan ahton wælstowe gewald.

———

AN 845 Her Eanulf aldorman gefeaht mid Sumursætum, ond Ealchstan biscep ond Osric aldorman mid Dornsætum gefuhton æt Pedridan muþan wiþ Deniscne here ond þær micel wæl geslogon ond sige namon.

———

AN 851 Her Ceorl aldormon gefeaht wiþ hæþene men mid Defenascire æt Wicganbeorge, ond þær micel wæl geslogon ond sige namon. Ond þy ilcan at Portland and for a good amount of time put the army to flight. However, the Danes were left in possession of the place of slaughter and killed that ealdorman.

AN 838 In this year Ealdorman Hereberht was killed by heathen men, and many with him among the people around Romney Marsh, and again later the same year, in Lindsey and among the East Angles and the inhabitants of Kent, many men were killed by the viking army.

AN 839 In this year there was great slaughter in London, and in Quentovic, and in Rochester.

AN 840 In this year King Æthelwulf fought against thirty-five ship's companies of vikings at Carhampton, and the Danes had possession of the place of slaughter.

AN 845 In this year Ealdorman Eanwulf, with the men of Somerset, and Bishop Ealhstan and Ealdorman Osric, with the men of Dorset, fought against a Danish force at the mouth of the River Parret and inflicted a great slaughter there, taking the victory.

AN 851 In this year Ealdorman Ceorl with the men of Devon fought against heathen men at *Wicganbeorg,* inflicted great slaughter, and took the geare Æþelstan cyning ond Ealchere *dux* micelne here ofslogon æt Sondwic on Cent ond IX scipu gefengun ond þa oþre gefliemdon. Ond hæþne men ærest ofer winter sæton. Ond þy ilcan geare cuom feorðe healf hund scipa on Temese muþan ond bræcon Contwaraburg ond Lundenburg ond gefliemdon Beorhtwulf, Miercna cyning, mid his fierde ond foron þa suþ ofer Temese on Suþrige. Ond him gefeaht wiþ Æþelwulf cyning ond Æþelbald his sunu æt Aclea mid Westseaxna fierde, ond þær þæt mæste wæl geslogon on hæþnum herige þe we secgan hierdon oþ þisne ondweardan dæg, ond þær sige namon.

AN 853 Her bæd Burgred, Miercna cyning, ond his wiotan Æþelwulf cyning þæt he him gefultumade þæt him Norþwalas gehiersumade. He þa swa dyde ond mid fierde for ofer Mierce on Norþwalas, ond hie him alle gehiersume dydon. Ond þy ilcan geare sende Æþelwulf cyning Ælfred his sunu to Rome. Þa was domne Leo papa on Rome, ond he hine to cyninge gehalgode ond hiene him to biscepsuna nam. Þa þy ilcan geare Ealhere, mid Cantwarum, ond Huda, mid Suþrigium, gefuhton on Tenet wiþ hæþnum herige ond ærest sige namon, ond þær wearþ monig mon ofslægen ond adruncen on gehwæþere hond. Ond þæs victory. And the same year King Æthelstan and Ealdorman Ealhhere destroyed an army at Sandwich in Kent, captured nine ships, and put the others to flight. And heathen men for the first time stayed over the winter. And the same year three hundred and fifty ships came into the mouth of the Thames and took Canterbury and London by storm, and they put to flight Beorhtwulf, king of the Mercians, with his levies, and then moved south over the Thames into Surrey. And King Æthelwulf and his son Æthelbald, with the West Saxon levies, fought against them at *Aclea,* and there inflicted the greatest slaughter on a heathen army that we have heard tell of up to this present day, and there took the victory.

AN 853 In this year Burgred, king of the Mercians, and his councilors asked King Æthelwulf to help them to subject the Welsh people to them. He did so, and with his levies he crossed Mercia into Wales, and they made all the people of that area subject to them. And the same year King Æthelwulf sent his son Alfred to Rome. At that time, the lord Leo was pope in Rome, and he consecrated the boy as king and took him as his godson. Then that same year Ealhhere, with the people of Kent, and Huda, with the men of Surrey, fought in Thanet against a heathen army, and at first were victorious, and there was many a man cut down or drowned on both sides. And ofer Eastron geaf Æþelwulf cyning his dohtor Burgrede cyninge of Wesseaxum on Merce.

AN 855 Her hæþne men ærest on Sceapige ofer winter sætun. Ond þy ilcan geare gebocude Æþelwulf cyning teoþan dæl his londes ofer al his rice Gode to lofe ond him selfum to ecere hælo. Ond þy ilcan geare ferde to Rome mid micelre weorþnesse ond þær was XII monaþ wuniende ond þa him hamweard for. Ond him þa Carl, Francna cyning, his dohtor geaf him to cuene, ond æfter þam to his leodum cuom, ond hie þæs gefægene wærun. Ond ymb II gear þæs ðe he of Francum com he gefor, ond his lic liþ æt Wintanceastre, ond he ricsode nigonteoþe healf gear.

2 Ond se Æþelwulf wæs Ecgbrehting, Ecgbryht Ealhmunding, Ealhmund Eafing, Eafa Eopping, Eoppa Ingilding. Ingild wæs Ines broþur, Westseaxna cyninges, þæs þe eft ferde to sancte Petre ond þær eft his feorh gesealde, ond hie wæron Cenredes suna. Cenred wæs Ceolwalding, Ceolwald Cuþaing, Cuþa Cuþwining, Cuþwine Ceaulining, Ceawlin Cynricing, Cynric Cerdicing, Cerdic Elesing, Elesa Esling, Esla Giwising, Giwis Wiging, Wig Freawining, Freawine Friþogaring, Friþogar Bronding, Brond Bældæging,

then after Easter, King Æthelwulf gave his daughter in marriage from the West Saxons to King Burgred of the Mercians.

AN 855 In this year heathen men for the first time overwintered in Sheppey. And the same year King Æthelwulf "booked" the tenth part of his land throughout all his kingdom for the glory of God and his own eternal salvation. And the same year he traveled to Rome in great state and remained there for twelve months before setting off homeward. And Charles the Bald, king of the Franks, gave him his daughter as queen, after which he returned to his own people and they were delighted at that. And two years after he returned from the land of the Franks, he died, and his body lies at Winchester; he had reigned for eighteen and a half years.

Now this Æthelwulf was Ecgberht's son, Ecg- 2
berht Ealhmund's son, Ealhmund Eafa's son, Eafa Eoppa's son, Eoppa Ingeld's son. Ingeld was the brother of Ine, the West Saxon king, who afterward went to Rome to Saint Peter's and there gave up his life, and they were sons of Cenred. Cenred was Ceolwald's son, Ceolwald Cutha's son, Cutha Cuthwine's son, Cuthwine Ceawlin's son, Ceawlin Cynric's son, Cynric Cerdic's son, Cerdic Elesa's son, Elesa Esla's son, Esla Gewis's son, Gewis Wig's son, Wig Freawine's son, Freawine Frithugar's son, Frithugar Brand's son,

Bældæg Wodening, Woden Friþowalding, Friþuwald Frealafing, Frealaf Friþuwulfing, Friþuwulf Finning, Fin Godwulfing, Godwulf Geating, Geat Tætwaing, Tætwa Beawing, Beaw Sceldwaing, Sceldwea Heremoding, Heremod Itermoning, Itermon Hraþraing (se wæs geboren in þære earce), Noe, Lamach, Matusalem, Enoh, Iaered, Maleel, Cainan, Enos, Sed, Adam, *primus homo, et pater noster est Christus, amen.*

3 Ond þa fengon Æþelwulfes suna twegen to rice, Æþelbald to Wesseaxna rice ond Æþelbryht to Cantwara rice ond to Eastseaxna rice ond to Suþrigea ond to Suþseaxna rice, ond þa ricsode Æþelbald v gear.

AN 860 Her Æþelbald cyng forþferde, ond his lic liþ æt Sciraburnan, ond feng Æþelbryht to allum þam rice his broþur, ond he hit heold on godre geþuærnesse ond on micelre sibsumnesse. Ond on his dæge cuom micel sciphere up ond abræcon Wintanceastre, ond wiþ þone here gefuhton Osric aldorman, mid Hamtunscire, ond Æþelwulf aldormon, mid Bearrucscire, ond þone here gefliemdon ond wælstowe gewald ahton. Ond se Æþelbryht ricsode v gear, ond his lic liþ æt Sciraburnan.

Brand Bældæg's son, Bældæg Woden's son, Woden Frithuwald's son, Frithuwald Frealaf's son, Frealaf Frithuwulf's son, Frithuwulf Finn's son, Finn Godwulf's son, Godwulf Geat's son, Geat Tætwa's son, Tætwa Beaw's son, Beaw Sceldwea's son, Sceldwea Heremod's son, Heremod Itermon's son, Itermon Hrathra's son (he was born in the ark), Noah, Lamech, Methuselah, Enoch, Jared, Mahalaleel, Cainan, Enos, Seth, Adam, *the first man, and our father is Christ, amen.*

And then Æthelwulf's two sons came to 3
power, Æthelbald taking the kingdom of the West Saxons, and Æthelberht the kingdoms of the people of Kent, and the East Saxons and the people of Surrey, and the South Saxons, and Æthelbald then reigned for five years.

AN 860 In this year King Æthelbald passed away—his body lies at Sherborne—and his brother Æthelberht succeeded to the entire kingdom and held it in good harmony and great peace. And in his day a large enemy fleet arrived and took Winchester by storm, but Ealdorman Osric, with the men of Hampshire, and Ealdorman Æthelwulf, with the men of Berkshire, fought against the raiding army and put them to flight and had control of the place of slaughter. And the above mentioned Æthelberht reigned for five years and his body lies at Sherborne.

AN 865 Her sæt hæþen here on Tenet ond genamon friþ wiþ Cantwarum, ond Cantware him feoh geheton wiþ þam friþe. Ond under þam friþe ond þam feohgehate se here hiene on niht up bestæl ond oferhergeade alle Cent eastewearde.

AN 866 Her feng Æþered Æþelbryhtes broþur to Wesseaxna rice, ond þy ilcan geare cuom micel here on Angelcynnes lond ond wintersetl namon on Eastenglum, ond þær gehorsude wurdon, ond hie him friþ wiþ namon.

AN 867 Her for se here of Eastenglum ofer Humbre muþan to Eoforwicceastre on Norþhymbre. Ond þær wæs micel unþuærnes þære þeode betweox him selfum, ond hie hæfdun hiera cyning aworpenne Osbryht ond ungecyndne cyning underfengon Ællan, ond hie late on geare to þam gecirdon þæt hie wiþ þone here winnende wærun. Ond hie þeah micle fierd gegadrodon ond þone here sohton æt Eoforwicceastre ond on þa ceastre bræcon, ond hie sume inne wurdon. Ond þær was ungemetlic wæl geslægen Norþanhymbra, sume binnan, sume butan, ond þa cyningas begen ofslægene, ond sio laf wiþ þone here friþ nam. Ond þy ilcan geare gefor

AN 865 In this year a heathen army stayed on in Thanet and made peace with the people of Kent, and in return for that peace, the people of Kent promised them money. However, under the cover of that peace and that promise of money, the army stole away by night and went raiding across the whole of the eastern part of Kent.

AN 866 In this year Æthelred, brother of Æthelberht, succeeded to the kingdom of the West Saxons, and that same year a large army invaded the land of the English and took winter quarters among the East Angles, and they were provided with horses there, and the East Angles made peace with them.

AN 867 In this year that army left East Anglia and crossed the mouth of the Humber to the city of York in Northumbria. And there was a great amount of discord among the people of that region, and they had cast out their king, Osberht, and accepted Ælle, a king not of royal blood, and it was late in the year by the time that they turned to fighting against the army. Nevertheless, they gathered a large levy of men and sought out the army at the city of York and broke into the city, and some of them got inside the fortifications. Immeasurable slaughter was inflicted on the Northumbrians there, some inside and some out, and both their rival kings were killed, and the survivors made peace with the army. And the same year Bishop Ealhstan departed this life; he

Ealchstan biscep, ond he hæfde þæt bisceprice L wintra æt Scireburnan, ond his lic liþ þær on tune.

AN 868 Her for se ilca here innan Mierce to Snotengaham ond þær wintersetl namon. Ond Burgræd Miercna cyning ond his wiotan bædon Æþered Westseaxna cyning ond Ælfred his broþur þæt hie him gefultumadon, þæt hie wiþ þone here gefuhton. Ond þa ferdon hie mid Wesseaxna fierde innan Mierce oþ Snotengaham ond þone here þær metton on þam geweorce. Ond þær nan hefelic gefeoht ne wearþ, ond Mierce friþ namon wiþ þone here.

AN 869 Her for se here eft to Eoforwicceastre ond þær sæt I gear.

AN 870 Her rad se here ofer Mierce innan Eastengle ond wintersetl namon æt Þeodforda, ond þy wintra Eadmund cyning him wiþ feaht, ond þa Deniscan sige namon ond þone cyning ofslogon ond þæt lond all geeodon. Ond þy geare gefor Ceolnoþ ærcebiscep.

AN 871 Her cuom se here to Readingum on Westseaxe, ond þæs ymb III niht ridon II eorlas up. Þa gemette hie Æþelwulf aldorman on Englafelda ond him þær wiþ gefeaht ond sige nam. Þæs ymb IV niht Æþered cyning ond Ælfred his broþur þær micle fierd to Readingum gelæddon ond wiþ had held the episcopal see at Sherborne for fifty years, and his body lies there in the town.

AN 868 In this year the same army moved into Mercia as far as Nottingham and took winter quarters there. And Burgred, king of the Mercians, and his councilors asked Æthelred, king of the West Saxons, and his brother Alfred to help them fight against that army. Then they went with the levies of the West Saxons into Mercian territory all the way to Nottingham and encountered the army there in the stronghold. But no serious fighting occurred there, and the Mercians made peace with the invaders.

AN 869 In this year the army returned to the city of York and stayed there for one year.

AN 870 In this year that army rode across Mercia into East Anglia and took winter quarters at Thetford, and that winter King Edmund fought against them, and the Danes took the victory and killed the king and conquered all that land. And this year Archbishop Ceolnoth departed this life.

AN 871 In this year the army moved on to Reading in Wessex, and three days after this two *jarls* rode up-country. Then Ealdorman Æthelwulf intercepted them at Englefield, fought against them there, and was victorious. Four days later, King Æthelred and Alfred, his brother, led a large levy of men to Reading and fought against the army, þone here gefuhton, ond þær wæs micel wæl geslægen on gehwæþre hond. Ond Æþelwulf aldormon wearþ ofslægen, ond þa Deniscan ahton wælstowe gewald. Ond þæs ymb IV niht gefeaht Æþered cyning ond Ælfred his broþur wiþ alne þone here on Æscesdune. Ond hie wærun on twæm gefylcum: on oþrum wæs Bachsecg ond Halfdene þa hæþnan cyningas, ond on oþrum wæron þa eorlas. Ond þa gefeaht se cyning Æþered wiþ þara cyninga getruman, ond þær wearþ se cyning Bagsecg ofslægen. Ond Ælfred his broþur wiþ þara eorla getruman, ond þær wearþ Sidroc eorl ofslægen se alda, ond Sidroc eorl se gioncga, ond Osbearn eorl, ond Fræna eorl, ond Hareld eorl, ond þa hergas begen gefliemde, ond fela þusenda ofslægenra. Ond onfeohtende wæron oþ niht. Ond þæs ymb XIV niht gefeaht Æþered cyning ond Ælfred his broður wiþ þone here æt Basengum, ond þær þa Deniscan sige namon. Ond þæs ymb II monaþ gefeaht Æþered cyning ond Ælfred his broþur wiþ þone here æt Meretune, ond hie wærun on tuæm gefylcium, ond hie butu gefliemdon ond longe on dæg sige ahton. Ond þær wearþ micel wælsliht on gehwæþere hond, ond þa Deniscan ahton wælstowe gewald. Ond þær wearþ Heahmund biscep ofslægen ond fela godra monna. Ond æfter þissum gefeohte cuom micel sumorlida. Ond þæs ofer Eastron gefor Æþered cyning, ond he ricsode v gear, ond his lic liþ æt Winburnan.

and there was much slaughter inflicted on each side. Ealdorman Æthelwulf was killed, and the Danes had control of the battlefield. And four days after that, King Æthelred and Alfred, his brother, fought against the army at Ashdown. It was in two troops: Bagsecg and Healfdene, the heathen kings, were in one troop, and in the other were the *jarls*. And King Æthelred fought against the kings' troops, and King Bagsecg was killed there. And Alfred his brother fought against the *jarls'* troops, and there *Jarl* Sidroc the Old was killed along with *Jarl* Sidroc the Young, and *Jarl* Osbearn, and *Jarl* Fræna, and *Jarl* Harold, and both of the enemy's forces were put to flight, and many thousands of people slaughtered. And they kept on fighting until night. And a fortnight later King Æthelred and Alfred, his brother, fought against the army at Basing and there the Danes took the victory. And two months later King Æthelred and Alfred, his brother, fought against the army at *Meretun* and this was again in two bands, and they put both to flight, and had that victory, long into the day. There was great slaughter on both sides, but the Danes had control of the battlefield. And Bishop Heahmund was killed there and many good men. And after this fight, a large summer fleet arrived. And then after Easter, King Æthelred departed this life; he had reigned for five years, and his body lies at Wimborne.

2 Þa feng Ælfred Æþelwulfing his broþur to Wesseaxna rice. Ond þæs ymb anne monaþ gefeaht Ælfred cyning wiþ alne þone here lytle werede æt Wiltune ond hine longe on dæg gefliemde, ond þa Deniscan ahton wælstowe gewald. Ond þæs geares wurdon ix folcgefeoht gefohten wiþ þone here on þy cynerice be suþan Temese, ond butan þam þe him Ælfred þæs cyninges broþur ond anlipig aldormon ond cyninges þegnas oft rade onridon þe mon na ne rimde. Ond þæs geares wærun ofslægene ix eorlas ond an cyning. Ond þy geare namon Westseaxe friþ wiþ þone here.

AN 872 Her for se here to Lundenbyrig from Readingum ond þær wintersetl nam, ond þa namon Mierce friþ wiþ þone here.

AN 873 Her for se here on Norþhymbre, ond he nam wintersetl on Lindesse æt Turecesiege, ond þa namon Mierce friþ wiþ þone here.

AN 874 Her for se here from Lindesse to Hreopedune ond þær wintersetl nam, ond þone cyning Burgræd ofer sæ adræfdon ymb xxii wintra þæs þe he rice hæfde ond þæt lond all geeodon. Ond he for to Rome ond þær gesæt, ond his lic liþ on sancta Marian ciricean on Angelcynnes scole. Ond þy ilcan geare hie sealdon anum unwisum cyninges þegne Miercna rice to haldanne, ond he

Then his brother Alfred, Æthelwulf's son, 2
succeeded to the kingdom of the West Saxons. And one month later, King Alfred, with a small band of men, fought at Wilton against the entire army, and long into the day put it to flight, and the Danes had control of the battlefield. And this year nine pitched battles were fought against the army in the kingdom to the south of the Thames, and that was apart from the forays which Alfred, the king's brother, and individual ealdormen and king's thegns frequently rode on, which were never counted. And during this year nine *jarls* were killed and one king. And this same year the West Saxons made peace with the army.

AN 872 In this year the army left Reading for London and took up winter quarters there, and the Mercians then made peace with the army.

AN 873 In this year the army moved to Northumbria, and took up winter quarters at Torksey in Lindsey, and the Mercians made peace with the army.

AN 874 In this year the army moved from Lindsey to Repton and took up winter quarters there, and they drove King Burgred across the sea, twenty-two years after he first came to power, and they subdued all that land. And he went to Rome and remained there, and his body lies in Saint Mary's Church in the English Quarter. And the same year the army gave the kingdom of the Mercians to a foolish king's thegn to hold, and he swore him aþas swor ond gislas salde þæt he him gearo wære swa hwelce dæge swa hie hit habban wolden, ond he gearo wære mid him selfum ond on allum þam þe him læstan woldon to þæs heres þearfe.

AN 875 Her for se here from Hreopedune, ond Healfdene for mid sumum þam here on Norþhymbre ond nam wintersetl be Tinan þære ei, ond se here þæt lond geeode ond oft hergade on Peohtas ond on Stræcledwalas. Ond for Godrum ond Oscytel ond Anwynd, þa III cyningas, of Hreopedune to Grantebrycge mid micle here ond sæton þær an gear. Ond þy sumera for Ælfred cyning ut on sæ mid sciphere ond gefeaht wiþ VII sciphlæstas ond hiera an gefeng ond þa oþru gefliemde.

AN 876 Her hiene bestæl se here into Werham Wesseaxna fierde, ond wiþ þone here se cyning friþ nam, ond him þa aþas sworon on þam halgan beage, þe hie ær nanre þeode noldon, þæt hie hrædlice of his rice foren, ond hie þa under þam hie nihtes bestælon þære fierde se gehorsoda here into Escanceaster. Ond þy geare Healfdene Norþanhymbra lond gedælde, ond ergende wæron ond hiera tilgende.

AN 877 Her cuom se here into Escanceastre from Werham. Ond se sciphere sigelede west ymbutan ond them oaths and gave hostages, that he would be ready for them, whatever day they should wish to have it back, and he himself would be ready, along with all those that would follow him to meet the needs of the army.

AN 875 In this year the army left Repton, and Healfdene went with part of it into Northumbria and took up winter quarters by the River Tyne; and the army overran that land and frequently went raiding among the Picts and the Strathclyde Britons. The three kings Guthrum, Oscetel, and Anund left Repton for Cambridge with a large army and stayed there for a year. And that summer King Alfred took an armed fleet out to sea and fought against seven ship's companies of vikings, capturing one of them and putting others to flight.

AN 876 In this year the army slipped away from the levies of the West Saxons into Wareham, and the king made peace with the army, and they swore him oaths on the sacred ring—something which earlier they had not wanted to do for any peoples—promising that they would speedily leave his kingdom; and under that cover at night, they slipped away from the levies into Exeter. And that year Healfdene shared out the lands of the Northumbrians, and they started plowing and tilling them.

AN 877 In this year the army now moved on to Exeter from Wareham. And the enemy fleet sailed west þa mette hie micel yst on sæ, ond þær forwearþ CXX scipa æt Swanawic. Ond se cyning Ælfred æfter þam gehorsudan here mid fierde rad oþ Exanceaster, ond hie hindan ofridan ne meahte ær hie on þam fæstene wæron, þær him mon to ne meahte. Ond hie him þær foregislas saldon, swa fela swa he habban wolde, ond micle aþas sworon ond þa godne friþ heoldon. Ond þa on hærfeste gefor se here on Miercna lond ond hit gedældon sum, ond sum Ceolwulfe saldon.

AN 878 Her hiene bestæl se here on midne winter ofer tuelftan niht to Cippanhamme ond geridon Wesseaxna lond ond gesæton ond micel þæs folces ofer sæ adræfdon, ond þæs oþres þone mæstan dæl hie geridon, ond him to gecirdon buton þam cyninge Ælfrede, ond he lytle werede unieþelice æfter wudum for ond on morfæstenum. Ond þæs ilcan wintra wæs Inwæres broþur ond Healfdenes on Westseaxum on Defenascire mid XXIII scipum, ond hiene mon þær ofslog ond DCCC monna mid him ond XL monna his heres. Ond þæs on Eastron worhte Ælfred cyning lytle werede geweorc æt Æþelingaeigge, ond of þam geweorce was winnende wiþ þone here ond Sumursætna se dæl, se þær niehst wæs.

along the coast, and a great storm at sea met them, and one hundred and twenty ships were lost there at Swanage. And King Alfred rode with his levies after the mounted army all the way to Exeter, and he could not overtake them before they were in the stronghold, where it was not possible to get at them. And they gave him preliminary hostages, as many as he wished to have, and swore great oaths, and held to a good peace. And then, in the autumn, the army moved into the land of the Mercians, dividing up some of it among themselves, and some they granted to Ceolwulf.

AN 878 In this year in midwinter after Twelfth Night the army stole away to Chippenham and rode all over the land of the West Saxons and occupied it, driving many of the population across the sea, and subduing the greatest part of the others, and these submitted to them, except for King Alfred, and he with a small band of men moved around with difficulty through woods and inaccessible marshland. And that same winter a brother of Inwær and Healfdene arrived in Wessex, in Devon, with twenty-three ships, and he was killed there, and eight hundred men with him, and forty other men of his army. And the following Easter, King Alfred, accompanied by a small band of men, built a fortification at Athelney, and from that fortification, he, with that part of the people of Somerset that lived nearest, proceeded to fight against the army.

2 Þa on þære seofoðan wiecan ofer Eastron, he gerad to Ecgbryhtes stane be eastan Sealwyda, ond him to comon þær ongen Sumorsæte alle, ond Wilsætan, ond Hamtunscir, se dæl se hiere behinon sæ was, ond his gefægene wærun. Ond he for ymb ane niht of þam wicum to Iglea, ond þæs ymb ane to Eþandune, ond þær gefeaht wiþ alne þone here ond hiene gefliemde ond him æfter rad oþ þæt geweorc ond þær sæt XIV niht. Ond þa salde se here him foregislas ond micle aþas þæt hie of his rice woldon ond him eac geheton þæt hiera kyning fulwihte onfon wolde, ond hie þæt gelæston swa. Ond þæs ymb III wiecan com se cyning to him, Godrum, þritiga sum þara monna þe in þam here weorþuste wæron, æt Alre, ond þæt is wiþ Æþelinggaeige, ond his se cyning þær onfeng æt fulwihte, ond his crismlising was æt Weþmor, ond he was XII niht mid þam cyninge, ond he hine miclum ond his geferan mid feo weorðude.

AN 879 Her for se here to Cirenceastre of Cippanhamme ond sæt þær an gear. Ond þy geare gegadrode an hloþ wicenga ond gesæt æt Fullanhamme be Temese. Ond þy ilcan geare aþiestrode sio sunne ane tid dæges.

AN 880 Her for se here of Cirenceastre on Eastengle ond gesæt þæt lond ond gedælde. Ond þy ilcan geare

Then in the seventh week after Easter he rode 2
to Ecgberht's Stone to the east of Selwood, and there came to join him all the people of Somerset and Wiltshire and that part of Hampshire which was on this side of the sea, and they rejoiced. And one day later he went from the camps to Iley, and the day after that to Edington, and there fought against the entire army and put it to flight, and he rode after it as far as its stronghold and put it under siege for fourteen days. And then the army gave him preliminary hostages and great oaths that they would depart from his kingdom, and they also promised him that their king would receive baptism; and they kept their word. And three weeks later King Guthrum, with thirty of the most highly regarded men in his army, came to him at Aller—and that is near Athelney—and there the king received him at baptism; and his *crismlysing* was at Wedmore; and he was twelve days with the king, who greatly honored him and his companions with valuable gifts.

AN 879 In this year the army moved from Chippenham to Cirencester and stayed there for a year. And that year a band of vikings gathered and settled at Fulham on the Thames. And the same year the sun grew dark for one hour of the day.

AN 880 In this year the army moved from Cirencester into East Anglia and settled that land and divided it up. And the same year the army that had earlier for se here ofer sæ þe ær on Fullanhomme sæt on Fronclond to Gend ond sæt þær an gear.

AN 881 Her for se here ufor on Fronclond, ond þa Francan him wiþ gefuhton, ond þær wearþ se here gehorsod æfter þam gefeohte.

AN 882 Her for se here up onlong Mæse feor on Fronclond ond þær sæt an gear. Ond þy ilcan geare for Ælfred cyning mid scipum ut on sæ ond gefeaht wiþ feower sciphlæstas Deniscra monna ond þara scipa tu genam. Ond þa men ofslægene wæron þe ðæron wæron, ond tuegen scipheras him on hond eodon, ond þa wæron miclum forslægene ond forwundode ær hie on hond eodon.

AN 883 Her for se here up on Scald to Cundoþ ond þær sæt an gear.

AN 884 Her for se here up on Sunnan to Embenum ond þær sæt an gear.

AN 885 Her todælde se foresprecena here on tu, oþer dæl east, oþer dæl to Hrofesceastre. Ond ymbsæton þa ceastre ond worhton oþer fæsten ymb hie selfe. Ond hie þeah þa ceastre aweredon oþþæt Ælfred com utan mid fierde. Þa eode se here to hiera scipum ond forlet þæt geweorc, ond hie stayed at Fulham went over the sea to Ghent in the land of the Franks and remained there for a year.

AN 881 In this year the army went further into the land of the Franks, and the Franks fought against them, and after the fight the army was provided with horses.

AN 882 In this year the army went up along the Meuse deep into the land of the Franks and stayed there for a year. And that same year King Alfred went out to sea with a naval force and fought against four ship's companies of Danes and captured two of the ships. The men that were on these were killed; and two shiploads surrendered to him, and they were badly beaten and severely wounded before they surrendered.

AN 883 In this year the army went up the Scheldt to Condé and stayed there for a year.

AN 884 In this year the army went up the Somme to Amiens and stayed there for a year.

AN 885 In this year the army just mentioned divided in two, one part going further east, the other part crossing over to Rochester. They besieged the city and built another stronghold around themselves. The inhabitants, however, defended the city until Alfred arrived from outside with his levy. Then the army went to their ships and abandoned their fortification and were divested of wurdon þær behorsude ond sona þy ilcan sumere ofer sæ gewiton. Ond þy ilcan geare sende Ælfred cyning sciphere on Eastengle. Sona swa hie comon on Sture muþan, þa metton hie xvi scipu wicenga ond wiþ ða gefuhton ond þa scipo alle geræhton ond þa men ofslogon. Þa hie þa hamweard wendon mid þære herehyþe, þa metton hie micelne sciphere wicenga ond þa wiþ þa gefuhton þy ilcan dæge, ond þa Deniscan ahton sige.

2 Þy ilcan geare ær middum wintra forþferde Carl, Francna cyning, ond hiene ofslog an efor. Ond ane geare ær his broður forþferde, se hæfde eac þæt westrice. Ond hie wæron begen Hloþwiges suna, se hæfde eac þæt westrice ond forþferde þy geare þe sio sunne aþiestrode. Se wæs Karles sunu þe Æþelwulf Westseaxna cyning his dohtor hæfde him to cuene. Ond þy ilcan geare gegadrode micel sciphere on Aldseaxum, ond þær wearþ micel gefeoht tua on geare. Ond þa Seaxan hæfdun sige, ond þær wæron Frisan mid. Þy ilcan geare feng Carl to þam westrice ond to allum þam westrice behienan Wendelsæ ond begeondan þisse sæ, swa hit his þridda fæder hæfde, butan Lidwiccium. Se Carl was Hloþwiges sunu, se Hloþwig was Carles broþur, se wæs Iuþyttan fæder þe Æþelwulf cyning hæfde, ond hie wæron Hloþwiges suna; se Hloþwig was þæs aldan

their horses there, and immediately that same summer they departed across the sea. The same year King Alfred sent a fleet to East Anglia. As soon as they came to the mouth of the Stour, they encountered sixteen ships of vikings and fought against them and seized all the ships and killed the men. Then when they were on their way home with their booty, they met a large fleet of vikings and then fought against them that same day, and the Danes had the victory.

The same year before midwinter, Carloman, 2
king of the Franks, passed away, killed by a wild boar. His brother, who also held power in the western kingdom, had passed away the previous year. They were both sons of the Louis who had also ruled the western kingdom and died in the year the sun darkened. He was the son of Charles the Bald, whose daughter Æthelwulf, king of the West Saxons, had as his queen. And the same year a large viking fleet assembled among the Old Saxons, and there was heavy fighting twice in the year. And the Old Saxons had the victory, and there were Frisians with them. That same year, Charles the Fat succeeded to that western kingdom and to all the western kingdom on this side of the Mediterranean and beyond this sea, as his great-grandfather Charlemagne had had it, apart from Brittany. This Charles was son of the Louis, who was the brother of the Charles who was father of Æthelwulf's wife, Judith, and they were both sons of the Louis the Pious who was

Carles sunu, se Carl was Pippenes sunu. Ond þy ilcan geare forþferde se goda papa Marinus, se gefreode Ongelcynnes scole be Ælfredes bene Westseaxna cyninges, ond he sende him micla gifa ond þære rode dæl þe Crist on þrowude. Ond þy ilcan geare se here on Eastenglum bræc friþ wiþ Ælfred cyning.

AN 886 Her for se here eft west þe ær east gelende ond þa up on Sigene ond þær wintersetl namon. Þy ilcan geare gesette Ælfred cyning Lundenburg ond him all Angelcyn to cirde þæt buton Deniscra monna hæftniede was, ond he þa befæste þa burg Æþerede aldormen to haldonne.

AN 887 Her for se here up þurh þa brycge æt Paris ond þa up andlang Sigene oþ Mæterne, oþ Cariei ond þa sæton þara ond innan Ionan tu winter on þam twam stedum. Ond þy ilcan geare forþferde Karl, Francna cyning, ond Earnulf his broþur sunu hine VI wicum ær he forþferde berædde æt þæm rice. Ond þa wearþ þæt rice todæled on V, ond V kyningas to gehalgode. Þæt wæs þeah mid Earnulfes geþafunge, ond hi cuædon þæt hie þæt to his honda healdan sceoldon, forþæm hira nan næs on fædren healfe to geboren buton him anum. Earnulf þa wunode on þæm londe be the son of the Charlemagne who was son of Pippin. And the same year there passed away the good pope Marinus who freed the English Quarter from taxes at the request of Alfred, king of the West Saxons, and also sent him great gifts and part of the cross on which Christ suffered. And the same year the army that had settled in East Anglia broke the peace with King Alfred.

AN 886 In this year the army that had earlier arrived in the east moved west again, and then went up the Seine and took winter quarters there. That same year King Alfred occupied London and all the English not in bondage to the Danes turned to him, and he then entrusted the town to Ealdorman Æthelred to hold.

AN 887 In this year the viking army went up through the bridge at Paris, and then up along the Seine to the Marne, as far as Chézy, and then stayed there and in the area of the Yonne for two years in those two places. And this same year Charles the Fat, king of the Franks, passed away, having six weeks earlier been dispossessed of his kingdom by Arnulf, his brother's son. And the kingdom was then divided into five, and five kings were consecrated as rulers. This was done with the consent of Arnulf, and they said it was right that they should hold it from his hands because none of them was born to it on the father's side except him alone. Arnulf then occupied the land to the eastan Rin, ond Roþulf þa feng to þæm middelrice, ond Oda to þæm westdæle, ond Beorngar ond Wiþa to Longbeardna londe ond to þæm londum on þa healfe muntes; ond þæt heoldun mid micelre unsibbe ond tu folcgefeoht gefuhton ond þæt lond oft ond gelome forhergodon, ond æghwæþer oþerne oftrædlice ut dræfde. Ond þy ilcan geare þe se here for forþ up ofer þa brycge æt Paris, Æþelhelm aldormon lædde Wesseaxna ælmessan ond Ælfredes cyninges to Rome.

AN 888 Her lædde Beocca aldormon Wesseaxna ælmessan ond Ælfredes cyninges to Rome, ond Æþelswiþ cuen, sio wæs Ælfredes sweostor cyninges, forþferde, ond hire lic liþ æt Pafian. Ond þy ilcan geare Æþered ercebiscep ond Æþelwold aldormon forþferdon on anum monþe.

AN 889 On þissum geare næs nan færeld to Rome, buton tuegen hleaperas Ælfred cyning sende mid gewritum.

AN 890 Her lædde Beornhelm abbud Westseaxna ælmessan to Rome ond Ælfredes cyninges. Ond Godrum se norþerna cyning forþferde, þæs fulluhtnama wæs Æþelstan, se wæs Ælfredes cyninges godsunu, ond he bude on Eastenglum ond þæt lond ærest gesæt. Ond þy ilcan geare for se here of Sigene to Sant Laudan, þæt is betueoh east of the Rhine, and Rudolf took control of the middle kingdom and Odo of the western part, and Berengar and Guido of the land of the Langobards and the territories on that side of the Alps; however, they held that with much discord, and they fought two general engagements and laid waste to that territory over and over again, each regularly driving the other out. And this, the same year that the viking army went up beyond the bridge at Paris, Ealdorman Æthelhelm conveyed the alms of the West Saxons and of King Alfred to Rome.

AN 888 In this year Ealdorman Beocca conveyed the alms of the West Saxons and King Alfred to Rome, and Queen Æthelswith, who was the sister of King Alfred, passed away, and her body lies at Pavia. And this same year Archbishop Æthelred and Ealdorman Æthelwald passed away in the same month.

AN 889 In this year there was no expedition to Rome, but King Alfred sent two couriers with letters.

AN 890 In this year Abbot Beornhelm conveyed the alms of the West Saxons and King Alfred to Rome. And Guthrum, the northern king, whose baptismal name was Æthelstan, passed away; he was King Alfred's godson, and he lived among the East Angles and was the first to settle in that land. And this same year the army moved from the Seine to Saint-Lô, which is on the border

Brettum ond Francum, ond Brettas him wiþ gefuhton ond hæfdon sige ond hie bedrifon ut on ane ea ond monige adrencton.

AN 891 Her for se here east, ond Earnulf cyning gefeaht wið ðæm rædehere ær þa scipu cuomon, mid Eastfrancum ond Seaxum ond Bægerum, ond hine gefliemde. Ond þrie Scottas comon to Ælfrede cyninge on anum bate butan ælcum gereþrum of Hibernia, þonon hi hi bestælon, forþon þe hi woldon for Godes lufan on elþiodignesse beon, hi ne rohton hwær. Se bat wæs geworht of þriddan healfre hyde þe hi on foron, ond hi namon mid him þæt hi hæfdun to seofon nihtum mete, ond þa comon hie ymb VII niht to londe on Cornwalum ond foron þa sona to Ælfrede cyninge. Þus hie wæron genemnde, Dubslane ond Maccbethu ond Maelinmun. Ond Swifneh, se betsta lareow þe on Scottum wæs, gefor.

2 Ond þy ilcan geare ofer Eastron, ymbe gangdagas oþþe ær, æteowde se steorra þe mon on boclæden hæt *cometa.* Sume men cweþaþ on Englisc þæt hit sie feaxede steorra, forþæm þær stent lang leoma of, hwilum on ane healfe, hwilum on ælce healfe.

AN 892 Her on þysum geare for se micla here þe we gefyrn ymbe spræcon eft of þæm eastrice westweard to Bunann ond þær wurdon gescipode, swa þæt hie asettan him on anne siþ ofer mid between the Bretons and the Franks; and the Bretons fought against them and had the victory, and forced them into a river and drowned many.

AN 891 In this year the army turned east, and King Arnulf, along with the East Franks, Saxons, and Bavarians, fought against the mounted army before the ships caught up with them, and put it to flight. And three Irishmen came to King Alfred from Ireland in a single boat without any oars, whence they had slipped away because they wished for the love of God to be in foreign parts, they did not care where. The boat that they traveled in was made of two and a half hides, and they took with them seven days' supply of food; and after seven days they came ashore in Cornwall and then went straight to King Alfred. Their names were Dubslane, Maccbethu, and Maelinmun. And Swifneh, the finest scholar there was among the Irish, departed this life.

After Easter that same year, around Rogation- 2
tide or earlier, there appeared the star that in
Latin is called *cometa.* Some people call it in
English a long-haired star, because a long beam
of light stands out from it, sometimes on one
side, sometimes on every side.

AN 892 In this year the great army that we spoke about earlier traveled back from the kingdom of the East Franks westward to Boulogne, and having been provided there with ships, they conveyed themselves over on a single occasion, horses and horsum mid ealle ond þa comon up on Limene muþan mid CCL scipa. Se muþa is on eastewerdre Cent æt þæs miclan wuda eastende þe we Andred hatað. Se wudu is eastlang ond westlang hund twelftiges mila lang oþþe lengra ond þritiges mila brad. Seo ea þe we ær ymbe spræcon lið ut of þæm wealda. On þa ea hi tugon up hiora scipu oþ þone weald IV mila fram þæm muþan uteweardum ond þær abræcon an geweorc inne on þæm fenne. Sæton feawa cirlisce men on ond wæs samworht. Þa sona æfter þæm com Hæsten mid LXXX scipa up on Temese muðan ond worhte him geweorc æt Middeltune, ond se oþer here æt Apuldre.

AN 893 On þys geare, þæt wæs ymb twelf monað þæs þe hie on þæm eastrice geweorc geworht hæfdon, Norþhymbre ond Eastengle hæfdon Ælfrede cyninge aþas geseald, ond Eastengle foregisla VI, ond þeh, ofer þa treowa, swa oft swa þa oþre hergas mid ealle herige ut foron, þonne foron hie, oþþe mid, oþþe on heora healfe an. Þa gegaderade Ælfred cyning his fierd ond for þæt he gewicode betwuh þæm twam hergum, þær þær he niehst rymet hæfde for wudufæstenne ond for wæterfæstenne, swa þæt he mehte ægþerne geræcan gif hie ænigne feld secan wolden. Þa foron all, and then came up into the estuary of the Lympne with two hundred and fifty ships. That estuary is in eastern Kent, at the east end of the great forest that we call the Andred. This forest is one hundred and twenty miles long from east to west or longer, and thirty miles broad. The river that we spoke about earlier flows out from that forest. On that river they towed their ships up as far as the forest, four miles from the outer part of the estuary and there destroyed a fortification within the marsh. A few rustics occupied it and it was half finished. Then immediately after that, Hæsten came with eighty ships up into the Thames estuary, and made himself a fortification at Milton; the other army did the same at Appledore.

AN 893 In this year, that was twelve months after they had constructed the fortification in the kingdom of the East Franks, the Northumbrians and East Angles had given oaths to King Alfred, and the East Angles had given six preliminary hostages, and yet, contrary to the agreement, as often as the other armies went out in full force, then they went out, either with them, or on their own. Then King Alfred gathered his levies and positioned himself between the two armies, where he was best placed with regard both to the fortification in the wood and the fortification by the water, so that he might reach either of them if they attempted to seek any open country. After hie siþþan æfter þæm wealda hloþum ond flocradum bi swa hwaþerre efes swa hit þonne fierdleas wæs, ond hi mon eac mid oþrum floccum sohte mæstra daga ælce oþþe on niht, ge of þære fierde, ge eac of þæm burgum. Hæfde se cyning his fierd on tu tonumen, swa þæt hie wæron simle healfe æt ham, healfe ute, butan þæm monnum þe þa burga healdan scolden.

2 Ne com se here oftor eall ute of þæm setum þonne tuwwa: oþre siþe þa hie ærest to londe comon, ær sio fierd gesamnod wære, oþre siþe þa hie of þæm setum faran woldon. Þa hie gefengon micle herehyð ond þa woldon ferian norþweardes ofer Temese in on Eastseaxe ongean þa scipu. Þa forrad sio fierd hie foran ond him wið gefeaht æt Fearnhamme ond þone here gefliemde ond þa herehyþa ahreddon. Ond hie flugon ofer Temese buton ælcum forda, þa up be Colne on anne iggað. Þa besæt sio fierd hie þær utan þa hwile þe hie þær lengest mete hæfdon. Ac hi hæfdon þa heora stemn gesetenne ond hiora mete genotudne, ond wæs se cyng þa þiderweardes on fære mid þære scire þe mid him fierdedon.

3 Þa he þa wæs þiderweardes ond sio oþeru fierd wæs hamweardes, ond ða Deniscan sæton þær behindan, forþæm hiora cyning wæs gewundod on þæm gefeohte, þæt hi hine ne mehton

that the enemy went through the forest in small groups and mounted bands, by whichever border was not watched over by the king's levies, and almost every day and also by night they were sought by other bands, both from the levies and also from the strongholds. The king had separated his levies into two, so that they were always half at home and half out, save for those that had to guard the strongholds.

2 The army did not all come out from the camps at the same time more than twice: once when they first came to land, before the levy was assembled, once when they wanted to leave the camps. Then, when they had seized much plunder, they wished to carry iṭ northward over the Thames into Essex to meet the ships. The levies then intercepted them and at Farnham fought against them and put the army to flight and recovered the plunder. And the survivors fled across the Thames without the help of a ford, then up along the river Colne onto an islet. There the levies besieged them for as long as they had food. But they had then completed their tour of duty and also consumed all their provisions, and the king was still on his way there with the division that was campaigning with him.

3 Then, when the king was on his way there and the other division of the levy was on its way home—though the Danes had remained there, their king having been wounded in the fight so that they could not transport him—the vikings

ferian, þa gegaderedon þa þe in Norþhymbrum bugeað ond on Eastenglum sum hund scipa ond foron suð ymbutan, ond sum feowertig scipa norþ ymbutan, ond ymbsæton an geweorc on Defnascire be þære norþsæ, ond þa þe suð ymbutan foron ymbsæton Exancester. Þa se cyng þæt hierde, þa wende he hine west wið Exanceastres mid ealre þære fierde, buton swiþe gewaldenum dæle easteweardes þæs folces.

4 Þa foron forð oþþe hie comon to Lundenbyrg ond þa, mid þæm burgwarum ond þæm fultume þe him westan com, foron east to Beamfleote. Wæs Hæsten þa þær cumen mid his herge þe ær æt Middeltune sæt, ond eac ṣe micla here wæs þa þærto cumen þe ær on Limene muþan sæt æt Apuldre. Hæfde Hæsten ær geworht þæt geweorc æt Beamfleote ond wæs þa ut afaren on hergaþ, ond wæs se micla here æt ham. Þa foron hie to ond gefliemdon þone here ond þæt geweorc abræcon ond genamon eal þæt þær binnan wæs, ge on feo, ge on wifum, ge eac on bearnum, ond brohton eall into Lundenbyrig, ond þa scipu eall oðþe tobræcon, oþþe forbærndon, oþþe to Lundenbyrig brohton, oþþe to Hrofesceastre. Ond Hæstenes wif ond his suna twegen mon brohte to þæm cyninge, ond he hi him eft ageaf, forþæm þe hiora wæs oþer his godsunu, oþer Æðeredes ealdormonnes: Hæfdon hi hiora onfangen ær Hæsten to Beamfleote come, ond he

who were living among the Northumbrians and East Angles gathered some hundred ships and went south around the coast, while some forty ships then went north round the coast and besieged a fortification in Devon by the North Sea, and those that had gone south along the coast besieged Exeter. When the king heard that, then he made his way west toward Exeter with all his levies, apart from a very small part that was active in the east.

This group continued on to London, and then, 4
with the people from the strongholds and what help came to them from the west, went east to Benfleet. Hæsten had arrived there with his army from Milton, and the great army which had earlier camped at Appledore on the mouth of the Lympne also joined him. On this occasion, Hæsten, having himself earlier constructed the fortification at Benfleet, had gone off on a raid, and the great army from Appledore was at home. Then the levies in the east got there and put the army to flight and destroyed the fortification and seized all that was inside it, both goods and women and also children, and brought all into London, and all the ships they either broke up or destroyed by fire, or brought to London or to Rochester. Hæsten's wife and his two sons were brought to the king, and he restored them to him, because one of them was his godson, the other Ealdorman Æthelred's: They had stood as godparents to them before Hæsten came to

him hæfde geseald gislas ond aðas, ond se cyng him eac wel feoh sealde, ond eac swa þa he þone cniht agef ond þæt wif. Ac sona swa hie to Beamfleote comon ond þæt geweorc geworht wæs, swa hergode he on his rice, þone ilcan ende þe Æþered his cumpæder healdan sceolde, ond eft oþre siþe he wæs on hergað gelend on þæt ilce rice, þa þa mon his geweorc abræc.

5 Þa se cyning hine þa west wende mid þære fierde wið Exancestres, swa ic ær sæde, ond se here þa burg beseten hæfde, þa he þærto gefaren wæs, þa eodon hie to hiora scipum. Þa he þa wið þone here þær wæst abisgod wæs, ond þa hergas wæron þa gegaderode begen to Sceobyrig on Eastseaxum ond þær geweorc worhtun, foron begen ætgædere up be Temese, ond him com micel eaca to, ægþer ge of Eastenglum ge of Norþhymbrum. Foron þa up be Temese oþþæt hie gedydon æt Sæferne, þa up be Sæferne.

6 Þa gegaderode Æþered ealdormon ond Æþelm ealdorman ond Æþelnoþ ealdorman, ond þa cinges þegnas þe þa æt ham æt þæm geweorcum wæron, of ælcre byrig be eastan Pedredan, ge be westan Sealwuda, ge be eastan, ge eac be norþan Temese, ond be westan Sæfern, ge

Benfleet, and he had given the king hostages and oaths, and the king had also granted him much wealth, and repeated this when he returned the boy and the woman. But as soon as they came to Benfleet and the fortification was made, Hæsten made raids on Alfred's kingdom—the same district which his son's godfather Æthelred had the task of controlling; and again a second time he was raiding in that same kingdom when his fortification was destroyed.

Now, as I reported earlier, the king had been 5
making his way west with his levies toward Exeter, troops from the Danelaw having besieged the stronghold; once he arrived there, they rejoined their ships. Then when he was occupied with the army in the west and the two other enemy forces had both gathered at Shoebury in the land of the East Saxons, they built a fortification there and went together up along the Thames, and great reinforcements came to them, both from the East Angles and from the Northumbrians. They continued up along the Thames until they arrived at the Severn, then up along the Severn.

Then there gathered Ealdorman Æthelred, 6
Ealdorman Æthelhelm, and Ealdorman Æthelnoth, and the king's thegns who were then at home in the fortifications, from every stronghold east of the Parret, both west and east of Selwood, and also north of the Thames and west of

eac sum dæl þæs Norðwealcynnes. Þa hie þa ealle gegaderode wæron, þa offoron hie þone here hindan æt Buttingtune on Sæferne staþe, ond hine þær utan besæton on ælce healfe on anum fæstenne. Þa hie ða fela wucena sæton on twa healfe þære e, ond se cyng wæs west on Defnum wiþ þone sciphere, þa wæron hie mid metelieste gewægde ond hæfdon micelne dæl þara horsa freten, ond þa oþre wæron hungre acwolen. Þa eodon hie ut to ðæm monnum þe on easthealfe þære e wicodon ond him wiþ gefuhton, ond þa Cristnan hæfdon sige, ond þær wearð Ordheh cyninges þegn ofslægen, ond eac monige oþre cyninges þegnas ofslægene, ond þara Deniscra þær wearð swiþe mycel geslegen, ond se dæl þe þær aweg com wurdon on fleame generede.

7 Þa hie on Eastseaxe comon to hiora geweorce ond to hiora scipum, þa gegaderade sio laf eft of Eastenglum ond of Norðhymbrum micelne here onforan winter ond befæston hira wif ond hira scipu ond hira feoh on Eastenglum, ond foron anstreces dæges ond nihtes, þæt hie gedydon on anre westre ceastre on Wirhealum, seo is Legaceaster gehaten. Þa ne mehte seo fird hie na hindan offaran ær hie wæron inne on þæm geweorce; besæton þeah þæt geweorc utan sume twegen dagas ond genamon ceapes eall þæt þær buton wæs ond þa men ofslogon þe hie foran forridan mehton butan geweorce ond þæt corn

the Severn, along with some portion of Welsh people. Then, when they had all assembled, they overtook the army from behind at Buttington on the bank of the Severn River, and besieged them on every side in a fortification there. When they had stayed for many weeks on the two sides of the river and the king was west in Devon confronting the enemy ships, the besieged were weighed down by lack of food and had eaten a large portion of the horses (the others had died of hunger). They then went out and fought against the men that were encamped on the east side of the river, and the Christians had the victory. Ordheah, the king's thegn, was killed there, and also many other king's thegns were killed, and very great slaughter was made there of the Danes; those that got away were saved by flight.

When they reached their fortification and 7
their ships in Essex, then before winter the remnant of the Danish army again assembled a great army from among the East Angles and the Northumbrians and secured their women and their ships and their possessions in East Anglia; they then traveled nonstop, day and night, until they arrived at a deserted city in the Wirral which is called Chester. Then the levies could not overtake them before they were inside the fortification; however, they besieged the fortification for some two days and took all the livestock that was outside it and killed the men outside the fortification that they could intercept on horseback

eall forbærndon ond mid hira horsum fretton on ælcre efenehðe. Ond þæt wæs ymb twelf monað þæs þe hie ær hider ofer sæ comon.

AN 894 Ond þa sona æfter þæm on ðys gere, for se here of Wirheale in on Norðwealas, forþæm hie ðær sittan ne mehton; þæt wæs forðy þe hie wæron benumene ægðer ge þæs ceapes ge þæs cornes ðe hie gehergod hæfdon. Þa hie ða eft ut of Norðwealum wendon mid þære herehyðe þe hie ðær genumen hæfdon, þa foron hie ofer Norðhymbra lond ond Eastengla, swa swa seo fird hie geræcan ne mehte, oþþæt hie comon on Eastseaxna lond easteweard, on an igland þæt is ute on þære sæ þæt is Meresig haten. Ond þa se here eft hamweard wende þe Exanceaster beseten hæfde, þa hergodon hie up on Suðseaxum neah Cisseceastre, ond þa burgware hie gefliemdon ond hira monig hund ofslogon ond hira scipu sumu genamon. Ða þy ilcan gere, onforan winter, þa Deniscan þe on Meresige sæton tugon hira scipu up on Temese ond þa up on Lygan. Þæt wæs ymb twa ger þæs þe hie hider ofer sæ comon.

AN 895 Ond þy ilcan gere worhte se foresprecena here geweorc be Lygan xx mila bufan Lundenbyrig. Þa þæs on sumera foron micel dæl þara burgwara ond eac swa oþres folces, þæt hie gedydon æt þara Deniscana geweorce ond þær wurdon gefliemde, ond sume feower cyninges þegnas and burned all the corn and with their horses stripped every surrounding area. And that was twelve months after they came here over the sea.

AN 894 And then immediately after that, in this year, the army moved from the Wirral into the territory of the Welsh; they could not stay there because they had been deprived both of the cattle and of the grain which they had plundered. Then when they returned from Wales with the plunder they had taken there, they traveled across the lands of the Northumbrians and the East Angles so that the levies could not get at them until they came into the eastern part of the land of the East Saxons, onto an island that is out in the sea, that is called Mersea. And when the army that had besieged Exeter turned homeward, then they went raiding in Sussex, near Chichester, and the townsfolk put them to flight and killed many hundreds of them and took some of their ships. Then this same year before winter the Danes that were staying on Mersea towed their ships up along the Thames and then up along the Lea. That was two years after they came here over the sea.

AN 895 In the same year the army mentioned above constructed a fortification by the Lea, twenty miles above London. Then in the summer a large part of the inhabitants, and also of other people, made their way to the Danish fortification and were put to flight there, and some four king's ofslægene. Þa þæs on hærfeste, þa wicode se cyng on neaweste þære byrig þa hwile þe hie hira corn gerypon, þæt þa Deniscan him ne mehton þæs ripes forwiernan. Þa sume dæge rad se cyng up bi þære eæ ond gehawade hwær mon mehte þa ea forwyrcan, þæt hie ne mehton þa scipu ut brengan. Ond hie ða swa dydon, worhton ða tu geweorc on twa healfe þære eas.

2 Þa hie ða þæt geweorc furþum ongunnen hæfdon ond þærto gewicod hæfdon, þa onget se here þæt hie ne mehton þa scipu ut brengan. Þa forleton hie hie ond eodon ofer land þæt hie gedydon æt Cwatbrycge be Sæfern ond þær gewerc worhton. Þa rad seo fird west æfter þæm herige, ond þa men of Lundenbyrig gefetedon þa scipu ond þa ealle þe hie alædan ne mehton tobræcon, ond þa þe þær stælwyrðe wæron binnan Lundenbyrig gebrohton. Ond þa Deniscan hæfdon hira wif befæst innan Eastengle ær hie ut of þæm geweorce foron. Þa sæton hie þone winter æt Cwatbrycge. Þæt wæs ymb þreo ger þæs þe hie on Limene muðan comon hider ofer sæ.

AN 896 Ða þæs on sumera on ðysum gere, tofor se here, sum on Eastengle, sum on Norðhymbre, ond þa þe feohlease wæron him þær scipu begeton ond suð ofer sæ foron to Sigene. Næfde se here, thegns killed. Then in harvesttime the king camped in the vicinity of the fortification while they reaped their corn, so that the Danish force could not prevent them from the reaping. Then one day the king rode up along the river and observed where the river might be obstructed so that they might not bring out their ships. And they then did so and made two fortifications on the two sides of the river.

Then as soon as they had begun that work and 2
had camped for that purpose, the army realized that they could not remove their ships. So then they abandoned them and went overland until they arrived at Bridgenorth by the Severn and made a fortification there. And the levies rode west after the army, and the men from London fetched the ships, and all those that they could not remove, they broke up, and those that were serviceable they brought into London. The Danes had secured their women in East Anglia before they left that fortification. Then they stayed at Bridgenorth for the winter. That was three years after they had come here across the sea into the mouth of the Lympne.

AN 896 Then in the summer of this year, the army dispersed, some to East Anglia, some to Northumbria, and those that were without property got themselves ships there and sailed south across the sea to the River Seine. Through God's mercy,

Godes þonces, Angelcyn ealles forswiðe gebrocod. Ac hie wæron micle swiþor gebrocede on þæm þrim gearum mid ceapes cwilde ond monna, ealles swiþost mid þæm þæt manige þara selestena cynges þegna þe þær on londe wæron forðferdon on þæm þrim gearum. Þara wæs sum Swiðulf biscop on Hrofesceastre, ond Ceolmund ealdormon on Cent, ond Beorhtulf ealdormon on Eastseaxum, ond Wulfred ealdormon on Hamtunscire, ond Ealhheard biscop æt Dorceceastre, ond Eadulf cynges þegn on Suðseaxum, ond Beornulf wicgefera on Winteceastre, ond Ecgulf cynges horsþegn, ond manige eac him, þeh ic ða geðungnestan nemde.

2 Þy ilcan geare drehton þa hergas on Eastenglum ond on Norðhymbrum Westseaxna lond swiðe be þæm suðstæðe mid stælhergum, ealra swiþust mid ðæm æscum þe hie fela geara ær timbredon. Þa het Ælfred cyng timbran langscipu ongen ða æscas. Þa wæron fulneah tu swa lange swa þa oðru. Sume hæfdon LX ara, sume ma. Þa wæron ægðer ge swiftran ge unwealtran ge eac hieran þonne þa oðru; næron nawðer ne on Fresisc gescæpene ne on Denisc, bute swa him selfum ðuhte þæt hie nytwyrðoste beon meahten.

3 Þa æt sumum cirre þæs ilcan geares comon þær sex scipu to Wiht ond þær micel yfel gedydon, ægðer ge on Defenum, ge welhwær be ðæm

the army did not too greatly afflict the English. But they had been much more severely afflicted in those three years by pestilence among cattle and men, most of all by the fact that many of the finest of the king's thegns who were there in the land passed away in those three years. Of these, one was Swithwulf, bishop in Rochester, and Ceolmund, ealdorman in Kent, and Beorhtwulf, ealdorman among the East Saxons, and Wulfred, ealdorman in Hampshire, and Ealhheard, bishop in Dorchester, and Eadwulf, king's thegn among the South Saxons, and Beornwulf, town reeve in Winchester, and Ecgwulf, king's horse thegn, and many in addition to them, though I have named the most distinguished.

The same year the armies in East Anglia and 2
Northumbria greatly harassed the land of the West Saxons along the south coast with predatory bands, most of all with the light, swift ships they had built many years before. Then King Alfred ordered longships to be built to oppose these light ships. These were very nearly twice as long as the others. Some had sixty oars, some more. They were both swifter and more stable, and also taller than the others; they were designed in neither a Frisian nor a Danish manner, but as it seemed to him that they might be most serviceable.

Then on a certain occasion in the same year 3
six ships came to the Isle of Wight and did great harm there, both among the people of Devon

særiman. Þa het se cyng faran mid nigonum to þara niwena scipa ond forforon him þone muðan foran on utermere. Þa foron hie mid þrim scipum ut ongen hie, ond þreo stodon æt ufeweardum þæm muðan on drygum: Wæron þa men uppe on londe of agane. Þa gefengon hie þara þreora scipa tu æt ðæm muðan uteweardum ond þa men ofslogon, ond þæt an oðwand. On þæm wæron eac þa men ofslægene buton fifum. Þa comon forðy onweg ðe ðara oþerra scipu asæton. Þa wurdon eac swiðe uneðelice aseten: Þreo asæton on ða healfe þæs deopes ðe ða Deniscan scipu aseten wæron, ond þa oðru eall on oþre healfe, þæt hira ne mehte nan to oðrum. Ac ða þæt wæter wæs ahebbad fela furlanga from þæm scipum, þa eodon ða Deniscan from þæm þrim scipum to þæm oðrum þrim þe on hira healfe beebbade wæron, ond hie þa þær gefuhton. Þær wearð ofslægen Lucumon, cynges gerefa, ond Wulfheard Friesa ond Æbbe Friesa ond Æðelhere Friesa ond Æðelferð cynges geneat, ond ealra monna Fresiscra ond Engliscra LXII ond þara Deniscena CXX.

4 Þa com þæm Deniscum scipum þeh ær flod to, ær þa Cristnan mehten hira ut ascufan, ond hie forðy ut oðreowon. Þa wæron hie to þæm gesargode þæt hie ne mehton Suðseaxna lond utan

and everywhere along the sea coast. Then the king ordered a sortie against them with nine of the new ships, and they obstructed the river mouth from the open sea. Then they went out with three ships against them, and three ships remained higher up the mouth on dry land: Their crews had gone up on land. Then the English captured two of the three ships at the outer part of the mouth and killed the men, and one escaped. In that one also the men were killed, except for five. They got away because the ships of the others had gone aground. They were also very awkwardly aground: Three were aground on the side of the channel that the Danish ships were aground, and the others all on the other side, so that none of them could get at the others. But, when the water had ebbed many furlongs from the ships, then the Danes went from their three remaining ships to the other three that were left aground on their side, and they then fought there. There Lucumon, king's reeve, was killed, and Wulfheard the Frisian, and Æbbe the Frisian, and Æthelhere the Frisian, and Æthelferth the king's *geneat,* and sixty-two of all the Frisian and English men, and one hundred and twenty of the Danes.

However, the tide then reached the Danish 4
ships first, before the Christians could push theirs out, and because of that they escaped by rowing. These had been so badly injured that they could not row past the land of the South

berowan, ac hira þær tu sæ on lond wearp, ond þa men mon lædde to Winteceastre to þæm cynge, ond he hie ðær ahon het, ond þa men comon on Eastengle þe on þæm anum scipe wæron swiðe forwundode. Þy ilcan sumera forwearð nolæs þonne xx scipa miḍ monnum mid ealle be þæm suðriman. Þy ilcan gere forðferde Wulfric cynges horsðegn, se wæs eac Wealhgerefa.

AN 897 Her on þysum gere gefor Æðelm Wiltunscire ealdormon, nigon nihtum ær middum sumere, ond her forðferde Heahstan, se wæs on Lundenne biscop.

———

AN 900 Her gefor Ælfred Aþulfing, syx nihtum ær ealra haligra mæssan, se wæs cyning ofer eall Ongelcyn butan ðæm dæle þe under Dena onwalde wæs, ond he heold þæt rice oþrum healfum læs þe xxx wintra, ond þa feng Eadweard his sunu to rice.

2 Þa gerad Æðelwald his fædran sunu þone ham æt Winburnan ond æt Tweoxneam butan ðæs cyninges leafe ond his witena. Þa rad se cyning mid firde þæt he gewicode æt Baddanbyrig wið Winburnan, ond Æðelwald sæt binnan þæm ham mid þæm monnum þe him to gebugon ond hæfde ealle þa geatu forworht in to him ond sæde þæt he wolde oðer oððe þær libban oððe þær licgan.

Saxons, but there the sea cast two of the ships ashore, and the men were taken to Winchester to the king, and he ordered them to be hanged there, and the men that were on the one ship arrived in East Anglia sorely wounded. That same summer no fewer than twenty ships perished, with men and all, along the south coast. The same year Wulfric, the king's horse thegn, who was also the Welsh reeve, passed away.

AN 897 In this year Æthelhelm, ealdorman of Wiltshire, departed this life, nine days before midsummer; and in this year Heahstan, who was bishop of London, passed away.

———

AN 900 In this year Alfred, Æthelwulf's son, departed this life, six days before All Saints' Day; he was king over all the English except the part that was under Danish control, and he ruled over that kingdom for twenty-eight and a half years, and his son, Edward, succeeded to the kingdom.

Then Æthelwold, Edward's brother's son, 2
seized the estates at Wimborne and at *Tweoxneam* without the permission of the king and his councilors. Then the king rode with his levies and camped at Badbury near Wimborne, and Æthelwold remained inside that estate with the men who had defected to him and had barricaded all the gates against him, and said that his intention was either to live or to die there. Then

Þa under þæm, þa bestæl he hine on niht onweg ond gesohte þone here on Norðhymbrum. Ond se cyng het ridan æfter, ond þa ne mehte hine mon ofridan. Þa berad mon þæt wif þæt he hæfde ær genumen butan cynges leafe ond ofer þara biscopa gebod, forðon ðe heo wæs ær to nunnan gehalgod. Ond on þys ilcan gere forðferde Æþered, wæs on Defenum ealdormon, feower wucum ær Ælfred cyning.

AN 902 Her gefor Aþulf ealdormon, Ealhswiðe broðor, ond Uirgilius, abbud of Scottum, ond Grimbald mæssepreost.

AN 903 Her com Æðelwald hider ofer sæ mid þæm flotan þe he mid wæs on Eastsexe.

AN 904 Her aspon Æðelwald þone here on Eastenglum to unfriðe, þæt hie hergodon ofer Mercna land oð hie comon to Creccagelade ond foron þær ofer Temese ond namon, ægðer ge on Brædene ge ðær ymbutan, eall þæt hie gehentan mehton, ond wendan ða eft hamweard. Þa for Eadweard cyning æfter, swa he raðost mehte his fird gegadrian, ond oferhergade eall hira land betwuh dicum ond Wusan, eall oð ða fennas norð.

2 Þa he ða eft þonan ut faran wolde, þa het he beodan ofer ealle þa fird þæt hie foron ealle ut

under cover of that, he stole away by night and joined the army in Northumbria. And the king ordered that he be pursued, but he could not be overtaken. However, horsemen seized the woman that he had earlier taken without the king's permission and against the command of the bishops, since she had previously been consecrated a nun. And in this same year Æthelred, who was ealdorman among the people of Devon, passed away four weeks before King Alfred.

AN 902 In this year Ealdorman Æthelwulf, brother of Ealhswith, departed this life, as did Virgilius, an abbot of the Scots, and the priest Grimbald.

AN 903 In this year Æthelwold sailed across the sea to Essex with the fleet he was with.

AN 904 In this year Æthelwold incited the army in East Anglia to break the peace so that they went raiding across the land of the Mercians as far as Cricklade, where they crossed the Thames, and, both in Braydon and there about, they took everything that they could seize, and afterward they turned back home. Then as soon as he could gather his levies, King Edward went after them and ravaged all their land between the dikes and the Ouse, right up to the fens in the north.

Then when he wished to withdraw, he ordered 2
it to be proclaimed throughout all his levies that they should all depart together. Then the

ætsomne. Þa ætsæton ða Centiscan þær beæftan ofer his bebod, ond seofon ærendracan he him hæfde to asend. Þa befor se here hie ðær, ond hie ðær gefuhton. Ond ðær wearð Sigulf ealdormon ofslægen, ond Sigelm ealdormon, ond Eadwold, cynges ðegen, ond Cenulf abbod, ond Sigebreht, Sigulfes sunu, ond Eadwald, Accan sunu, ond monige eac him, þeh ic ða geðungnestan nemde; ond on ðara Deniscena healfe wearð ofslægen Eohric hira cyng ond Æðelwald æðeling, ðe hine to þæm unfriðe gespon, ond Byrhtsige, Beornoðes sunu æðelinges, ond Ysopa hold ond Oscytel hold ond swiðe monige eac him þe we nu genemnan ne magon, ond þær wæs on gehwæðre hond micel wæl geslægen, ond þara Deniscena þær wearð ma ofslægen, þeh hie wælstowe gewald ahton. Ond Ealhswið gefor þy ilcan geare.

AN 905 Her on þys geare gefor Ælfred, wæs æt Baðum gerefa, ond on þæm ilcan gere mon fæstnode þone frið æt Yttingaforda, swa swa Eadweard cyng gerædde, ægðer wið Eastengle ge wið Norðhymbre.

AN 908 Her gefor Denulf, se wæs on Winteceastre biscop.

Kentish contingent remained behind there against his command, and he had sent out seven messengers to them. Then the army took them by surprise, and they fought there. And Ealdorman Sigewulf was killed there, and Ealdorman Sigehelm, and Eadwald, king's thegn, and Abbot Cenwulf, and Sigeberht, son of Sigewulf, and Eadwald, son of Acca, and many others in addition to them, although I have named the most distinguished; and on the side of the Danes was killed their king, Eohric, and the ætheling Æthelwold, who had incited him to that hostility, and Byrhtsige, son of the ætheling Beornoth, and *Hold* Ysopa, and *Hold* Oscetel, and very many in addition to them that we cannot now name, and there was much slaughter on both sides, and a greater number of the Danes were killed there, although they had possession of the place of slaughter. And Ealhswith departed this life the same year.

AN 905 In this year in this year Alfred, who was reeve at Bath, departed this life, and in the same year peace was ratified at Tiddingford with both the East Angles and the Northumbrians just as King Edward had determined.

AN 908 In this year Denewulf, who was bishop in Winchester, departed this life.

AN 909 Her feng Friðestan to biscopdome on Winteceastre, ond Asser biscop gefor æfter ðæm, se wæs æt Scireburnan biscop. Ond þy ilcan gere sende Eadweard cyng firde ægðer ge of Westseaxum ge of Mercum, ond heo gehergade swiðe micel on þæm norðhere, ægðer ge on mannum ge on gehwelces cynnes yrfe, ond manega men ofslogon þara Deniscena, ond þær wæron fif wucan inne.

AN 910 Her bræc se here on Norðhymbrum þone frið, ond forsawon ælc frið þe Eadweard cyng ond his witan him budon ond hergodon ofer Mercna lond. Ond se cyng hæfde gegadrod sum hund scipa ond wæs þa on Cent, ond þa scipu foran be suðan east andlang sæ togenes him. Þa wende se here þæt his fultumes se mæsta dæl wære on þæm scipum ond þæt hie mehten faran unbefohtene þær þær hie wolden. Þa geascade se cyng þæt, þæt hie ut on hergað foron, þa sende he his fird ægðer ge of Westseaxum ge of Mercum, ond hie offoron ðone here hindan, þa he hamweard wæs, ond him þa wið gefuhton ond þone here gefliemdon ond his fela þusenda ofslogon, ond þær wæs Eowils cyng ofslægen.

AN 911 Her gefor Æðered ealdormon on Mercum, ond Eadweard cyng feng to Lundenbyrg ond to Oxnaforda ond to ðæm landum eallum þe þærto hierdon.

AN 909 In this year Frithestan succeeded to the episcopal see in Winchester, and after that Asser, who was bishop at Sherborne, died. And the same year King Edward sent off levies of both West Saxons and Mercians, and they made very heavy raids on the northern army, both in men and cattle of every kind, and they killed many men of Danish origin, and remained in that area for five weeks.

AN 910 In this year the army in Northumbria broke the peace, and they scorned every offer of peace that King Edward and his councilors offered them, and they went raiding across Mercia. And the king, who was at that time in Kent, had assembled a hundred or so ships, and these were then sailing east along the south coast to join him. Then the army believed that the largest part of his military support was in those ships and that they might go unopposed wherever they wished. When the king learned that they had gone out on a raid, then he dispatched his levies of both West Saxons and Mercians, and they intercepted the army when it was on its way home and then fought against it and put the army to flight, and they killed many thousands, including King Eowils.

AN 911 In this year Æthelred, ealdorman of the Mercians, died, and King Edward took control of London and Oxford and all the lands that belonged to them.

AN 912 Her on þys geare ymb Martines mæssan het Eadweard cyning atimbran þa norðran burg æt Heorotforda betweox Memeran ond Beneficcan ond Lygean. Ond þa æfter þam þæs on sumera, betweox gangdagum ond middum sumera, þa for Eadweard cyning mid sumum his fultume on Eastseaxe to Mældune ond wicode þær þa hwile þe man þa burg worhte ond getimbrede æt Witham, ond him beag god dæl þæs folces to þe ær under Deniscra manna anwalde wæron. Ond sum his fultum worhte þa burg þa hwile æt Heorotforda on suþhealfe Lygean.

AN 913 Her on þys gere rad se here ut ofer Eastron of Hamtune ond of Ligeraceastre ond bræcon þone friþ ond slogon monige men æt Hocneratune ond þær onbutan. Ond þa swiðe raþe æfter þæm, swa þa oþre ham comon, þa fundon hie oþre flocrade þæt rad ut wið Lygtunes. Ond þa wurdon þa landleode his ware ond him wiþ gefuhton ond gebrohton hie on fullum fleame ond ahreddon eall þæt hie genumen hæfdon, ond eac hira horsa ond hira wæpna micelne dæl.

AN 914 Her on þysum geare com micel sciphere hider ofer suþan of Lidwiccum ond twegen eorlas mid, Ohtor ond Hroald, ond foron west onbutan þæt hie gedydon innan Sæferne muþan, ond hergodon on Norþwealas æghwær be þam sæ þær hie

AN 912 Here, in this year around Martinmas, King Edward ordered the construction of the northern fortification at Hertford between the rivers Maran, Beane, and Lea. And then after that, during the summer, between Rogation Days and midsummer, King Edward went with some of his forces into Essex to Maldon and camped there while the fortification at Witham was constructed and built, and a good number of the people who were earlier under the domination of the Danes submitted to him. And meanwhile some of his forces built a fortification at Hertford on the south side of the Lea.

AN 913 In this year after Easter, the army rode out from Northampton and Leicester, and they broke the peace and killed many men at Hook Norton and thereabouts. And then very shortly after that, as the one group came home, they met up with a second mounted band that rode out toward Luton. And then the people of the area became aware of it and fought against them and brought them to full flight and recovered everything that they had taken as well as a large part of their horses and weapons.

AN 914 In this year a great hostile fleet came over here from the south, from Brittany, and with it two *jarls,* Ohtor and Hroald, and they went around west until they arrived within the mouth of the Severn; they then raided everywhere they pleased among the Welsh along the coast, and þonne onhagode, ond gefengon Cameleac biscop on Ircingafelda ond læddon hine mid him to scipum, ond þa aliesde Eadweard cyning hine eft mid XL pundum.

2 Þa æfter þam, þa for se here eall up ond wolde faran þa giet on hergaþ wið Ircingafeldes. Þa gemetton þa men hie of Hereforda ond of Gleaweceastre ond of þam niehstum burgum ond him wið gefuhton ond hie gefliemdon ond ofslogon þone eorl Hroald ond þæs oþres eorles broþor, Ohteres, ond micel þæs heres, ond bedrifon hie on anne pearruc ond besæton hie þær utan, oþþe hie him sealdon gislas, þæt hie of Eadweardes cyninges anwalde afaran woldon. Ond se cyng hæfde funden þæt him mon sæt wiþ on suþhealfe Sæfernmuþan, westan from Wealum, east oþ Afene muþan, þæt hie ne dorston þæt land nawer gesecan on þa healfe. Þa bestælon hie hie þeah nihtes upp æt sumum twam cirron, æt oþrum cierre be eastan Wæced, ond æt oþrum cierre æt Portlocan. Þa slog hie mon æt ægþrum cirre, þæt hira feawa onweg comon, buton þa ane þe þær ut ætswummon to þam scipum. Ond þa sæton hie ute on þam iglande æt Bradan Relice, oþ þone first þe hie wurdon swiþe metelease, ond monige men hungre acwælon, forþon hie ne meahton nanne mete geræcan.

3 Foran þa þonan to Deomodum ond þa ut to Irlande, ond þis wæs on hærfest. Ond þa æfter

they seized Cyfeiliog, bishop in Archenfield, and took him back with them to the ships; and then King Edward ransomed him for forty pounds.

Then after that, the entire army went up in- 2
land and wanted to go raiding toward Archenfield. Then the men from Hereford and Gloucester and from the nearest fortifications met and fought against them and put them to flight and killed the *jarl* Hroald and the brother of the other *jarl,* Ohtor, and a large part of the army, and drove the survivors into an area of enclosed land, and they besieged them until they gave them hostages promising they would leave King Edward's dominion. And the king had arranged that men were stationed against them on the southern side of the Severn estuary, from Cornwall on the west, and east as far as the mouth of the Avon, so that they dared not attack that land anywhere on that side. Then they stole ashore by night on two occasions, on one occasion east of Watchet, and on the other at Porlock. On each occasion they were attacked, so that few of them got away apart from the ones that swam out there to the ships. And these then stayed out on the island of Flat Holm until the time that they became short of provisions, and many men died of hunger because they could not obtain any food.

Then they moved from there to Dyfed and 3
then out to Ireland, and this was in the autumn. And then after that, in that same year, before

þam on þam ilcan gere foran to Martines mæssan, ða for Eadweard cyning to Buccingahamme mid his firde ond sæt þær feower wucan ond geworhte þa burga buta on ægþere healfe eas ær he þonon fore. Ond Þurcytel eorl hine gesohte him to hlaforde, ond þa holdas ealle, ond þa ieldstan men ealle mæste ðe to Bedanforda hierdon ond eac monige þara þe to Hamtune hierdon.

AN 915 Her on þys gere Eadweard cyng for mid fierde to Bedanforda foran to Martines mæssan ond beget þa burg, ond him cirdon to mæst ealle þa burgware þe hie ær budon. Ond he sæt þær feower wucan ond het atimbran þa burg on suþhealfe þære eas ær he þonan fore.

AN 916 Her on þys gere, foran to middum sumera, for Eadweard cyning to Mældune ond getimbrede þa burg ond gestaðolode ær he þonon fore. Ond þy ilcan geare for Þurcytel eorl ofer sæ on Francland mid þam mannum þe him gelæstan woldon mid Eadweardes cynges friþe ond fultume.

AN 917 Her on þysum gere foran to Eastron, Eadweard cyning het gefaran þa burg æt Tofeceastre ond hie getimbran, ond þa eft æfter þam on þam ilcan geare to gangdagum, he het atimbran þa burg æt Wigingamere. Þy ilcan sumera betwix hlafmæssan ond middum sumera, se here bræc þone friþ of Hamtune ond of Ligeraceastre ond þonan

Martinmas, King Edward went to Buckingham with his levy and stayed there for four weeks and built both of the two fortifications, one on each side of the river, before he left there. And *Jarl* Thurcytel sought him as lord, along with all the *holds* and almost all the principal men who belonged to Bedford, and also many of those who belonged to Northampton.

AN 915 In this year, before Martinmas, King Edward went with a levy to Bedford and took possession of the fortification there, and almost all the inhabitants who lived there submitted to him. And he stayed there for four weeks, and before he left there, he ordered the fortification for the south bank of the river to be built.

AN 916 In this year, before midsummer, King Edward went to Maldon and constructed the fortification and made it secure before he left. And the same year, *Jarl* Thurcytel, with the promise of peace and support from King Edward, crossed the sea to the land of the Franks with those men who wished to follow him.

AN 917 In this year, before Easter, King Edward ordered the stronghold at Towcester to be occupied and fortified; and then after that, at Rogationtide in the same year, he ordered the construction of the fortification at *Wigingamere*. That same summer, between Lammas and midsummer, the army broke the peace in Northampton and Leicester norþan ond foron to Tofeceastre ond fuhton on þa burg ealne dæg ond þohton þæt hie hie sceolden abrecan. Ac hie þeah awerede þæt folc þe þærbinnan wæs oþ him mara fultum to com, ond hie forleton þa þa burg ond foron aweg. Ond þa eft, swiðe raþe æfter þam, hie foron eft ut mid stælherge nihtes ond comon on ungearwe men ond genomon unlytel, ægþer ge on mannum ge on ierfe, betweox Byrnewuda ond Æglesbyrig.

2 Þy ilcan siþe for se here of Huntandune ond of Eastenglum ond worhton þæt geweorc æt Tæmeseforda ond hit budon ond bytledon ond forleton þæt oþer æt Huntandune, ond þohton þæt hie sceoldon þanon of mid gewinne ond mid unfriðe eft þæs landes mare geræcan, ond foran þæt hie gedydon æt Bedanforda. Ond þa foran þa men ut ongean þe þærbinnan wæron ond him wiþ gefuhton ond hie gefliemdon ond hira godne dæl ofslogon. Þa eft æfter þam þa giet gegadorode micel here hine of Eastenglum ond of Mercna lande ond foran to þære byrig æt Wigingamere ond ymbsæton hie utan ond fuhton lange on dæg on ond namon þone ceap onbutan, ond þa men aweredon þeah þa burg þe þærbinnan wæron, ond þa forleton hie þa burg ond foron aweg.

3 Þa æfter þam þæs ilcan sumeres gegadorode micel folc hit on Eadweardes cynges anwalde of

and the northward, and they went to Towcester and attacked that fortification all day, and they thought that they would be able to break into it. However, the people that were inside nevertheless defended it until more help came to them; and the attackers then left the fortification and departed. And then again very soon after that, they went out again by night with predatory bands, and they came upon men that were unprepared and seized no small amount of people and property, between Bernwood Forest and Aylesbury.

At the same time the army left Huntingdon 2
and East Anglia and constructed a new fortification at Tempsford and occupied it, built it up, and abandoned the other at Huntingdon; and they thought that from there they might then acquire further territory with war and with hostility, and traveled to Bedford to accomplish that. And the men who were within went out against them and fought against them and put them to flight and killed a good proportion of them. Then yet again after that, a large army assembled from East Anglia and from Mercia and went to the fortification at *Wigingamere* and surrounded it and attacked it long into the day and seized the cattle round about; and the men who were inside defended the fortification, and then the army left it and went away.

Then after that, the same summer, there as- 3
sembled in King Edward's domain a large band of

þam niehstum burgum þe hit ða gefaran mehte, ond foron to Tæmeseforda ond besæton ða burg ond fuhton ðæron oð hi hie abræcon ond ofslogon þone cyning ond Toglos eorl ond Mannan eorl, his sunu, ond his broþor, ond ealle þa þe þærbinnan wæron ond hie wergan woldon, ond namon þa oþre ond eal þæt þærbinnan wæs. Þa æfter þam þæs forhraþe gegadorode micel folc hit on hærfest, ægþer ge of Cent, ge of Suþrigum, ge of Eastseaxum, ge æghwonan of þam nihstum burgum, ond foron to Colneceastre ond ymbsæton þa burg ond þæron fuhton oþ hie þa geeodon, ond þæt folc eall ofslogon, ond genamon eal þæt þærbinnan wæs buton þam mannum þe þær oþflugon ofer þone weall.

4 Þa æfter þam þa giet þæs ilcan hærfestes, gegadorode micel here hine of Eastenglum, ægþer ge þæs landheres ge þara wicinga þe hie him to fultume aspanen hæfdon, ond þohton þæt hie sceoldon gewrecan hira teonan, ond foron to Mældune ond ymbsæton þa burg ond fuhton þæron oþ þam burgwarum com mara fultum to utan to helpe, ond forlet se here þa burg ond for fram. Ond þa foron þa men æfter ut of þære byrig, ond eac þa þe him utan comon to fultume, ond gefliemdon þone here ond ofslogon hira monig hund, ægþer ge æscmanna ge oþerra.

men that might reach it from the nearest fortifications, and they went to Tempsford and besieged the fortification and fought until they broke in and killed the king, and *Jarl* Toglos, and his son, *Jarl* Manna, and his brother, and everyone inside who wished to defend themselves, and seized the others and everything that was inside there. Then very quickly after that, in autumn, a great multitude assembled both from Kent and from the people of Surrey and from the East Saxons, and from the nearest fortifications on all sides, and they went to Colchester and besieged the fortification there and attacked it until they took it, and except for the men who fled away over the wall, they killed all the people and took everything inside.

Then after that yet again that same autumn a 4
great army assembled from East Anglia, both from the local army and from those vikings that they had persuaded to help them, and they thought to avenge their injuries, and they went to Maldon and besieged the fortification and attacked it until more reinforcements came from outside to help the inhabitants, and the army left the fortification and went away. Then the inhabitants came out of the fortification and also those that had come from outside to help, and they put the enemy force to flight and killed many hundreds of them, both the shipmen and others.

Þa þæs forhraþe þæs ilcan hærfestes for Eadweard cyning mid Westsexna fierde to Passanhamme ond sæt þær þa hwile þe mon worhte þa burg æt Tofeceastre mid stanwealle. Ond him cirde to Þurferþ eorl, ond þa holdas, ond eal se here þe to Hamtune hierde norþ oþ Weolud, ond sohton hine him to hlaforde ond to mundboran. Ond þa se firdstemn for ham, þa for oþer ut ond gefor þa burg æt Huntandune, ond hie gebette ond geedneowade þær heo ær tobrocen wæs be Eadweardes cyninges hæse, ond þæt folc—eal þæt þær to lafe wæs þara landleoda—beag to Eadwearde cyninge, ond sohton his friþ ond his mundbyrde. Þa giet æfter þam þæs ilcan geres foran to Martines mæssan, for Eadweard cyning mid Westsexna fierde to Colneceastre ond gebette þa burg ond geedneowade þær heo ær tobrocen wæs. Ond him cirde micel folc to, ægþer ge on Eastenglum, ge on Eastseaxum þe ær under Dena anwalde wæs, ond eal se here on Eastenglum him swor annesse, þæt hie eal þæt woldon þæt he wolde ond eall þæt friþian woldon þæt se cyng friþian wolde, ægþer ge on sæ, ge on lande. Ond se here þe to Grantanbrycge hierde hine geces synderlice him to hlaforde ond to mundboran, ond þæt fæstnodon mid aþum swa swa he hit þa ared.

Then very quickly after this that same autumn, King Edward went with a levy of the West Saxons to Passenham and stayed there while the fortification at Towcester was built with a stone wall. And *Jarl* Thurferth, and the *holds,* and all the army from Northampton, north as far as the Welland submitted to him, and they sought him as their lord and protector. And then when the levy on duty went home, the other levy went out and captured the fortification at Huntingdon and at King Edward's command repaired and restored it where it had been damaged earlier; and all the people of the locality that were left submitted to King Edward, and sought his peace and protection. Then after that, the same year, before Martinmas, King Edward went with a levy of West Saxons to Colchester and repaired and renewed the fortification where it previously had been damaged. And a large number of people submitted to him, from among both the East Angles and the East Saxons, that were earlier under the control of the Danes, and the entire army of the East Angles swore him a covenant, saying that they wanted everything that he wanted and would keep peace with all those that the king wished to keep peace with, both on sea and on land. And the army based in Cambridge separately chose him as their lord and protector and confirmed that with oaths just as he determined.

AN 918 Her on ðysum gere, betweox gangdagum ond middan sumera, for Eadweard cing mid firde to Stanforda ond het gewyrcan ða burg on suðhealfe ðære eas, ond ðæt folc eal ðe to ðære norþerran byrig hierde him beah to ond sohtan hine him to hlaforde. Ond þa on þæm setle ðe he þær sæt, þa gefor Æþelflæd, his swystar, æt Tameworþige XII nihtum ær middum sumera, ond þa gerad he þa burg æt Tameworþige, ond him cierde to eall se þeodscype on Myrcna lande þe Æþelflæde ær underþeoded wæs, ond þa cyningas on Norþwealum, Howel, ond Cledauc, ond Ieoþwel, ond eall Norþweallcyn hine sohton him to hlaforde. Þa for he þonan to Snotingaham ond gefor þa burg ond het hie gebetan ond gesettan, ægþer ge mid Engliscum mannum ge mid Deniscum, ond him cierde eall þæt folc to þe on Mercna lande geseten wæs, ægþer ge Denisc ge Englisce.

AN 919 Her on þysum geare for Eadweard cyning mid fierde onufan hærfest to Þelwæle ond het gewyrcan þa burg ond gesettan ond gemannian, ond het oþre fierd eac of Miercna þeode, þa hwile þe he þær sæt, gefaran Mameceaster on Norþhymbrum ond hie gebetan ond gemannian.

AN 920 Her on þysum gere, foran to middum sumera, for Eadweard cyning mid fierde to Snotingaham ond

AN 918 In this year, between the Rogation Days and midsummer, King Edward went with the levy to Stamford and ordered a new fortification to be made on the south side of the river, and all the people attached to the existing more northerly fortification submitted to him and sought him as their lord. And then during the period that he stayed there, his sister Æthelflæd departed this life at Tamworth twelve days before midsummer; and he then rode and took control of the fortification at Tamworth, and the entire population of the land of the Mercians that was earlier subject to Æthelflæd submitted to him, and the kings of the Welsh, Howel, Cledauc, and Ieothwel, and all the Welsh sought him as their lord. Then from there he went to Nottingham and captured the fortification there and ordered it to be improved and occupied with both Englishmen and Danes, and the whole population that was settled in the land of the Mercians, both Danish and English, submitted to him.

AN 919 In this year, after autumn, King Edward went with a levy to Thelwall and ordered the fortification to be made, occupied, and manned, and while he remained there, he ordered another levy, also from the people of the Mercians, to take Manchester in Northumbria and improve and man it.

AN 920 In this year, before midsummer, King Edward went to Nottingham with a levy and ordered a het gewyrcan þa burg on suþhealfe þære eas ongean þa oþre ond þa brycge ofer Treontan betwix þam twam burgum, ond for þa þonan on Peaclond to Badecanwiellon ond het gewyrcan ane burg þær on neaweste ond gemannian. Ond hine geces þa to fæder ond to hlaforde Scotta cyning ond eall Scotta þeod ond Rægnald ond Eadulfes suna ond ealle þa þe on Norþhymbrum bugeaþ, ægþer ge Englisce, ge Denisce, ge Norþmen, ge oþre, ond eac Stræcledweala cyning, ond ealle Stræcledwealas.

———

AN 924 Her Eadweard cing forþferde, and Æþelstan his sunu feng to rice.

———

AN 931 Her mon hadode Byrnstan bisceop to Wintanceastre IV *kalendas Iunii,* and he heold þridde healf gear bisceopdom.

AN 932 Her forþferde Fryþestan bisceop.

AN 933 Her for Æþelstan cyning in on Scotland, ægþer ge mid landhere ge mid scyphere, and his micel oferhergade. And Byrnstan bisceop forþferde on Wintanceastre to *Omnium sanctorum.*

AN 934 Her feng Ælfheah bisceop to bisceopdome.

———

fortification to be made on the south side of the river opposite the other one and also a bridge over the Trent between the two fortifications, and then he went from there into the Peak District to Bakewell and ordered a single fortification to be made in the neighborhood and manned. And then the king of the Scots and all the people of the Scots, and Ragnald, and the sons of Eadwulf, and everyone living in Northumbria—English and Danish and Northmen and others—and the king of the Strathclyde Britons and all the Strathclyde Britons chose him as father and lord.

———

AN 924 In this year King Edward passed away, and Æthelstan, his son, succeeded to the kingdom.

———

AN 931 In this year, on the twenty-ninth of May, Byrnstan was ordained bishop of Winchester, and he held the see for two and a half years.

AN 932 In this year Bishop Frithestan passed away.

AN 933 In this year King Æthelstan went into Scotland with both a land and a naval force and laid waste much of it. And Bishop Byrnstan passed away in Winchester on All Saints' Day.

AN 934 In this year Bishop Ælfheah succeeded to the episcopal see.

———

AN 937 Her Æþelstan cyning, eorla dryhten,
beorna beah-gifa, and his broþor eac,
Eadmund æþeling, ealdor-langne tir
geslogon æt sæcce sweorda ecgum
ymbe Brunanburh. Bord-weal clufan,
heowan heaþo-linde, hamora lafan,
afaran Eadweardes, swa him geæþele wæs
from cneo-mægum, þæt hi æt campe oft
wiþ laþra gehwæne land ealgodon,
hord and hamas. Hettend crungun,
Sceotta leoda and scip-flotan
fæge feollan, feld dynede
secgas hwate, siððan sunne up
on morgen-tid, mære tungol,
glad ofer grundas, Godes condel beorht,
eces Drihtnes, oð sio æþele gesceaft
sah to setle. Þær læg secg mænig
garum ageted, guma norþerna,
ofer scild scoten, swilce Scittisc eac,
werig, wiges sæd. Wesseaxe forð
ondlongne dæg eorod-cistum
on last legdun laþum þeodum,
heowan here-fleman hindan þearle
mecum mylen-scearpan. Myrce ne wyrndon
heardes hond-plegan hæleþa nanum
þe mid Anlafe ofer æra gebland

AN 937 In this year King Æthelstan, lord of men,
ring-giver to warriors, and his brother also,
the ætheling Edmund, with the edges of swords,
won lasting glory in battle
around Brunanburh. With their blades, the leavings of hammers,
the offspring of Edward cut through the shield wall,
hacked at the linden battle shields, as was instilled in them
by their kinfolk, so that often in battle they
protected their land, treasure, and homes
against every foe. Enemies died by violence,
people of the Scots and seafarers,
brave men fell doomed,
the field of battle resounded, from the time the sun,
glorious star, bright candle of God,
the eternal Lord, rose in the morning,
glided over the depths, until the noble creation
sank to its rest. There lay many a man
struck down by spears, a northerner
shot over his shield, a Scot, too,
weary, sated with battle. Throughout the day,
the West Saxons in bands of chosen men
continuously laid low the hated people,
cut down the fugitives from behind
with grindstone-sharpened swords. The Mercians did not withhold
hard handplay from any of the warriors
that had sought the land with Olaf,

on lides bosme land gesohtun,
fæge to gefeohte. Fife lægun
on þam camp-stede cyninges giunge,
sweordum aswefede, swilce seofene eac
eorlas Anlafes, unrim heriges,
flotan and Sceotta. Þær geflemed wearð
Norðmanna bregu, nede gebeded,
to lides stefne, litle weorode.
Cread cnear on flot, cyning ut gewat
on fealene flod, feorh generede.
Swilce þær eac se froda mid fleame com
on his cyþþe norð, Costontinus,
har hilde-rinc, hreman ne þorfte
mæcan gemanan. He wæs his mæga sceard,
freonda gefylled on folc-stede,
beslagen æt sæcce, and his sunu forlet
on wæl-stowe, wundun forgrunden,
giungne æt guðe. Gelpan ne þorfte
beorn blanden-feax bil-geslehtes,
eald in-widda, ne Anlaf þy ma;
mid heora here-lafum hlehhan ne þorftun
þæt heo beadu-weorca beteran wurdun
on camp-stede cumbol-gehnastes,
gar-mittinge, gumena gemotes,
wæpen-gewrixles, þæs hi on wæl-felda

over the tumult of waves, on the bosom of the sea,
doomed men to the battle. Five young kings
lay in the place of battle,
put to the sleep of death by swords; likewise seven
of Olaf's *jarl*s, and countless seafarers
and Scots from the army. There the leader of the Northmen,
constrained by necessity, was forced to flee
to the ship's prow, with a small band.
The viking ship pushed forward into deep water and the king departed
on the yellow-gray flood, saved his life.
Likewise the venerable Constantine,
gray-haired warrior, escaped north
in flight to his kin; he had no occasion to exult
in the clash of swords. Bereft of his kinsmen,
deprived of his friends slain in conflict
on the battlefield, he left his son
in the place of slaughter, the young man ground down
by wounds in battle. The gray-haired warrior,
that old adversary, had no cause to boast—
nor Olaf either—at that clash of swords;
with the remains of their army they had no cause to exult
that they were better at battle
in deeds of war, the clash of banners,
meeting of spears, encounter of men,
exchange of weapons, after they played

wiþ Eadweardes afaran plegodan.
Gewitan him þa Norþmen nægled-cnearrum,
dreorig daraða laf, on Dingesmere
ofer deop wæter Difelin secan,
and eft Iraland, æwisc-mode.
Swilce þa gebroþer begen ætsamne
cyning and æþeling, cyþþe sohton,
Wesseaxena land, wiges hremige.
Letan him behindan hræw bryttian
saluwig-padan, þone sweartan hræfn,
hyrned-nebban, and þane hasewan padan,
earn æftan hwit, æses brucan,
grædigne guð-hafoc and þæt græge deor,
wulf on wealde. Ne wearð wæl mare
on þis eiglande æfer gieta
folces gefylled beforan þissum,
sweordes ecgum, þæs þe us secgað bec,
ealde uðwitan, siþþan eastan hider
Engle and Seaxe up becoman,
ofer brad brimu Brytene sohtan,
wlance wig-smiþas, Wealas ofercoman,
eorlas ar-hwate eard begeatan.

AN 940 Her Æþelstan cyning forðferde on VI *kalendas Nouembris* ymbe XL wintra butan anre niht þæs þe Ælfred cyning forþferde, and Eadmund æþeling

with the sons of Edward on the field of slaughter.
The Northmen, the wretched remnant of
spears, left
on *Dingesmere* in their nail-studded ships,
to seek Dublin over the deep sea
and, ashamed at heart, Ireland.
So too the two brothers, the king and the
ætheling,
sought out their homeland together,
the land of the West Saxons, exulting in war.
They left behind them to share the corpses,
to enjoy the slaughter, the dark-coated raven,
black and horny beaked,
and the dusky-coated one, the eagle, white from
behind,
the greedy hawk of war, and that gray animal,
the wolf in the forest. There has never yet
on this island before this
been a greater slaughter of people felled
by the edges of swords, as books tell us,
ancient sages, since here
over the broad sea, Angles and Saxons,
proud smiths of war, came from the east
seeking Britain, overcame the Britons,
active and glorious men obtained the land.

AN 940 In this year King Æthelstan passed away on the twenty-seventh of October, just one day short of the forty years since King Alfred passed away, and Ætheling Edmund succeeded to the feng to rice, and he wæs þa XVIII wintre. And Æþelstan cyning rixade XIV gear and X wucan.

AN 942 Her Eadmund cyning,   Engla þeoden,
maga mund-bora,   Myrce geeode,
dyre dæd-fruma,   swa Dor scadeþ,
Hwitanwylles geat   and Humbra ea,
brada brim-stream: burga fife,
Ligoraceaster,   and Lindcylene,
and Snotingaham,   swylce Stanford,
eac Deoraby.   Dæne wæran ær
under Norðmannum   nyde gebegde
on hæþenra   hæfte-clommum
lange þraga,   oþ hie alysde eft
for his weorþscipe   wiggendra hleo,
afera Eadweardes,   Eadmund cyning.

Eadmund cyning onfeng Anlafe cyninge æt fulluhte, and þy ylcan geare ymb tela micel fæc he onfeng Rægenolde cyninge æt bisceopes handa.

AN 944 Her Eadmund cyning geeode eal Norþhymbra land him to gewealdan and aflymde ut twegen cyningas, Anlaf, Syhtrices sunu, and Rægenald, Guðferþes sunu.

AN 945 Her Eadmund cyning oferhergode eal Cumbra land and hit let to eal Malculme Scotta cyninge kingdom, and he was then eighteen years old. And King Æthelstan ruled for thirteen years and ten weeks.

AN 942 In this year King Edmund, lord of the English,
protector of kinsmen, dear lord,
overran Mercia to where the River Dore
divides it,
Whitwell Gate, and the River Humber,
broad stream: five boroughs,
Leicester, and Lincoln,
and Nottingham, Stamford
and Derby. The Danes, forced by necessity,
had previously, under the Northmen,
been in the heathens' fetters
a long time, until to his honor,
King Edmund, the protector of warriors,
son of Edward, later released them.

King Edmund received Olaf in baptism, and in the same year, after a very long interval, he also received King Ragnald at the bishop's hand.

AN 944 In this year King Edmund brought all the land of the Northumbrians under his control and drove out two kings, Olaf, son of Sihtric, and Ragnald, Guthferth's son.

AN 945 In this year King Edmund laid waste all the land of the Cumbrians and granted it all to Malcolm, on þæt gerad þæt he wære his midwyrhta ægþer ge on sæ ge on lande.

AN 946 Her Eadmund cyning forðferde on sanctes Agustinus mæssedæge, and he hæfde rice seofoþe healf gear, and þa feng Eadred æþeling, his broþor, to rice and gerad eal Norþhymbra land him to gewealde. And Scottas him aþas sealdan, þæt hie woldan eal þæt he wolde.

AN 951 Her forðferde Ælfheah Wintanceastres bisceop on sancte Gregories mæssedæg.

AN 955 Her forþferde Eadred cining on sancte Clementes mæssedæg on Frome, and he rixsade teoþe healf gear, and þa feng Eadwig to rice, Eadmundes sunu cinges.

AN 958 Her forðferde Eadwig cyng on *kalendas Octobris,* and Eadgar his broðor feng to rice.

AN 962 Her forðferde Ælfgar, cinges mæg on Defenum, and his lic rest on Wiltune, and Sigferð cyning hine offeoll, and his lic ligð æt Wimburnan. And king of the Scots, on condition that he collaborated with him both at sea and on land.

AN 946 In this year King Edmund passed away on Saint Augustine's Day, and he reigned for six and a half years, and then his brother, the ætheling Eadred, succeeded to the kingdom and got the whole of the land of the Northumbrians under his control. And the Scots gave him oaths that they would do everything that he wanted.

——

AN 951 In this year on Saint Gregory's Day, Ælfheah, bishop of Winchester, passed away.

——

AN 955 In this year on Saint Clement's Day, King Eadred passed away in Frome, and he had reigned for nine and a half years, and then King Edmund's son Eadwig succeeded to the kingdom.

——

AN 958 In this year on the first of October, King Eadwig passed away, and his brother Edgar succeeded to the kingdom.

——

AN 962 In this year Ælfgar, the king's kinsman, passed away in Devon, and his body rests in Wilton, and King Sigeferth killed himself, his body lying at Wimborne. Then during that year a great þa on geare wæs swiðe micel mancwealm, and se micela manbryne wæs on Lundene, and Paules mynster forbarn and þy ilcan geare wearð eft gestaþelad. On þys ilcan geare for Aþelmod mæssepreost to Rome and þær forðferde XVIII *kalendas Septembris.*

AN 963 Her forðferde Wulfstan diacon on cilda mæssedæge, and æfter þon forðferde Gyric mæssepreost. On þys ilcan geare feng Aþelwold abbod to þæm bisceoprice to Wintanceastre, and hine mon gehalgode *in uigilia sancti Andree,* wæs Sunnandæg on dæg.

AN 964 Her dræfde Eadgar cyng þa preostas on ceastre of Ealdan Mynstre and of Niwan Mynstre and of Ceortesige and of Middeltune and sette hy mid munecan, and he sette Æþelgar abbod to Niwan Mynstre to abbode, and Ordbirht to Ceortesige, and Cyneweard to Middeltune.

AN 971 Her forþferde Eadmund æþeling, and his lic liþ æt Rumesige.

AN 973 Her Eadgar wæs, Engla waldend,
corðre micelre to cyninge gehalgod
on ðære ealdan byrig, Acemannesceastre
eac hi ig-buend oðre worde
beornas Baðan nemnaþ. Þær wæs blis micel

pestilence occurred, and there was that great conflagration in London, when Saint Paul's monastery burned down and that same year was restored. And this same year the priest Æthelmod went to Rome and there passed away on the fifteenth of August.

AN 963 In this year on the feast of the Holy Innocents, the deacon Wulfstan passed away, and after that the priest Gyric passed away. And this year Abbot Æthelwold succeeded to the episcopal see at Winchester, and he was consecrated on the vigil of Saint Andrew, which was on a Sunday.

AN 964 In this year King Edgar drove the priests in the city from the Old Minster and the New Minster, and from Chertsey and from Milton and replaced them with monks, and he appointed Abbot Æthelgar as abbot at New Minster and Ordberht to Chertsey and Cyneweard to Milton.

———

AN 971 In this year the ætheling Edmund passed away, and his body lies at Romsey.

———

AN 973 In this year Edgar, ruler of the English,
with a large entourage, was consecrated king
in the ancient town known as *Acemannesceaster,*
which men, island dwellers, also call
by another word, Bath. There on that blessed day,

on þam eadgan dæge eallum geworden,
þone niða bearn nemnað and cigað
Pentecostenes dæg. Þær wæs preosta heap,
micel muneca ðreat, mine gefrege,
gleawra gegaderod. And ða agangen wæs
tyn hund wintra geteled rimes
fram gebyrd-tide bremes Cyninges,
leohta hyrdes, buton ðær to lafe þa gen
wæs winter-geteles, þæs ðe gewritu secgað,
seofon and twentig; swa neah wæs sigora Frean
ðusend aurnen, ða þa ðis gelamp.
And him Eadmundes eafora hæfde
nigon and xx, nið-weorca heard,
wintra on worulde, þa þis geworden wæs,
and þa on ðam xxx wæs ðeoden gehalgod.

AN 975 Her geendode eorðan dreamas
Eadgar, Engla cyning, ceas him oðer leoht,
wlitig and wynsum, and þis wace forlet,
lif þis læne. Nemnað leoda bearn,
men on moldan, þæne monað gehwær
in ðisse eðel-tyrf, þa þe ær wæran
on rim-cræfte rihte getogene,
Iulius monoð, þæt se geonga gewat

which the children of men name and call
Pentecost, great rejoicing was
experienced by all. There was gathered together
a crowd of priests, a great band of monks and of wise men,
as I have heard. And ten hundred years
had passed, counted
from the birth of the glorious King,
the guardian of light, except that there still remained,
in number of years, twenty-seven
as the records say, so near had a thousand years passed
for the Lord of victories, when this happened.
And the son of Edmund, bold
in deeds of conflict, had had twenty-nine
years in the world when this came to pass,
and then in the thirtieth was the lord consecrated.

AN 975 In this year, Edgar, king of the English, reached the end
of earth's joys, chose another light for himself,
fair and delightful, and abandoned this weak
and transitory life. The children of men,
people on the earth, everywhere on this noble turf,
those that have previously been
correctly instructed in the craft of numbers,
name as July this month in which the young

on þone eahteðan dæg   Eadgar of life,
beorna beah-gyfa,   and feng his bearn syððan
to cyne-rice,   cild unweaxen,
eorla ealdor,   þam wæs Eadweard nama.
And him tir-fæst hæleð   tyn nihtum ær
of Brytene gewat,   bisceop se goda,
þurh gecyndne cræft,   ðam wæs Cyneweard nama.
Ða wæs on Myrceon,   mine gefræge,
wide and wel-hwær   waldendes lof
afylled on foldan.   Fela wearð todræfed
gleawra Godes ðeowa;   þæt wæs gnornung micel
þam þe on breostum wæg   byrnende lufan
metodes on mode.   Þa wæs mærða fruma
to swiðe forsewen,   sigora waldend,
rodera rædend,   þa man his riht tobræc.
And þa wearð eac adræfed   deor-mod hæleð,
Oslac, of earde   ofer yða gewealc,
ofer ganotes bæð,   gamol-feax hæleð,
wis and word-snotor,   ofer wætera geðring,
ofer hwæles eðel,   hama bereafod.
And þa wearð ætywed   uppe on roderum
steorra on staðole,   þone stið-ferhþe,
hæleð hige-gleawe,   hatað wide

Edgar, ring-giver of men, departed from life
on the eighth day, and his son,
an ungrown child by the name of Edward,
lord of men, succeeded to the kingdom.
And ten days before him, a glorious hero,
a bishop, good through natural disposition,
whose name was Cyneweard, departed from Britain.
Then among the Mercians, as I have heard,
the praise of the ruler was widely and everywhere
cast down to the ground. Many wise servants
of God were driven out; that was great grief
for whoever bore in his breast, in his heart,
burning love of the creator. Then the author of marvels,
ruler of victories, ruler of the heavens
was too greatly despised when people broke his laws.
And then too the stouthearted hero, Oslac,
was driven from the land, over the tossing of the waves,
over the gannet's bath, the press of the waters,
over the whale's homeland, and the gray-haired hero,
wise and prudent of words, was bereft of his estates.
And then up in the heavens set in the firmament,
there was revealed a star,
which stouthearted heroes, learned men,

cometa be naman,   cræft-gleawe men,
wise soð-boran.   Wæs geond wer-ðeode
waldendes wracu   wide gefrege,
hungor ofer hrusan;   þæt eft heofona weard
gebette, brego engla: geaf eft blisse gehwæm
eg-buendra   þurh eorðan westm.

———

AN 978 Her wearð Eadweard cyning ofslegen. On þis ylcan geare feng Æðelred æðeling, his broðor, to rice.

———

AN 983 Her forðferde Ælfhere ealdorman.

AN 984 Her forðferde se welwillenda bisceop Aðelwold, and seo halgung þæs æfterfilgendan bisceopes Ælfheages, se ðe oðran naman wæs geciged Godwine, wæs XIV *kalendas Nouembris,* and he gesæt þone bisceopstol an þara twegra apostola dæge, Simonis and Iudæ, on Wintanceastre.

———

AN 993 Her on ðissum geare com Unlaf mid þrim and hund nigontigon scipum to Stane and forhergedon þæt onytan and for ða ðanon to Sandwic and swa ðanon to Gipeswic and þæt eall ofereode and swa to Mældune, and him ðær com togeanes

wise truth-bearers, widely call
comet by name. The vengeance of the ruler
was widely known throughout mankind,
hunger across the earth; the guardian of heaven,
lord of angels, repaired that: he gave back joy to each
of the islanders through the produce of the earth.

AN 978 In this year King Edward was killed. And in the same year his brother the ætheling Æthelred succeeded to the kingdom.

AN 983 In this year Ealdorman Ælfhere passed away.

AN 984 In this year the benevolent bishop Æthelwold passed away, and the consecration of his successor, Ælfheah, who was called Godwine by his other name, was on the nineteenth of October, and he took his place on the bishop's throne in Winchester on the day of the two apostles, Simon and Jude.

AN 993 In this year Olaf came with ninety-three ships to Folkestone and plundered all round that place and then went from there to Sandwich and so on to Ipswich and overran all that region and so to Maldon; and there came against them there

Byrhtnoð ealdorman mid his fyrde and him wið gefeaht, and hy þone ealdorman þær ofslogon and wælstowe geweald ahtan, and him man nam syððan frið wið, and hine nam se cing syððan to bisceopes handa.

AN 994 Her forðferde Sigeric arcebisceop, and feng Ælfric Wiltunscire bisceop to ðam arcebisceoprice.

AN 1001 Her on ðysum geare wæs micel unfrið on Angelcynnes londe þurh sciphere, and welgehwær hergedon and bærndon, swa þæt hy upp asetton on ænne siþ þæt hy coman to Æþelingadene, and þa com þær togeanes Hamtunscir and him wið gefuhton, and ðær wearð Æþelweard, cinges heahgerefa, ofslegen, and Leofric æt Hwitciricean, and Leofwine, cinges heahgerefa, and Wulfhere, bisceopes ðegn, and Godwine æt Worðige, Ælfsiges bisceopes sunu, and ealra manna an and hund eahtatig, and þær wearð þara Denescra micle ma ofslegenra, þeah ðe hie wælstowe geweald ahtan. And foran ða þanon west oþ þæt hy coman to Defenan—and him þær togeanes com Pallig mid þan scipan ðe he gegaderian mihte, forþam þe he asceacen wæs fram Æðelrede cyncge ofer ealle ða getrywða ðe he him geseald hæfde, and eac se cyng him wel gegifod hæfde on hamon and on golde and seolfre—and forbærndon Tegntun and eac fela oðra

Ealdorman Byrhtnoth with his levy and fought against them there, and they killed the ealdorman and gained possession of the place of slaughter, and peace was afterward made with them, and the king received Olaf at the bishop's hands.

AN 994 In this year Archbishop Sigeric passed away, and Ælfric, bishop of Wiltshire, succeeded to the archiepiscopal see.

AN 1001 In this year there was much disruption in the land of the English caused by an enemy fleet, and they plundered and burned almost everywhere, until they made their way in a single journey to *Æþelingadene,* and the levies of Hampshire intercepted them and fought against them, and there Æthelweard, king's high reeve was killed, and Leofric from Whitchurch, and Leofwine, king's high reeve, and Wulfhere, bishop's thegn, and Godwine from Worthy, the son of Bishop Ælfsige, and eighty-one men all told, and there were far more of the Danes killed, although they had control over the place of slaughter. And they then went west until they came to Devon, where they were met by Pallig with such ships as he could muster, because he had deserted King Æthelred in spite of all the pledges he had given him, and also the king had endowed him well with estates, and gold and silver; they then burned Kingsteignton and also many good godra hama þe we genemnan ne cunnan, and heom man syððan þær frið wið nam. And hy foran þa þanon to Exan muðan, swa þæt hy asettan him upp on ænne sið oð hy coman to Peonho, and þær wæs Kola, ðæs cyninges heahgerefa, and Eadsige, þæs cynincges gerefa, togeanes him mid ðære fyrde ðe hy gegaderian mihtan. And hy ðær aflymede wurdon, and ðær wearð fela ofslegenra, and ða Denescean ahtan wælstowe geweald, and ðæs on mergen forbærndon þone ham æt Peonho and æt Glistune, and eac fela godra hama þe we genemnan na cunnan, and foran ða eft east ongean oð hy coman to Wiht, and þæs on mergen forbærndon ðone ham æt Wealtham and oðra cotlifa fela. And hiom man raþe þas wið þingode, and hy namon frið.

estates that we are unable to name, and peace was afterward made with them. And from there they moved to the mouth of the River Exe, and all crossed over at the same time, and proceeded to Pinho, and Kola the king's high reeve and Eadsige the king's reeve came to meet them with the levies that they were able to assemble. And they were put to flight there and many men were killed and the Danes had control of the place of slaughter; and the next day they burned the estates at Pinho and at Clyst and also many other good estates that we are unable to name, and they went back east again as far as the Isle of Wight, and the following morning they burned down the hamlet at Waltham and many other smallholdings. And negotiations were speedily held with them, and they made peace.

THE DEATH OF ALFRED

The Death of Alfred

1036 Her com Ælfred, se unsceððiga æþeling, Æþelrædes sunu cinges, hider inn and wolde to his meder, þe on Wincestre sæt, ac hit him ne geþafode Godwine eorl ne ec oþre men þe mycel mihton wealdan, forðan hit hleoðrode þa swiðe toward Haraldes, þeh hit unriht wære.

Ac Godwine hine þa gelette and hine on hæft sette,
and his geferan he todraf and sume mislice ofsloh.
Sume hi man wið feo sealde, sume hreowlice acwealde,
sume hi man bende, sume hi man blende,
sume hamelode, sume hættode.
Ne wearð dreorlicre dæd gedon on þison earde
syþþan Dene comon and her frið namon.
Nu is to gelyfenne to ðan leofan Gode
þæt hi blission bliðe mid Criste
þe wæron butan scylde swa earmlice acwealde.
Se æþeling lyfode þa gyt; ælc yfel man him gehet
oð þæt man gerædde þæt man hine lædde
to Eligbyrig swa gebundenne.

The Death of Alfred

1036 In this year, Alfred, the guiltless ætheling, son of King Æthelred, came into this country and wished to go to his mother, who lived in Winchester, but Earl Godwine did not allow him, nor also other men who had much power, because sentiment leaned very much toward Harold, although it was not right.

But Godwine detained him and put him in bonds
and drove away his companions and killed some of them in various ways.
Some were sold for money, some were killed wretchedly,
some were put in bonds, some were blinded,
some mutilated, some scalped.
There was not a crueler deed done in this land
since the Danes came and made peace here.
Now we should trust in beloved God
that they rejoice happily with Christ
who guiltless were killed so grievously.
The ætheling still lived; he was threatened with every evil
until they were advised that he be led
in bonds to Ely.

Sona swa he lende   on scype man hine blende
and hine swa blindne   brohte to ðam munecon,
and he þar wunode   ða hwile þe he lyfode.
Syððan hine man byrigde,   swa him wel gebyrede,
ful wurðlice   swa he wyrðe wæs,
æt þam west-ende   þam styple ful gehende
on þam suð-portice.   Seo saul is mid Criste.

As soon as he landed he was blinded on the ship,
and thus blind he was brought to the monks,
and he remained there while he lived.
Afterward, he was buried entirely worthily,
as became him well, since he was worthy,
at the west end near the tower,
in the south *portic.* His soul is with Christ.

THE DEATH OF EDWARD

The Death of Edward

[1065] Her Eadward kingc, Engla hlaford,
sende soþfæste sawle to Criste
on Godes wæra, gast haligne.
He on worulda her wunode þrage
on kyne-þrymme, cræftig ræda;
XXIV freolic wealdend
wintra gerimes weolan brytnode
and healfe tid. Hæleða wealdend
weold wel geþungen Walum and Scottum
and Bryttum eac, byre Æðelredes,
Englum and Sexum, oret-mægcum,
swa ymbclyppað cealde brymmas,
þæt eall Eadwarde æðelum kinge
hyrdon holdlice hage-stealde menn.
Wæs a bliðe-mod bealuleas kyng,
þeah he lang ær lande bereafod
wunode wræc-lastum wide geond eorðan,
syððan Cnut ofercom kynn Æðelredes,
and Dena weoldon deore rice
Engla landes XXVIII
wintra gerimes welan brytnodan.
Syððan forð becom freolice in geatwum
kyningc kystum god, clæne and milde,

The Death of Edward

1065 In this year, King Edward, lord of the English,
sent his faithful soul, his holy spirit,
to Christ into God's protection.
He lived here in the world for a time
in royal majesty, wise in his counsels;
a noble ruler, he distributed riches
for twenty-four and a half
years by count. A ruler of warriors,
a very excellent son of Æthelred, he ruled
the Welsh, the Scots, and the British also,
Angles and Saxons, warriors
as far as the cold sea waters encompass,
so that all the young men
obeyed him, that noble king Edward, loyally.
An innocent king, he was always happy in spirit,
although for a long time before, deprived of land,
he had dwelled on earth far and wide in the tracks of exile
after Cnut conquered Æthelred's people,
and the Danes controlled the noble kingdom,
land of the English, for twenty-eight
years by count, distributed riches.
Afterward, glorious Edward came forth, noble in his armor,
a king good in his virtues, chaste and merciful;

Eadward se æðela;   eðel bewerode
land and leode,   oðþæt lungre becom
deað se bitera   and swa deore genam
æþelne of eorðan.   Englas feredon
soþfæste sawle   innan swegles leoht.
And se froda swa þeah   befæste þæt rice
heah-þungenum menn   Harolde sylfum,
æþelum eorle,   se in ealle tid
hyrde holdlice   hærran sinum
wordum and dædum;   wihte ne agælde
þæs þe þearf wæs   þæs þeod-kyninges.

he protected his ancestral domain,
the land and the people, until bitter death
came quickly and took so excellent
a nobleman from the earth. Angels carried
his faithful soul into the light of glory.
And the wise one, however, had entrusted that kingdom
to an excellent man, Harold himself,
noble earl, who in all his time
had obeyed loyally his lord
in words and deeds; he did not neglect at all
what was of service to the king.

THE BATTLE OF MALDON

The Battle of Maldon

. . . brocen wurde.
Het þa hyssa hwæne   hors forlætan,
feor afysan   and forð gangan,
hicgan to handum   and to hige godum.
Þa þæt Offan mæg   ærest onfunde,
þæt se eorl nolde   yrhðo geþolian,
he let him þa of handon   leofne fleogan
hafoc wið þæs holtes,   and to þære hilde stop.
Be þam man mihte oncnawan   þæt se cniht nolde
wacian æt þam wige,   þa he to wæpnum feng.
Eac him wolde Eadric   his ealdre gelæstan,
frean to gefeohte,   ongan þa forð beran
þa hwile þe he mid handum   healdan mihte
bord and brad-swurd;   beot he gelæste
þa he ætforan his frean   feohtan sceolde.
Ða þær Byrhtnoð ongan   beornas trymian,
rad and rædde,   rincum tæhte
hu hi sceoldon standan   and þone stede healdan,
and bæd þæt hyra randas   rihte heoldon
fæste mid folman,   and ne forhtedon na.
Þa he hæfde þæt folc   fægere getrymmed,
he lihte þa mid leodon   þær him leofost wæs,
þær he his heorð-werod   holdost wiste.

The Battle of Maldon

. . . was broken. He then ordered a certain one among the young warriors to leave his horse behind, drive it away, and go forward on foot, to concentrate on the work of hands and on good courage. As soon as it came to the attention of Offa's kinsman that the nobleman was not minded to tolerate idling, he let his dear hawk fly from his hands toward the woods, and he strode toward the battle. By that, one could know the young man would not weaken in the strife, once he had taken up weapons.

Like him, Eadric was determined to stand by his lord, his chief, in the fight; he began then to go forward with his spear, toward the conflict. He had a good heart as long as he could grip with his hands shield and broadsword. He accomplished his vow when it was his turn to fight in the sight of his lord.

Then Byrhtnoth began there to exhort his warriors; he circulated on horseback and gave instructions, demonstrated to the men how they should stand and defend the place; and he ordered that they should hold their shields correctly, firmly in their hands, and that they should never fear. When he had thoroughly arranged his force, he alighted amid men dearest to him, there where he knew his war band to be most loyal.

Þa stod on stæðe, stiðlice clypode
wicinga ar, wordum mælde,
se on beot abead brim-liþendra
ærænde to þam eorle, þær he on ofre stod:
"Me sendon to þe sæ-men snelle,
heton ðe secgan þæt þu most sendan raðe
beagas wið gebeorge; and eow betere is
þæt ge þisne gar-ræs mid gafole forgyldon,
þonne we swa hearde hilde dælon.
Ne þurfe we us spillan, gif ge spedaþ to þam;
we willað wið þam golde grið fæstnian.
Gyf þu þat gerædest, þe her ricost eart,
þæt þu þine leoda lysan wille,
syllan sæ-mannum on hyra sylfra dom
feoh wið freode, and niman frið æt us,
we willaþ mid þam sceattum us to scype gangan,
on flot feran, and eow friþes healdan."
Byrhtnoð maþelode, bord hafenode,
wand wacne æsc, wordum mælde,
yrre and an-ræd ageaf him andsware:
"Gehyrst þu, sæ-lida, hwæt þis folc segeð?
Hi willað eow to gafole garas syllan,
ættrynne ord and ealde swurd,
þa here-geatu þe eow æt hilde ne deah.
Brim-manna boda, abeod eft ongean,
sege þinum leodum miccle laþre spell,
þæt her stynt unforcuð eorl mid his werode,
þe wile gealgean eþel þysne,
Æþelredes eard, ealdres mines,
folc and foldan. Feallan sceolon
hæþene æt hilde! To heanlic me þinceð

At that point, a messenger of the vikings took his stand on the bank, called out loudly, put his speech into words; he announced the seafarers' message as a proposition to the nobleman, there where he stood on the shore: "Bold seamen have sent me to you, ordered me to tell you that you have the opportunity quickly to send rings in return for protection; and it will be better for all of you that you buy off this spear-storm with tribute than that we share such hard battle. We have no need to kill each other if you all have such resources; in return for that gold, we will establish a binding truce. If you, who are the most noble here, decide that you want to spare your people, to pay out to the seafarers at their own discretion property in return for peace, and to accept protective peace from us, then we intend to depart to ship with that reward, to set out on the sea, and to hold the peace with you all."

Byrhtnoth made a speech, raised up his shield, shook his pliant ash spear, and spoke out in words; angry and resolute, he gave him his answer: "Do you hear, seafarer, what this army replies? They are minded to donate spears for tribute, poisoned points and ancient swords, a tribute of war gear that will do you no good in battle. Messenger of the seamen, take this announcement back again, say to your people a much more hostile message, that here, with his war band, stands a warrior of unstained reputation who intends to defend this soil, the land of my lord Æthelred, his people, and his territory. Heathens must fall in battle! Too demeaning it

þæt ge mid urum sceattum   to scype gangon
unbefohtene,   nu ge þus feor hider
on urne eard   in becomon.
Ne sceole ge swa softe   sinc gegangan:
Us sceal ord and ecg   ær geseman,
grim guð-plega,   ær we gofol syllon."
  Het þa bord beran,   beornas gangan,
þæt hi on þam ea-steðe   ealle stodon.
Ne mihte þær for wætere   werod to þam oðrum:
Þær com flowende   flod æfter ebban,
lucon lagu-streamas.   To lang hit him þuhte,
hwænne hi togædere   garas beron.
Hi þær Pantan stream   mid prasse bestodon,
East-Seaxena ord   and se æsc-here;
ne mihte hyra ænig   oþrum derian,
buton hwa þurh flanes flyht   fyl gename.
Se flod ut gewat.   Þa flotan stodon gearowe,
wicinga fela,   wiges georne.
  Het þa hæleða hleo   healdan þa bricge
wigan wig-heardne;   se wæs haten Wulfstan,
cafne mid his cynne   —þæt wæs Ceolan sunu—
þe ðone forman man   mid his francan ofsceat
þe þær baldlicost   on þa bricge stop.
Þær stodon mid Wulfstane   wigan unforhte,
Ælfere and Maccus,   modige twegen,
þa noldon æt þam forda   fleam gewyrcan,
ac hi fæstlice   wið ða fynd weredon
þa hwile þe hi wæpna   wealdan moston.
Þa hi þæt ongeaton   and georne gesawon
þæt hi þær bricg-weardas   bitere fundon,
ongunnon lytegian þa   laðe gystas:

seems to me that you all should go to your ships with our money but without a fight, now that you have come so far up on our land. You must not so easily get our treasure: Point and edge, the grim game of battle, shall settle things between us before we give up tribute."

He then ordered men to bear shields, to advance so that they all were standing at the edge of the water. Neither armed band could get at the other there on account of the water: After the ebb, the flood tide had come flowing; streams of the current flowed together. It seemed to them too long until they might bring their spears together. There, in military pride, they stood on both sides of the River Pante, the front rank of the East Saxons and the shipborne invaders; no man of them could do harm to another unless someone should be felled by the flight of an arrow. The high tide went out. The seamen were standing ready then, a host of vikings eager for the fight.

The protector of warriors then ordered a war-hardened fighter to hold the ford; he was named Wulfstan, a man of courage and lineage—he was the son of Ceola—who, with his Frankish spear, shot down the first man who stepped out boldly there into the ford. There stood with Wulfstan Ælfhere and Maccus, warriors without fear, a spirited pair who did not intend to make a retreat from that ford; rather they defended firmly against the enemy as long as they could hold their weapons. When they noticed and clearly perceived that they had found there grim guardians of the ford, then the hateful strangers began to use a trick: They asked

Bædon þæt hi up-gangan agan moston,
ofer þone ford faran, feþan lædan.
Þa se eorl ongan for his ofer-mode
alyfan landes to fela laþere ðeode.
Ongan ceallian þa ofer cald wæter
Byrhtelmes bearn (beornas gehlyston):
"Nu eow is gerymed: Gað ricene to us,
guman to guþe. God ana wat
hwa þære wæl-stowe wealdan mote."
Wodon þa wæl-wulfas (for wætere ne murnon),
wicinga werod, west ofer Pantan,
ofer scir wæter, scyldas wegon,
lid-men to lande linde bæron.
Þær ongean gramum gearowe stodon
Byrhtnoð mid beornum. He mid bordum het
wyrcan þone wi-hagan and þæt werod healdan
fæste wið feondum. Þa was feohte neh,
tir æt getohte: Wæs seo tid cumen
þæt þær fæge men feallan sceoldon.
Þær wearð hream ahafen; hremmas wundon,
earn æses georn; wæs on eorþan cyrm.
Hi leton þa of folman feol-hearde speru,
grimme gegrundene garas fleogan.
Bogan wæron bysige; bord ord on feng.
Biter wæs se beadu-ræs, beornas feollon
on gehwæðere hand, hyssas lagon.
Wund wearð Wulfmær, wæl-ræste geceas,
Byrhtnoðes mæg; he mid billum wearð,
his swuster sunu, swiðe forheawen.
Þær wearð wicingum wiþer-lean agyfen:
Gehyrde ic þæt Eadweard anne sloge

that they might have passage, might go over the ford, and lead their infantry up on land.

Then, in his hubris, that nobleman granted too much land to the hateful people. The son of Byrhthelm began to call then over the cold water (the warriors listened): "Now space is cleared for you: Come quickly to us, fighters to the fight. God alone knows who will be granted control of the killing field."

Then the slaughter-wolves, the viking force, strode forward (they did not trouble themselves about the water) west over the Pante, over the bright water, carried their shields, seamen bore linden shields to the land. There stood Byrhtnoth together with his warriors, ready against the angry ones. He commanded them to make the battle-hedge with their shields and the troop to hold firm against the enemy. Then was battle near, glory in war: The time had come when doomed men would have to fall there. Noise arose there; ravens were circling, the eagle eager for carrion; there was a clamor upon the earth. From their hands they let fly spears as hard as files, grimly sharpened javelins. Bows were busy; the shield intercepted the arrow point. The rush of battle was bitter, warriors fell on every side, young fighters lay dead.

Wulfmær, kinsman of Byrhtnoth, was wounded, lay down at rest among the dead; he had been badly hacked with swords, his sister's son. Retaliation was delivered there to the vikings: I heard that Edward struck one hard with his

swiðe mid his swurde, swenges ne wyrnde,
þæt him æt fotum feoll fæge cempa.
Þæs him his ðeoden þanc gesæde,
þam bur-þene, þa he byre hæfde.
Swa stemnetton stið-hicgende
hysas æt hilde, hogodon georne
hwa þær mid orde ærost mihte
on fægean men feorh gewinnan,
wigan mid wæpnum. Wæl feol on eorðan.
Stodon stæde-fæste; stihte hi Byrhtnoð,
bæd þæt hyssa gehwylc hogode to wige
þe on Denon wolde dom gefeohtan.
Wod þa wiges heard, wæpen up ahof,
bord to gebeorge, and wið þæs beornes stop.
Eode swa an-ræd eorl to þam ceorle:
Ægþer hyra oðrum yfeles hogode.
Sende ða se sæ-rinc suþerne gar,
þæt gewundod wearð wigena hlaford;
he sceaf þa mid ðam scylde, þæt se sceaft tobærst,
and þæt spere sprengde, þæt hit sprang ongean.
Gegremod wearð se guð-rinc; he mid gare stang
wlancne wicing, þe him þa wunde forgeaf.
Frod wæs se fyrd-rinc: He let his francan wadan
þurh ðæs hysses hals, hand wisode
þæt he on þam fær-sceaðan feorh geræhte.
Ða he oþerne ofstlice sceat,
þæt seo byrne tobærst; he wæs on breostum wund
þurh ða hring-locan, him æt heortan stod
ætterne ord. Se eorl wæs þe bliþra:
Hloh þa, modi man, sæde Metode þanc
ðæs dæg-weorces þe him Drihten forgeaf.

sword, did not hold back the blow, so that the fated warrior fell at his feet. For that his lord said thanks to him, to the chamber attendant, as soon as he had a chance. Thus the strong-minded young fighters fell silent in the midst of battle, contemplated keenly who, with his weapon, with his sword, might first take the life of a fated man, of a warrior. The dead fell to the earth. They stood steadfast; Byrhtnoth encouraged them, commanded that each of the young fighters who wanted to achieve fame at the expense of the Danes keep his mind on the fight.

Then one hardened in battle came striding, raised up his weapon, his shield for protection, and stalked toward the man. Equally resolved, the nobleman advanced toward the yeoman: Each of them had in mind harm for the other. Then the seaman threw his southern spear so that the lord of warriors was wounded; he then shoved with the shield so that the shaft broke in two and freed the spear head such that it sprang out again. The warrior was furious; with his spear he pierced the proud viking who had given him the wound. Experienced was that warrior: He caused his Frankish spear to pass through that young man's throat; his hand guided it so that he reached the life of that fearsome attacker.

Then he quickly shot another man so that his armor burst; he was wounded in the breast through the ring-mail vest, the deadly point lodged in his heart. The nobleman was happier for that: The bold man laughed then, said thanks to God for the day's work the Lord had granted him.

Forlet þa drenga sum daroð of handa,
fleogan of folman, þæt se to forð gewat
þurh ðone æþelan Æþelredes þegen.
Him be healfe stod hyse unweaxen,
cniht on gecampe, se full caflice
bræd of þam beorne blodigne gar,
Wulfstanes bearn, Wulfmær se geonga;
forlet forheardne faran eft ongean;
ord in gewod, þæt se on eorþan læg
þe his þeoden ær þearle geræhte.
Eode þa gesyrwed secg to þam eorle;
he wolde þæs beornes beagas gefecgan,
reaf and hringas and gerenod swurd.
Þa Byrhtnoð bræd bill of sceðe,
brad and brun-eccg, and on þa byrnan sloh.
To raþe hine gelette lid-manna sum,
þa he þæs eorles earm amyrde.
Feoll þa to foldan fealo-hilte swurd;
ne mihte he gehealdan heardne mece,
wæpnes wealdan. Þa gyt þæt word gecwæð
har hilde-rinc, hyssas bylde,
bæd gangan forð gode geferan;
ne mihte þa on fotum leng fæste gestandan.
He to heofenum wlat:
"Ic geþance þe, ðeoda waldend,
ealra þæra wynna þe ic on worulde gebad.
Nu ic ah, milde Metod, mæste þearfe
þæt þu minum gaste godes geunne,
þæt min sawul to ðe siðian mote
on þin geweald, Þeoden engla,
mid friþe ferian. Ic eom frymdi to þe
þæt hi hel-sceaðan hynan ne moton."

Then one of the viking warriors launched a javelin from his hand, let it fly from his grip, so that it went too straight, through that noble officer of Æthelred. By his side was standing a young fighter, a boy on the battlefield, son of Wulfstan, Wulfmær the Young, who very bravely pulled the bloody spear out of that warrior; he made the hard-tempered spear travel back again; the point went in so that the one who before had harshly reached his lord lay stretched on the earth.

Then a well-armed man came toward the nobleman; he intended to take that warrior's armbands, his armor and his gold rings, and his ornamented sword. Byrhtnoth then drew that blade, broad and dark edged, from its scabbard and aimed a stroke at the mail coat. Too quickly one of the sea-farers hindered him as he disabled the nobleman's arm. The yellow-hilted sword then fell to the ground; he could no longer hold the hard sword, wield the weapon. And yet the gray-haired warrior spoke a word, encouraged the young fighters, exhorted the good comrades to advance; he could then no longer stand firm on his feet. He looked up to heaven: "I thank you, ruler of peoples, for all those pleasures that I experienced in the world. Now, generous God, I have the greatest need that you grant good to my spirit so that my soul be permitted to travel to you, into your control, O Lord of angels, that it journey in peace. I am petitioning to you that attackers from hell may not afflict it."

Ða hine heowon hæðene scealcas
and begen þa beornas þe him big stodon;
Ælfnoð and Wulmær begen lagon,
ða onemn hyra frean feorh gesealdon.
Hi bugon þa fram beaduwe þe þær beon noldon.
Þær wurdon Oddan bearn ærest on fleame,
Godric from guþe, and þone godan forlet
þe him mænigne oft mear gesealde;
he gehleop þone eoh þe ahte his hlaford,
on þam gerædum þe hit riht ne wæs,
and his broðru mid him begen ærndon,
Godwine and Godwig, guþe ne gymdon,
ac wendon fram þam wige and þone wudu sohton,
flugon on þæt fæsten and hyra feore burgon—
and manna ma þonne hit ænig mæð wære,
gyf hi þa geearnunga ealle gemundon
þe he him to duguþe gedon hæfde.
Swa him Offa on dæg ær asæde
on þam meþel-stede, þa he gemot hæfde,
þæt þær modiglice manega spræcon
þe eft æt þearfe þolian noldon.
Þa wearð afeallen þæs folces ealdor,
Æþelredes eorl; ealle gesawon
heorð-geneatas þæt hyra heorra læg.
Þa ðær wendon forð wlance þegenas,
unearge men efston georne;
hi woldon þa ealle oðer twega,
lif forlætan oððe leofne gewrecan.
Swa hi bylde forð bearn Ælfrices,
wiga wintrum geong, wordum mælde;
Ælfwine þa cwæð; he on ellen spræc:

Then heathen warriors cut him down and both the men who had stood beside him; Ælfnoth and Wulfmær both lay dead, who had given up their life beside their lord.

Then those who did not want to be there turned from the battle. The sons of Odda were the first in flight; Godric turned from the fight and left that good man who had often given him many a horse. He leaped onto the horse that had belonged to his lord, onto that riding gear where he had no right to be. And both his brothers, Godwine and Godwig, ran away with him, cared nothing for the battle, but rather turned from the fight and sought the woods, fled to that safety and saved their lives—and many more men than would have been at all fitting if they had remembered all the honors which he had bestowed on them for their profit. Earlier on that very day, when he had held a meeting at the place of assembly, Offa had predicted just such a thing, that many a man was speaking boldly in that place who would not, when his turn came, endure in need.

The leader of the army, Æthelred's nobleman, lay fallen then; all the attendants of the inner circle saw that their lord lay dead. Then the courageous subjects, the uncowardly men, turned to face the front, hastened eagerly; all of them then wanted one of two things: to lose their life or else to avenge the dear man.

So the son of Ælfric, a warrior young in winters, urged them forward, spoke plainly; Ælfwine then spoke; he spoke

"Gemunaþ nu þæra mæla   þe we oft æt meodo spræcon,
þonne we on bence   beot ahofon,
hæleð on healle,   ymbe heard gewinn.
Nu mæg cunnian   hwa cene sy.
Ic wylle mine æþelo   eallum gecyþan,
þæt ic wæs on Myrcon   miccles cynnes;
wæs min ealda fæder   Ealhelm haten,
wis ealdor-man,   woruld-gesælig.
Ne sceolon me on þære þeode   þegenas ætwitan
þæt ic of ðisse fyrde   feran wille,
eard gesecan,   nu min ealdor ligeð
forheawen æt hilde.   Me is þæt hearma mæst:
He wæs ægðer min mæg   and min hlaford."
Þa he forð eode,   fæhðe gemunde,
þæt he mid orde   anne geræhte
flotan on þam folce,   þæt se on foldan læg
forwegen mid his wæpne.   Ongan þa winas manian,
frynd and geferan,   þæt hi forð eodon.
Offa gemælde,   æsc-holt asceoc:
"Hwæt þu, Ælfwine, hafast   ealle gemanode
þegenas to þearfe.   Nu ure þeoden lið,
eorl on eorðan,   us is eallum þearf
þæt ure æghwylc   oþerne bylde
wigan to wige,   þa hwile þe he wæpen mæge
habban and healdan,   heardne mece,
gar and god-swurd.   Us Godric hæfð,
earh Oddan bearn,   ealle beswicene:
Wende þæs formoni man—   þa he on meare rad,
on wlancan þam wicge—   þæt wære hit ure hlaford;
forþan wearð her on felda   folc totwæmed,
scyld-burh tobrocen.   Abreoðe his angin
þæt he her swa manigne   man aflymde!"

out with courage: "Remember now those occasions when we would often make speeches over the mead cups, when on the benches, as warriors in the hall, we declared our vow about the hard fight. Now it can be tested who may be brave. I want to make known my lineage to all, that I came of a great family among the Mercians; my grandfather was called Ealhhelm, a wise nobleman, prosperous in the world. Officers in that folk shall not criticize me, that I would desert this army, seek out my home, now that my leader lies cut down in battle. For me the injury is greatest: He was both my kinsman and my lord."

Then he advanced, kept his mind on the grievance, with the result that he reached with his point one seaman in that force so that he was lying on the ground, slain by his weapon. He began then to exhort his comrades, friends, and fellows that they should go forward.

Offa made a speech, shook his ash spear: "Well, Ælfwine, you have exhorted all the supporters in our moment of need. Now that our lord lies dead, the nobleman on the earth, it is necessary for us all that each one of us encourage the other, encourage the warrior in battle, as long as he may be able to have and hold his weapon, his hard saber, spear, and good sword. Godric, the cowardly son of Odda, has betrayed us all: Too many a man believed—when he rode on the horse, on that proud steed—that it was our lord; for that reason the army was split in two here on the field, the shield wall broken. May his deed be damned that he put to flight so many a man here."

Leofsunu gemælde and his linde ahof,
bord to gebeorge; he þam beorne oncwæð:
"Ic þæt gehate, þæt ic heonan nelle
fleon fotes trym, ac wille furðor gan,
wrecan on gewinne minne wine-drihten.
Ne þurfon me embe Sturmere stedefæste hælæð
wordum ætwitan, nu min wine gecranc,
þæt ic hlafordleas ham siðie,
wende fram wige, ac me sceal wæpen niman,
ord and iren." He ful yrre wod,
feaht fæstlice; fleam he forhogode.
Dunnere þa cwæð, daroð acwehte,
unorne ceorl, ofer eall clypode,
bæd þæt beorna gehwylc Byrhtnoð wræce:
"Ne mæg na wandian se þe wrecan þenceð
frean on folce, ne for feore murnan."
Þa hi forð eodon, feores hi ne rohton;
ongunnon þa hired-men heardlice feohtan,
grame gar-berend, and God bædon
þæt hi moston gewrecan hyra wine-drihten
and on hyra feondum fyl gewyrcan.
Him se gysel ongan geornlice fylstan;
he wæs on Norð-hymbron heardes cynnes;
Ecglafes bearn, him wæs Æscferð nama.
He ne wandode na æt þam wig-plegan,
ac he fysde forð flan genehe;
hwilon he on bord sceat, hwilon beorn tæsde;
æfre embe stunde he sealde sume wunde,
þa hwile ðe he wæpna wealdan moste.

Leofsunu made a speech and he lifted up the linden wood, his shield for protection; he gave answer to that man: "I make this promise: that I will not flee one footstep from this place; rather, I will go forward, will avenge my loving lord in the struggle. Steadfast warriors around Sturmere Lake will have no need to blame me with words, that I journeyed home lordless, turned from the fight, now that my leader has fallen; but rather, the weapon, the point and the iron shall take me." In great wrath he strode, fought without yielding; he scorned retreat.

Dunnere, a simple freeman, spoke then, shook his javelin, called out over all, urged each of the men to avenge Byrhtnoth: "Whoever thinks to avenge his lord among the troops can never turn back nor care about his life." Then they stepped forward, had no concern for their life; the men of the hearth watch, angry spear-bearers, began to fight fiercely and prayed God that they might avenge their beloved lord and cause death among their enemies.

The hostage began keenly to help them; he came of a tough clan among the Northumbrians; son of Ecglaf, his name was Æscferth. He never turned aside from that battle play; rather he sent forth arrow after arrow; sometimes his shot hit a shield, sometimes he pierced a man; ever and again he dealt out some wound as long as he could wield his weapons.

Þa gyt on orde stod Eadweard se langa,
gearo and geornful, gylp-wordum spræc
þæt he nolde fleogan fot-mæl landes,
ofer bæc bugan, þa his betera leg.
He bræc þone bord-weall and wið þa beornas feaht,
oðþæt he his sinc-gyfan on þam sæ-mannum
wurðlice wrec, ær he on wæle læge.
Swa dyde Æþeric, æþele gefera,
fus and forð-georn, feaht eornoste,
Sibyrhtes broðor, and swiðe mænig oþer.
Clufon cellod bord; cene hi weredon;
bærst bordes lærig, and seo byrne sang
gryre-leoða sum.
Þa æt guðe sloh
Offa þone sæ-lidan, þæt he on eorðan feoll,
and ðær Gaddes mæg grund gesohte.
Raðe wearð æt hilde Offa forheawen;
he hæfde ðeah geforþod þæt he his frean gehet,
swa he beotode ær wið his beah-gifan
þæt hi sceoldon begen on burh ridan,
hale to hame, oððe on here crincgan,
on wæl-stowe wundum sweltan.
He læg ðegenlice ðeodne gehende.
Ða wearð borda gebræc. Brim-men wodon,
guðe gegremode. Gar oft þurhwod
fæges feorh-hus.
Forð þa eode Wistan,
Þurstanes sunu, wið þas secgas feaht.
He wæs on geþrange hyra þreora bana,
ær him Wigelmes bearn on þam wæle læge.

Edward the Tall still stood in the front rank; keen and eager, he spoke out in the words of a vaunt that he would not give up the measure of one foot of land, would not turn back, since his superior lay dead. He crashed through the shield wall and fought against the warriors until he had wreaked proper vengeance for his treasure-giving lord against those seamen, before he lay among the dead.

Ætheric, the noble companion, did the same; battle-eager and ready to advance, the brother of Sibyrht fought earnestly, and very many another. They cleft the decorated shield; the daring men defended themselves; the shield rim burst, and the mail coat sang a song of terror.

Then in the fight Offa struck that sea traveler so that he fell to the earth, and there also the kinsman of Gadd sought the ground. Offa was quickly cut down in the battle; however, he had carried out that which he promised his lord when previously he uttered the vow before his ring-giver that they should both ride into the fortress, ride home unharmed, or else fall amid the army, die of wounds in the place of carnage. He lay beside his lord as a warrior should.

Then there was a clashing of shields. Seafarers, infuriated by the fight, came striding. Often the spear passed through the life house of the fated.

Then Wigstan, son of Thurstan, stepped forward, fought against the warriors. In the melee he was the death of three of them before he himself, descendant of Wighelm, should lie down among the slaughtered.

Þær wæs stið gemot. Stodon fæste
wigan on gewinne. Wigend cruncon,
wundum werige. Wæl feol on eorþan.
Oswold and Eadwold ealle hwile,
begen þa gebroþru, beornas trymedon,
hyra wine-magas wordon bædon
þæt hi þær æt ðearfe þolian sceoldon,
unwaclice wæpna neotan.
Byrhtwold maþelode, bord hafenode—
se wæs eald geneat— æsc acwehte;
he ful baldlice beornas lærde:
"Hige sceal þe heardra, heorte þe cenre,
mod sceal þe mare, þe ure mægen lytlað.
Her lið ure ealdor eall forheawen,
god on greote. A mæg gnornian
se ðe nu fram þis wig-plegan wendan þenceð.
Ic eom frod feores; fram ic ne wille,
ac ic me be healfe minum hlaforde,
be swa leofan men, licgan þence."
Swa hi Æþelgares bearn ealle bylde,
Godric to guþe. Oft he gar forlet,
wæl-spere windan on þa wicingas,
swa he on þam folce firmest eode,
heow and hynde, oð þæt he on hilde gecranc.
Næs þæt na se Godric þe ða guðe forbeah . . .

There was a stern meeting there. Warriors stood fast in the struggle. Fighters fell, weary with their wounds. Dead flesh fell to the ground.

All the while Oswold and Eadwold, both those brothers, rallied the troops, vocally urged their beloved kinsmen that they should endure there in the time of need, should ply their weapons without weakening.

Byrhtwold made a speech, raised up his shield—he was an old comrade—shook his ash spear; he instructed the men very boldly: "Thought must be the tougher, heart the keener, spirit must be the greater, the more our strength declines. Here lies our leader, cut down completely, the good man in the grit. He must ever grieve who now considers turning away from this battle play. I am old in terms of life; I do not wish to get away; rather, I intend to lie by the side of my lord, by the man so dear."

In the same way, the son of Æthelgar, Godric, incited them all to the fight. Often he released a spear, let a deadly javelin fly into the vikings; in the same way, he strode foremost into that army, hacked, and brought them low until he sank in battle. By no means was that the Godric who fled the battle . . .

Abbreviations

The Anglo-Saxon Chronicle: A Collaborative Edition:

A, A-text = Volume 3, *MS. A,* ed. Janet Bately (Cambridge, 1986)

B, B-text = Volume 4, *MS. B,* ed. Simon Taylor (Cambridge, 1983)

C, C-text = Volume 5, *MS. C,* ed. Katherine O'Brien O'Keeffe (Cambridge, 2001)

D, D-text = Volume 6, *MS. D,* ed. G. P. Cubbin (Cambridge, 1996)

E, E-text = Volume 7, *MS. E,* ed. Susan Irvine (Cambridge, 2004)

Asser, *Life of King Alfred* = William Henry Stevenson, ed., *Asser's Life of King Alfred: Together with the Annals of Saint Neots Erroneously Ascribed to Asser,* new impression with an article by Dorothy Whitelock (Oxford, 1959; originally published, Oxford, 1904)

CCCC = Cambridge, Corpus Christi College

DOE = *Dictionary of Old English: A to Le,* ed. Angus Cameron, Ashley Crandell Amos, Antonette diPaolo Healey, and others (Toronto, 2024), https://doe.artsci.utoronto.ca/

EETS s.s. = Early English Text Society supplementary series

EH = *Bede's Ecclesiastical History of the English People,* ed. and trans. Bertram Colgrave and R. A. B. Mynors (Oxford, 1969; reprinted with corrections, Oxford, 1991)

OE = Old English

Recap. = *Recapitulatio,* book 5, chapter 24 of Colgrave and Mynors, *Bede's Ecclesiastical History,* pp. 560–67

s.a. = *sub anno* (under the year)

Swanton, *Chronicle* = Michael Swanton, ed. and trans., *The Anglo-Saxon Chronicle* (London, 1996)

Wiley Blackwell Encyclopedia = *The Wiley Blackwell Encyclopedia of Anglo-Saxon England,* ed. Michael Lapidge, John Blair, Simon Keynes, and Donald Scragg, 2nd ed. (Chichester, West Sussex, 2014)

Note on the Texts

The Old English Chronicle, the A-Text to 1001

Annals 1 to 1001 of the A-text survive in a single manuscript, Cambridge, Corpus Christi College MS 173, known as the Parker manuscript, after its most famous owner, Archbishop Matthew Parker, who acquired it in 1575 from the dean of Christ Church, Canterbury. In the early eleventh century, the A-text was copied into London, British Library, Cotton MS Otho B. xi, now known as the G-text. This manuscript was almost totally destroyed in the Cotton Library fire of 1731, though not before a transcript of it had been made by Laurence Nowell in 1562 (London, British Library, MS Add. 43703, fols. 200–232). The great value of the G-text is its witness against the changes to the A-text made after the Norman Conquest by the scribe of another Chronicle text, manuscript F, who heavily revised the A-text up to the annal for 784, with further interpolations at annals 924 and 940. It has thus been possible to use the witness of G as reconstructed in the edition by Angelika Lutz, *Die Version G der angelsächsischen Chronik: Rekonstruktion und Edition* (Munich, 1981), to restore readings now partly or wholly illegible in the A-text. These readings are incorporated in the semidiplomatic text, volume 3 of David N. Dumville and Simon

Keynes's *Collaborative Edition,* on which the present edition is based.

In line with the practice adopted in previous editions of Old English texts in this series, only variants that significantly affect the translation or its interpretation are indicated in the Notes to the Texts. The edited text is made up of those entries in the A-text that were copied before the Norman Conquest, with input, in the case of substantial damage, from the readings of its copy, manuscript G. (Additions and alterations in post-Conquest hands are not reported.) Since the differences between the A-text and the other manuscripts of the Chronicle have been identified and their possible significance exhaustively discussed in the volumes devoted to them in *The Anglo-Saxon Chronicle: A Collaborative Edition,* these will normally not be listed. As a result, the Notes to the Texts refer almost exclusively to those readings in the A-text that have been corrected.

Following the editorial conventions of the *Collaborative Edition,* accents have not been recorded, and abbreviations are silently expanded—including the ubiquitous Tironian *nota,* "⁊," printed here either as *ond* or *and,* depending on the date and dialect of the section in which the abbreviation occurs. Capitalization, punctuation, and word division are modern and conventional. Arabic numerals replace the Roman numerals that appear in the manuscript for each annal year (but not the Roman numerals in the entries themselves). Annal numbers with no accompanying entry in the manuscript are omitted, their absence marked by a long dash. In the case of those parts of the A-text that share material with the B/C group of Chronicle manuscripts, readings from these latter manuscripts are only very exceptionally reported in the notes.

The Death of Alfred *and* The Death of Edward

The C-text of the Old English Chronicles is found in London, British Library, Cotton MS Tiberius B. i, fols. 115v–64r, a composite manuscript. For a discussion of the manuscript and its contents, see Katherine O'Brien O'Keeffe, ed., *MS. C,* vol. 5 of *The Anglo-Saxon Chronicle: A Collaborative Edition,* ed. David N. Dumville and Simon Keynes (Cambridge, 2001), xv–xxvi. Folios 3r–111v of the manuscript preserve a text of the Old English translation of Orosius's *History,* copied some time in the first half of the eleventh century. Folios 112–64 are a mid-eleventh century addition to the earlier manuscript and contain the C-text and two Old English poems, the *Menologium* (fols. 112r–14v) and *Maxims II* (fol. 115r–v). Annals for the C-text begin at 60 BCE and end with an incomplete entry for the events of 1066, breaking off at the Battle of Stamford Bridge. There are eight hands at work in the C-text, and the two poems edited here, *The Death of Alfred* and *The Death of Edward,* were the work of Hands 2 (annals 491 through 1048) and 6 (1065 and 1066 to *sandwic*), respectively (O'Brien O'Keeffe, *MS. C,* xxvi–xxxvii). The C-text transmits all of the Old English Chronicle poems edited in Elliot Van Kirk Dobbie, ed., *The Anglo-Saxon Minor Poems,* vol. 6 of *The Anglo-Saxon Poetic Records* (New York, 1942), 16–26. Of these, *The Death of Alfred* and *The Death of Edward* are preserved only in the C-text and the D-text (London, British Library, Cotton MS Tiberius B. iv); the

E-text (Oxford, Bodleian Library, Laud Misc. 636) omits all mention of the murder of Alfred in its annal for 1036 and is silent for 1065.

The editorial conventions for these two poems from the C-text generally follow those outlined above. The text is based on that in the *Collaborative Edition,* vol. 5, though emending on occasion and offering more generous punctuation than that followed in the *Collaborative* series. The Notes to the Texts that follow are selective and ignore the numerous minor scribal errors that have been silently corrected by the editor.

The Battle of Maldon

The Battle of Maldon was transmitted to postmedieval times in London, British Library, Cotton MS Otho A. xii, a manuscript burned in its entirety in the fire of 1731. Before the manuscript was destroyed, a transcript of the poem was made by David Casley, probably in 1725 (Oxford, Bodleian Library, Rawlinson MS B. 203, fols. 7r–12v). In the destroyed Cotton manuscript, the poem was already a fragment bound together with other Old English texts in the seventeenth century. Casley's transcript evinces what appear to be some fairly typical errors made in modern copies of Old English texts, such as confusion of *a* and *u,* of *ð* and *d,* and of *c* and *t,* and these have been corrected with some confidence in the present text. This text agrees in most particulars with the edition of Elliott Van Kirk Dobbie, with minor differences adduced chiefly on the basis of the findings of Donald Scragg in his edition, and to a lesser extent of John C. Pope, as well as the edition of Mark Griffith (see the Bibliography for these references). Abbreviations have been silently expanded and spacing and punctuation made to conform to modern standards for the editing of Old English poetry. As in other poetic texts edited in this series, a hyphen has been supplied between the constituents of genuine compounds.

The Notes to the Texts are a listing of textual variants. Variants, listed after the colon, are the readings of Casley's transcript. An ellipsis (. . .) is Casley's own indication of missing material, the number of points presumably corresponding to the number of missing characters.

Notes to the Texts

The Old English Chronicle, the A-Text to 1001

Genealogical and Regnal List

1 æt: *added above the line in another hand*

2 Westseaxna rice: seaxna rice; *for the insertion of* west, *see David N. Dumville, "The West Saxon Genealogical Regnal List: Manuscripts and Texts," Anglia 104 (1986): 1–32, at 32*

Ceaulining: celming

Ceawlin: celm

3 Westseaxna lond: wesseaxna lond, *with* t *added above the line in a different hand (the predominant spelling in A is* ss; *see Janet Bately, ed., MS. A, vol. 3 of The Anglo-Saxon Chronicle: A Collaborative Edition, ed. David N. Dumville and Simon Keynes [Cambridge, 1986], clx)*

geeodon: geodon

Annals

640 Eadbald *E:* [R]edbald *(with* R *erased)*

653 Middelengle: Middelseaxe

655 Peada: Penda

668 Þeodorus: Þeodorius *(with* i *erased)*

676 oferhergeade: oferhergeada

687 forhergeade: forhergeada

731 Tatwine wæs: Tatwine ond wæs

741 gehalgod: gehalgode

790 ærcebiscepe: biscepe

796 Coenwulf: Ceolwulf

830 Feologild: Feologid

855.2 Friþuwald Frealafing: Friþuwald Freawining
Cainan: Camon

866 friþ wiþ: friþ

878.1 ond micel þæs folces: micel þæs folces ond

879 an hloþ: on hloþ

885.1 Sture: Stufe

893.6 þegnas ofslægene: þegn *(with* as *in another hand)* ofslægen
ond þara Deniscra . . . geslegen: *added from BC*

896.1 þegna *BC (s.a. 897)*: þena

896.4 Wealhgerefa *BC (s.a. 897)*: Wealhgefera

900.2 þæt he gewicode: þæt he *from G*; *original reading erased*

910 Eowils *BC (s.a. 911)*: Ecwils

918 Stanforda: Steanforda

937.12 dynede *G*: dæn\n/ede

937.26 þe mid: þæmid

937.39 hilde-rinc: hildering

937.43 forgrunden: fergrunden

937.49 cumbol-gehnastes: culbodgehnades

937.56 Iraland: hira land

937.72 Wealas: weealles

942 ylcan: ylecan

973.13 þa gen: þa agan

The Death of Alfred

20 suð-portice: suð postice *C*; suð portice *D*

The Death of Edward

1 Her *D*: er *with space left for a capital* H *C*

2 soþfæste: soþfæ *with loss of letters where the edge of the page has flaked away C*; soðfeste *D*; soðfæst *Laurence Nowell, in London, British Library, MS Add. 43704*

7 weolan *D*: weolm *C*
brytnode: brytnode *corrected to* brytnodo\n/ *C*; britnode *D*

12 cealde: ceald *C*; cealda *D*

21 brytnodan: brynodan *C*; brytnodon *D*

25 lungre *Elliott Van Kirk Dobbie, The Anglo-Saxon Minor Poems, vol. 6 of The Anglo-Saxon Poetic Records (New York, 1942)*: lunger *CD*

The Battle of Maldon

4 to hige: t hige

5 Þa: þ

33 þonne: þon

hilde: ..ulde

61 we: þe

113 wearð: weard

116 wearð: wærd

171 gestandan: ge stundan

173 Ic: *not in David Casley's transcript*

191 ærndon: ærdon

192 Godwine: godrine

200 modiglice: modelice

201 þearfe: þære

208 forlætan: for lætun

212 gemunaþ nu þæra mæla: ge munu þa mæla

224 ægðer: ægder

292 crincgan: crintgan

297 Forð þa: forða

298 sunu: suna

299 geþrange: geþrang

300 Wigelmes: wigelines

324 oð: od

325 guðe: gude

Notes to the Translations

The Old English Chronicle, the A-Text to 1001

Genealogical and Regnal List

1–3 *In this year . . . from the Britons*: The Genealogical and Regnal List (often referred to as the "Genealogical Preface") is a narrative pedigree of King Æthelwulf (King Alfred's father), and is a document meant to support the claims of Æthelwulf and his sons as members of the dynasty descended from Cerdic. The dates of reigns in the Genealogical and Regnal List do not always accord with the dates given in Æthelwulf's pedigree at AN 855.2. For an analysis of the list and its witness to the history of Wessex, see David N. Dumville, "The West Saxon Genealogical Regnal List and the Chronology of Early Wessex," *Peritia* 4 (1985): 21–66. For an edition with variants from all witnesses, see David N. Dumville, "The West Saxon Genealogical Regnal List: Manuscripts and Texts," *Anglia* 104 (1986): 1–32.

2 *son of Ceawlin, Ceawlin*: The A-text and all other witnesses to the West Saxon Genealogical and Regnal List read "Celming, Celm." AN 855.2, giving King Æthelwulf's lineage, reads instead "Ceaulining, Ceawlin," which has been adopted at this point in the OE text. Dumville, "West Saxon Genealogical Regnal List: Manuscripts and Texts," 19, argues persuasively that the correct Anglian form is "Celining, Celin" and emends accordingly (25).

Annals

[60 BCE] *the emperor Gaius Julius*: The source of this entry is Bede, *Recapitulatio (Recap.)*, the list of dated events that concludes his *Ec-*

clesiastical History (EH), ed. and trans. Bertram Colgrave and R. A. B. Mynors, *Bede's Ecclesiastical History of the English People,* Oxford Medieval Texts (Oxford, 1969; repr., Oxford, 1991), 560–61. The OE text uses the early loan word *casere* as "emperor, ruler," rather than as the cognomen *Caesar.*

the first of the Romans: The chronicler here follows the syntax of the entry for 60 BCE in Bede, *Recap.* to refer to Gaius Julius Caesar as "the first Roman to make war on Britain."

1 *AN 1*: The abbreviation *AN* in the text of Chronicle stands for Latin *annus* (year), or more likely *anno* (in the year). The annal numbers, given as Arabic numerals in this text and translation, were written as Roman numerals in the manuscript.

fifty-six years . . . fifty-second: Octavian Caesar did not become emperor of the Romans, with the title Augustus, until 27 BCE. However, as great-nephew to Julius Caesar and his adopted son and heir, he is described in a number of Latin texts as ruling from the date of the latter's assassination on the Ides of March, 44 BCE—that is to say, for fifty-six years. The figure is later produced in the A-text by a revising scribe, along with an accompanying figure of forty-two for A's fifty-two, as the time of Christ's birth. These correct figures of fifty-six and forty-two are found also in the OE renderings of Bede and Orosius, as well as in a range of early medieval Latin texts.

2 *The astrologers*: The Magi who followed the star to find Christ. See Matthew 2:1.

3 *Herod died, having stabbed himself*: A claim found also in the *Old English Martyrology* and in an OE version of the *Vindicta Salvatoris,* which describes the weapon as a spear. Compare Matthew 2:19 and Acts 12:21–23.

12 *Lycia*: A misreading of the personal name Lysanias (the tetrarch of Abilene) for a form of the place-name Lycia.

30 *the twelve apostles*: Having just named five of the apostles listed in Matthew 10:2–4, the annalist should have referred here to "*the rest of* the twelve apostles." On Christ's baptism, see Luke 3:1.

34 *Paul*: The conversion of Saul (later, as here, known as Paul), first described in Acts 9, is generally assigned to the years 33 to 36.

Stephen: The stoning of the protomartyr Saint Stephen is described in Acts 7:58–59.

39 *Gaius*: Gaius Caesar, nicknamed Caligula (Latin *caligula* is a small military boot), actually became emperor in 37 and was assassinated in 41.

45 *Herod*: See Acts 12:2.

71 *Jerusalem*: The Romans' siege of Jerusalem ended in the year 70.

81 *Titus*: Vespasian's son in fact succeeded his father in 79, with 81 being the year of his death, aged forty-one. The reference to what Titus said comes ultimately from Suetonius but has been handed down in a number of different forms, another of which is used in the OE translation of Orosius 6.8, ed. Janet Bately, *The Old English Orosius,* EETS s.s. 6 (London, 1980), 139.

83 *Domitian*: Roman emperor, correct dates 81 to 96.

90 *John the evangelist went to his rest in Ephesus*: Literally, "rested himself." A translation of the Latin verb *requiescere,* used of Saint John's death in a range of Latin texts, reflecting a belief in the early Church that the saint was in fact only resting, awaiting the Second Coming of Christ. This information was originally entered as AN 90, subsequently erased, and added by a later hand as AN 99.

110 *Ignatius*: The precise year of the martyrdom of the bishop of Antioch is uncertain.

167 *To him Lucius, king of the Britons, sent a letter*: The date and the details of the supposed correspondence between Eleutherius, bishop of Rome, and Lucius, king of the Britons, come via Bede, *Recap.,* 562–63. Modern research, however, has shown that the Lucius in question was in fact not a Briton but a king of Edessa in the province of Syria. See Alan Smith, "Lucius of Britain: Alleged King and Church Founder," *Folklore* 90, no. 1 (1979): 29–36, at 29.

189 *a dike*: *EH* 1.5, pp. 24–27, gives this date of accession for Severus and comments that this dike was accompanied by a very strong rampart with a large number of towers. It was a rebuilding of an earlier fortification constructed by the emperor Hadrian, under whose name the wall is still known today.

381 *born in the land of Britain*: A misconstrual of the statement in Bede, *Recap.*, 562–63, that Maximus (not, as here, "Maximianus") was made emperor by the army in Britain.

430 *Palladius*: Who Palladius was is not known.

the Irish: Bede, *Recap.*, 562–63, has "Scottos," translated in the A-text by "Scottum," a term used up to at least the turn of the ninth century to refer to both the people of Ireland and the Irish immigrants who settled in Iona and on mainland Britain. See Introduction, "Names of Peoples, Ethnic Groups, or Political Entities." For OE *Irland* and *Iraland,* see below, annals 914.3 and 937.56.

449 *Mauricius and Valentinus*: Manuscript A's reading "Mauricius" was later altered to "Martianus"; A's reading "Ualentines" for "Ualentinus" refers to Emperor Valentinianus III.

succeeded to the kingdom and ruled for seven years: The OE translator's verbal alterations make nonsense of the facts. Marcianus was Byzantine emperor from 450 to 457. Valentinian was Roman emperor from 425 to 455: the two emperors overlapped only for the years 450 to 455.

the Britons: OE *Brettas,* a people of Celtic origin, speaking British, a Brittonic language that survives today as Cornish, Welsh, and Breton.

455 *Hengest and Horsa*: War leaders, described by *EH* 1.15, pp. 50–51, as *duces* (leaders, commanders, chiefs), arriving in longships. As OE common nouns, *hengest* and *horsa* both mean "horse" and may here have been bynames.

457 *London*: OE *Lunden* (Latin *Londinium*) is here collocated with the word *burg,* a term found in a wide range of contexts in OE place-names, still surviving in modern English *-borough, -bury, -burgh.* With *burg*'s basic sense of "fortified place," used to refer to a stronghold, fort, fortress, or fortification, and extended to cover towns and cities, *Lunden,* despite being described as *ceaster* in the *Old English Bede,* meets the criteria for the title *burg* in the A-text. (The remains of the surrounding defensive walls are still to be seen today.)

465 *Britons*: The OE *Walas* may seem misapplied, since *wealh* is a word

in other contexts normally translated as "foreigner, stranger, slave," with names for the native inhabitants of a place including *inlenda* and *inlendisc.* In the Chronicle's account of events in fifth-century Britain, however, it was the *indigini* of Bede, the indigenous population, who, from the ninth-century English point of view, were the ones from another nation—the *walas.* In the law code of Ine (promulgated 688–694 and appended to Alfred's *Domboc*), they were allotted a status inferior to that of the English. The use of the word "Welsh" throughout this section in the translations of Benjamin Thorpe, G. M. Garmonsway, Michael Swanton, and others is inaccurate.

leaders: For the terms *ealdormann* (initially applied to a range of high-ranking men) and *thegn,* see Introduction, "Names of Peoples, Ethnic Groups, or Political Entities."

477 *Andredesleag*: In the A-text, OE *leag* is used in its earliest sense, "woodland." In this annal, *Andredesleag* refers to the area in Kent now known as the Weald (from OE *weald,* "forest, wood"), with first component *Andred,* derived from Latin *Anderida,* the Roman fort at Pevensey. See *Andredesceaster,* AN 491.

495 *chieftains*: The OE version again uses the word *ealdormann* here in a nonspecific sense, but this time the people involved are leading an invasion force.

501 *Portsmouth*: Not a reference to the present-day city of Portsmouth, which is mainly located on Portsea (OE *Portes ieg,* "Port's island"), in Hampshire. The designation may well go back to Roman times, with the *Portus Ardaoni* (or *Adurni*), a fortress now part of a medieval castle in present-day Porchester.

530 *Wihtgaraburg*: Manuscript A's puzzling reading "Wihtgarabyrg" (repeated in AN 544) is best explained as the result of confusion on the part of a scribe copying a group of three annals, connecting the personal name Wihtgar, first used in AN 514, with the place-name *Wiht* (Isle of Wight), first used in AN 530, the problem being how to account for the anomalous "Wihtgarabyrg." Dorothy Whitelock, in her translation, *The Anglo-Saxon Chronicle,* with David C. Douglas and Susie I. Tucker (London, 1961), prints without comment the OE of texts A, B, and C,

while Swanton replaces *Wihtgara* with the genitive of *Wihtgar* (OE *Wihtgares*) to read "Wihtgar's stronghold"; Michael Swanton, ed. and trans., *The Anglo-Saxon Chronicle* (London, 1996), 16. Swanton, *Chronicle,* 16n4, also suggests an emendation to *Wihtwarabyrg* (*burg* of the inhabitants of the Isle of Wight). In these circumstances, this edition leaves readers free to draw their own conclusions as to the most plausible solution.

538 *sixteenth of February*: Literally, "fourteen days before the calends of March."

from daybreak until nine in the morning: The third hour of the day, OE *undern,* is our 9:00 a.m.

540 *twentieth of June*: Literally, "twelve days before the calends of July."

547 *Ida*: In 547, the Northumbrians were still divided between two kingdoms, Bernicia and Deira, with Ida the first king of Bernicia.

Eoppa's son . . . Bældæg's son: This is the first of a series of genealogies of Anglo-Saxon kings inserted in this part of the A-text with the suffix *-ing* conveying filial relationship. For Ida as progenitor, see AN 670, 685, and 731.

556 *Barbury*: Barbury Castle (Wiltshire) is the site of a great Iron Age hill fort, hence the use of the term *burg,* "fortification."

568 *Æthelberht*: King of the people of Kent, with a Christian Frankish wife, Bertha, Æthelberht was the first Anglo-Saxon ruler to convert to Christianity and the third to be called "Bretwalda."

noblemen: On the range of the term *ealdormann,* see Introduction, "Names of Peoples, Ethnic Groups, or Political Entities."

571 *four settlements*: The OE term here is *tun,* found in this annal in composition in the place-name *Benningtun.* Given the range of possible renderings (for example, "homestead, manor, village, and town"), the term "settlement," employed by archaeologists, seems a practical compromise both here and for the suffix *-ham* (homestead, manor, estate, village).

Limbury: *Lygeanburg* was a settlement on the Roman road known as the Icknield Way, developed on a site already in use by the Iron Age. Its first component, *Lyge,* is a river name of British origin.

Aylesbury: Excavations in 1985 produced evidence of the town having had its roots within an Iron Age hill fort, the ditch of which was still in use in the sixth century, not being replaced until the eighth.

577 *Gloucester, Cirencester*: Both names have second component *ceaster*. Romano-British *Glevum* was a legionary fort on the River Severn, while Cirencester's addition of *ceaster* to the original name presumably acknowledges the contribution of the Romans, providers of a fort and defensive walls. The capture of these two key settlements, along with Bath, would have opened up the Severn valley to the attackers and separated from each other the areas still held by the Britons in the north and the west.

592 *Woden's Barrow*: The OE reads *Woddesbeorge,* with second element, *beorg,* meaning "barrow, hill, mound, tumulus." It is also mentioned in AN 715. In the E-text, the place-name is given as Woden's *(Wodnes)* Barrow. The tumulus in question is now known as "Adam's Grave," a Neolithic long barrow at Alton Priors, Wiltshire.

596 *sent Augustine to Britain*: This entry compresses into a single annal material that Bede, *Recap.,* enters in two, with *anno* 596 referring to the sending of Augustine (a monk and prior of a monastery in Rome) with a few monks to England, and (in *anno* 597) their arrival. According to Bede, Augustine and his companions, having set out on their mission, were overcome by fear at the thought of going to a "barbarous, fierce, and unbelieving nation whose language they did not even understand" (*EH* 1.23, p. 69). After a papal rebuke, Augustine, with nearly forty companions and some Frankish interpreters, finally arrived in Kent.

601 *pallium*: A band of white wool in the gift of the pope, worn round the shoulders, and at this date not yet automatically bestowed on archbishops.

spiritual instructors: Among the teachers sent from Rome, *EH* 1.29, pp. 104–5, names Paulinus, Justus, and Mellitus. Mellitus was consecrated bishop of London, later succeeding another of Augustine's colleagues, Laurentius, in Canterbury. Justus was initially bishop of Rochester, but on Mellitus's death was appointed archbishop of Canterbury (*EH* 2.7–8, pp. 156–59).

Edwin, king of the Northumbrians: Son of Ælle, he lived in exile at the court of Rædwald, king of the East Angles, during the reign of Æthelferth, until the latter was killed by the East Angles in 616. Edwin gained control of both Bernicia and Deira, accepted Christianity in 627, and died in battle with Cadwallon of Gwynedd and the Mercian king, Penda, in 633.

603 *Degsa's Stone*: *EH* 1.34, pp. 116–17, reports that in the battle at *Degsastan* (which Bede translates "the stone of Degsa") the Northumbrians defeated a force led by the king of the Irish people that had settled in northern Britain. The OE text gives the name as *Egesanstane.*

614 *Cwichelm*: Son of Cynegils and coupled with him again in AN 628, possibly as his joint heir. Described in *EH* 2.9, pp. 164–65, as a king of the West Saxons who, in 626, sent an assassin to murder Edwin of Northumbria. An unarmed thegn, one Lilla, died saving the king, who survived the attack.

626 *Penda*: This first reference in the text to Penda, king of the Mercians, is a clumsy summary of his subsequent career. Book 3 of *EH* describes Penda as a heathen, a barbarous and evil enemy, who, whether attacking the Northumbrians, or, later, the East Angles, cruelly devastated their territories, destroying everything he could with fire and sword. The lifespan attributed to him in the text is clearly an exaggeration, with the most likely date of his accession either 626 or 632.

632 *Eorpwald*: The true date of the conversion of Eorpwald, king of the East Angles and son of Rædwald, is uncertain. *EH* 2.15, pp. 188–90, reports that he was killed by a heathen, shortly after he had been persuaded by King Edwin to accept the Christian faith, an event calculated to have occurred in 627 or 628.

633 *Paulinus returned*: *EH* 2.20, pp. 204–5, describes how Paulinus, after the death of King Edwin, fled to Kent, taking with him Edwin's widow and children, along with much treasure. He then served as bishop of Rochester until his death in 644.

634 *Bishop Birinus*: *EH* 3.7, pp. 232–33, reports that Birinus came to

England on the advice of Pope Honorius. Finding the entire West Saxon nation to be heathen, he decided to preach the word there, rather than to go further afield. First bishop of the West Saxons, his see was at Dorchester on Thames.

635 *Dorchester*: Site of a Roman town with a neighboring Iron Age hill fort.

Oswald: Oswald was king, first of Bernicia, later of all the Northumbrians, when, on defeating Cadwallon, king of Gwynedd, he reunited his kingdom and neighboring Deira. One of the reasons for the visit to Dorchester appears to be the cementing of relations with Cynegils, the king of the West Saxons. After his death in battle against Penda, king of the Mercians, he was venerated as the first Anglo-Saxon royal saint. See *EH* 3.9–13, pp. 240–55.

636 *Felix*: According to *EH* 2.15, pp. 190–91, and 3.17, pp. 268–69, Felix, born in Burgundy, was sent by the archbishop of Canterbury, Honorius, to the kingdom of the East Angles, where, as bishop of Dunwich, he helped Sigeberht, their new king returned from exile in Gaul, to establish "a school where boys could be taught letters" (p. 269).

639 *Cuthred*: He is described as king by texts B, C, and F. Cuthred may have been associated with Cynegils in exercising royal power after the death of Cwichelm in 636. See the note for 648.

643 *Winchester*: On the site of the former Roman city, *Venta Belgarum*. The description *ceaster* reflected the city's status as the former site of a Roman fort that was subsequently provided with stone walls.

644 *York*: OE *Eoforwic* (the city of the boar), derived from Latin *Eboracum*. Under Scandinavian influence (after 866) the name later became *Jorvik*, modern York. The added suffix *ceaster* in the A-text *(Eoforwicceastre)* recognizes the existence of a city already important in Roman times, with its fortress greatly extended and its walls made of stone.

645 *driven out*: Unusually, the explanation for this event is not given until AN 658.

648 *his kinsman Cuthred*: According to the genealogy of Cerdic that precedes the A-text, Cenwalh was Cynegils's son, making Cuthred, as son of Cwichelm and grandson of Cynegils, his nephew.

hides: The word is supplied from versions B and C. The hide provided the basis for rough estimates of the size of large areas of land, according to the number of households they could be expected to support. It was later used to determine the number of men to be called up from a specific area by the king to provide his levies.

Ashdown: The first of three instances of the name *Æscesdun*.

650 *Agilbert*: *EH* 3.25, pp. 298–309, describes the role Agilbert (OE *Ægelbryht*) played in 664 at the Synod of Whitby, where he supported the Roman position on the handling of Easter against that of the Irish.

651 *Oswine*: After Oswald's death, the kingdom of the Northumbrians was once more split in two. Oswine, made king of Deira, was later betrayed and killed on the orders of Oswiu, king of neighboring Bernicia.

653 *Middle Angles*: The OE text incorrectly calls them "Middle Saxons." According to *EH* 3.21, pp. 278–79, Peada, son of Penda, had been put in control of the Middle Angles by his father.

654 *Anna*: Successor of Sigeberht as king of the East Angles, Anna was killed by Penda. *EH* 3.7, pp. 234–35, reports that the Christian Anna had harbored the exiled Cenwalh for three years.

Icanho: Possibly Iken, Suffolk, an area where Botwulf is believed to have founded his monastery.

655 *Peada . . . succeeded*: Although Peada is here said to have succeeded his father, it was the victor in the battle, Oswiu, king of the Northumbrians and seventh Bretwalda, who, according to *EH* 3.24, pp. 292–95, ruled the kingdom of the Mercians for the three years after Penda's death. Peada, who had accepted Christianity as a condition for marrying Oswiu's daughter, was given the kingdom of southern Mercia, holding it for one year.

657 *Peada passed away*: According to *EH* 3.24, pp. 294–95, Peada was "most foully murdered," apparently due to treachery on the part of his wife during the Easter festival.

Wulfhere: According to *EH* 3.24, pp. 294–95, Wulfhere, a young son of Penda's, had been kept concealed after his father's death by three Mercian ealdormen in rebellion against Oswiu. They now set him up as their king. Ruling over the Mercians for seventeen years, Wulfhere gradually acquired power over most of the southern kingdoms.

658 *Peonnum*: Usually identified as Penselwood, Somerset. *Peonn* is assumed to be a garbled form of the British name *Penn* (hilltop, headland); the name of the forest, Selwood, was added in the fourteenth century to distinguish it from the name *Pendomer.*

660 *Agilbert departed*: According to *EH* 3.7, pp. 234–35, the Gaul had acted as archbishop of Canterbury for a number of years, until the king split the diocese into two, and, "without consulting him," introduced into the kingdom Wine, a cleric also consecrated in Gaul, but one who this time "spoke the king's own tongue." Offended, Agilbert returned to Gaul, later taking up a see in Paris.

Wine: Having been given Winchester as his see, Wine was some years later expelled by Cenwalh, taking refuge with King Wulfhere in Mercia. *EH* 3.7, pp. 234–35, relates that for a sum of money he purchased from the latter the see of London.

661 *Posentesburg*: Possibly Posbury, Devon. The criteria for what is now a small hamlet to have qualified—in this text at least—for the designation *burg* are met by the presence of an Iron Age hill fort, now known as Posbury Camp, and, south of the hamlet, the remains of a Roman road.

King Coenberht: A West Saxon, described in a genealogy in AN 685 as father of Cædwalla and great-grandson of Ceawlin. It has been suggested that if the attribution of the title of king is correct, his role could have been that of sub-king.

Æthelwald: So also versions B, C, and E, for Æthelwalh. *EH* 4.13, p. 372, spells *Aediluualch.*

Eoppa: Abbot of Selsey, in West Sussex. According to *EH* 4.13, p. 372, his name was Eappa, and it was the South Saxons that he was sent to convert at this time.

Wilfrid: Bishop of the Northumbrians (d. 709). In spite of the enormous amount of detail about *Uilfridus* provided in *EH* 5.19, with Stephen of Ripon's *Vita sancti Wilfrithi* as its major source, the annalist provides no more than three very brief entries. See the note for 678.

664 *Colman*: He was an Irishman from Iona, who became bishop of Lindisfarne, a see at that time following the Irish observation of Easter, not the Roman one used in most parts of the country. The main spokesman at the Synod of Whitby for the adoption of the Irish model, when his case was rejected, Colman left Britain with his Irish followers (*EH* 3.25–26, pp. 296–308). See further Wesley M. Stevens, "Easter Controversy," in *The Wiley Blackwell Encyclopedia of Anglo-Saxon England,* ed. Michael Lapidge, John Blair, Simon Keynes, and Donald Scragg, 2nd ed. (Chichester, West Sussex, 2014), 160–61.

Chad: Saint Chad (OE *Ceadda*), recalled after his retirement in his own monastery of Lastingham, was appointed bishop of the Mercians and of Lindsey. He had been consecrated long before by the Irish, and at the Synod of Whitby had, according to Bede, acted as a careful interpreter for both parties.

Deusdedit: A West Saxon, Deusdedit was the sixth archbishop of Canterbury.

668 *Theodore*: A Greek from Tarsus in what is now Turkey, Theodore was consecrated by Pope Vitalis and sent to England when Deusdedit's designated successor, Wigheard, died of the plague shortly after arriving in Rome to receive his pallium. A scholar of exceptional learning, the fruits of his surviving biblical commentaries illuminate the teaching that he and his no-less erudite colleague Hadrian (not mentioned in the A-text) gave to the students in their school at Canterbury.

670 *Oswiu*: Son of King Æthelfrith and seventh Bretwalda, he convened a synod at Whitby in 664 to resolve the contemporary controversy over the method for determining the correct dates for celebrating Easter.

Ecgfrith: As king, according to *EH* 4.21, pp. 400–401, Ecgfrith inherited his father Oswiu's troubles with the Mercians. He had previously spent some time as their hostage. Peace was restored through the mediation of Archbishop Theodore.

Hlothhere: Bishop of the West Saxons. An anglicized version of a Frankish name given in *EH* 3.7, p. 236, as *Leutherius.* Agilbert, refusing an invitation by Cenwalh to return, recommended his nephew, Leuthere, in place of himself.

673 *In this year . . . Ely*: The source for both events is Bede, *Recap.*, 565. The text of the decisions of the Council of Hertford is given in *EH* 4.5, pp. 348–55.

Æthelthryth: Also known as Etheldreda or Audrey. The daughter of Anna, king of the East Angles, she was, as a widow of Tondberht, ealdorman of the South Gyrwas, given in a never-consummated second marriage to Ecgfrith, king of the Northumbrians. *EH* 4.19, pp. 390–97, relates how Æthelthryth, finally permitted to take the veil, founded a double monastery at Ely and became its abbess.

675 *Biedanheafde*: Literally, "Bede's head." The second component, *heafde* (head), has acquired a wide range of meanings in modern English place-names. Here the sense is "projecting piece of land."

Æthelred: Bede, *Recap.*, 566, reports that after thirty-one years on the throne (in fact, it was twenty-nine) Æthelred retired to Bardney monastery as a monk and later became its abbot.

678 *Wilfrid was driven from his see*: The tension between Wilfrid and Ecgfrith, king of the Northumbrians, had to do with Wilfrid's encouragement of Queen Æthelthryth to become a nun at Coldingham monastery. She later founded the monastery at Ely (see AN 673). For a modern assessment of Wilfrid's life and achievements, see Alan Thacker, "St Wilfred," in *Wiley Blackwell Encyclopedia*, 495–96.

679 *Ælfwine*: The eighteen-year-old brother of King Ecgfrith of the Northumbrians, Ælfwine was killed in battle against Æthelred, king of the Mercians. *EH* 4.21, pp. 400–401, relates how further hostilities were avoided through the mediation of Archbishop Theodore and the payment of the appropriate financial

compensation (wergild) to the king to whom the duty of vengeance belonged.

680 The Synod of Hatfield was convened in 679 (see *EH* 4.17, pp. 384–85 and n. 3) to affirm the orthodoxy of the English churches.

Hild: Connected to the Northumbrian royal line, Hild had decided at the age of thirty-three to adopt the monastic life. She became abbess of Hartlepool (between 647 and 651), later founding the monastery at Whitby, location for the synod in 664 on the dating of Easter. *EH* 4.24, pp. 414–20, reports that Hild, as abbess, recognized the gift of song possessed by a layman called Cædmon and encouraged him to take monastic vows.

Whitby: The OE name for the site of the abbey was *Streoneshealh*. Its second component, *healh*, meant "nook or corner of land"; its first component, possibly OE *streon*, would mean "property, gain, treasure." The name is preserved today as neighboring Strenshall.

685 *Cædwalla*: An exile from the kingdom of the West Saxons, with a British name and, although a great-great-grandson of Ceawlin, otherwise unrelated to either Æscwine or Centwine. Cædwalla's first step toward gaining power was to attack the kingdom of the South Saxons, later getting control of the kingdom of the West Saxons. Promising to give one fourth of the still-pagan Isle of Wight to the Lord upon its capture, he subsequently gave three hundred hides there to Bishop Wilfrid. He abdicated in 688, went to Rome to be baptized, and died there in 689.

688 *Ine*: Very little is reported of Ine's thirty-seven years as king of the West Saxons. The A-text makes no mention of Ine's law code, the earliest known laws of the West Saxons, which King Alfred appended to his *Domboc*.

690 *Beorhtwald*: The date of his accession given in the A-, B-, and C-texts is incorrect. *EH* 5.8, pp. 474–75, gives the date of Beorhtwald's election as July 692 and his consecration as June 693. He was also not, as reported here, the first English appointee, since despite his Latin name, Deusdedit, the sixth, was West Saxon.

694 *thirty thousand sceattas*: Versions A and E leave the denomination unexpressed, B and C read "xxx punda" (thirty pounds); Dorothy Whitelock suggests "pence": *English Historical Documents,* ed. David C. Douglas, 2nd ed., vol. 1, *c. 500–1042,* ed. Dorothy Whitelock (London, 1979), p. 169 and note. In the early Kentish laws, the "ordinary" punishment by payment of wergild for causing death is given in shillings. If in *sceattas,* as Swanton, *Chronicle,* 40n3, suggests, it "would be approximately equal to a king's wergild according to the Law of the Mercians." The name *sceattas* is generally given to the earliest silver pennies minted in England from the late seventh century.

Wihtred: Issuer of a law code that still survives.

705 *Seaxwulf*: It is more likely he died in approximately 692, the year Wilfrid was exiled to Mercia. See Swanton, *Chronicle,* 40n4.

709 *Aldhelm*: Abbot of Malmesbury, Aldhelm was made bishop of the new see of Sherborne when the diocese of the West Saxons was divided into two. Today his considerable renown rests on his writings, some of which are listed in *EH* 5.18, pp. 514–15, along with praise for his remarkable learning and his polished style.

Ceolred became king . . . and Coenred went to Rome: Two apparently straightforward facts, but ones that relate to events with a complicated background. Ceolred and Coenred were cousins. When their grandfather Penda died, it was Ceolred's father, Æthelred, who succeeded him. However, in 704, when Æthelred became a monk, it was not to his son but to Coenred that, in the words of Bede, *Recap.,* 567, he "left" the throne. And it was not until 709, when Coenred decided to follow the same path as his uncle, that Ceolred finally became king.

Offa: Son of the king of the East Saxons, Sigehere. Traveling to Rome with Cenred, Offa too received the tonsure, but, according to the *Liber pontificalis,* died soon after his arrival. Simon Keynes, "Appendix I: Rulers of the English, c. 495–1066," in *Wiley Blackwell Encyclopedia,* 511, describes Offa as having succeeded his father in approximately 694, "though not certainly a full king."

714 *Guthlac*: An anchorite living in the fens near Crowland (d. 714), Guthlac is celebrated in a Latin *vita,* ed. Bertram Colgrave, *Felix's Life of St. Guthlac* (Cambridge, 1956); in a translation of the *vita,* ed. Paul Gonser, *Das angelsächsischen Prosa-Leben der hl. Guthlac* (Heidelberg, 1909); in two anonymous Old English poems, *Guthlac A* and *Guthlac B,* ed. Philip Krapp and Elliott Van Kirk Dobbie, *The Exeter Book,* vol. 3 of *The Anglo-Saxon Poetic Records* (New York, 1936), 49–88; and in an entry in the Old English *Martyrology,* ed. Christine Rauer, *The Old English Martyrology: Edition, Translation and Commentary,* Anglo-Saxon Texts 10 (Cambridge, 2013), 80.

716 *Osred*: According to *EH* 5.18, p. 512n3, Osred became king when he was about eight years old and was killed eleven years later, at the age of nineteen.

Lichfield: The element *Licit* is drawn from Romano-British *Letocetum,* the name of an important Roman military staging post, the remains of which are preserved at Wall (Staffordshire), a couple of miles from Lichfield itself, where *EH* 4.3, pp. 336–37, reports that the episcopal seat of the Mercians was established by Bishop Chad.

Æthelbald: The correct date of Æthelbald's death as 757 is supported by the reference to a forty-one-year reign.

722 *the exile Ealdberht*: A West Saxon prince, banished by Ine. Henry of Huntingdon, *Historia Anglorum: The History of the English People,* ed. and trans. Diana Greenway, Oxford Medieval Texts (Oxford, 1996), section 4.9, p. 226, explains that it was the destruction of the fortification at Taunton that forced Ealdberht to flee eastward.

728 *Æthelheard*: All other versions of the Chronicle report 726 as the date of his accession. Bede, "Continuations" (*EH,* p. 572), reports his date of death as 739. Æthelheard's ancestry is not reported. However, in the genealogy that precedes the A-text, he is entered as descended from Cerdic.

Oswald: Described as *æþeling* ("prince" or "lord"), a term in the chronicles frequently used of a prince of the blood royal. However, the genealogical details show that Oswald was not a close relative of the current king. On the application of *æþeling* as a title, see David N. Dumville, "The Ætheling: A Study in Anglo-Saxon Constitutional History," *Anglo-Saxon England* 8 (1979): 1–33.

731 *Osric . . . was killed*: The correct year is 729, given in texts D, E, and F and Bede, *Recap.*

Ceolwulf: King Ceolwulf of Northumbria is the addressee of Bede's Preface to his *EH* (p. 2). Of Ceolwulf's seven-year reign, beginning, in fact, two years earlier, in 729, the annalist tells us nothing. Bede, "Continuations" (*EH,* pp. 572–73), reports that, in 731, Ceolwulf was seized and tonsured before being restored to his kingdom. Ceolwulf resigned in 737 and ended his life in Lindisfarne, in approximately 764.

Tatwine: *EH* 5.23, pp. 558–59, describes Tatwine, a Mercian, as a scholar renowned for his devotion, wisdom, and knowledge of the scriptures. Two works of his survive: a collection of forty *aenigmata* (riddles) and a grammar, *Ars de partibus orationis.* On the *aenigmata,* see Andy Orchard, ed. and trans., *The Old English and Anglo-Latin Riddle Tradition,* Dumbarton Oaks Medieval Library 69 (Cambridge, MA, 2021), 110–39.

734 *Bede*: A Northumbrian, Bede spent his life from the age of seven in the monastery of Wearmouth and Jarrow. Bede's large body of writings in Latin includes biblical commentaries, homilies, hymns, poems, letters, hagiography, the *Historia abbatum,* and the *Historia ecclesiastica.* The *Historia ecclesiastica* was one of the handful of books translated into Old English in the second half of the ninth century.

738 *Eadberht*: Resigning in 758 in favor of his son Oswulf (who was shortly afterward murdered by his own thegns), Eadberht became a monk and died in York (768).

743 *Britons*: As also Whitelock, for OE *Walas.* Swanton's more specific rendering is "Welsh," but in spite of the relatively late date, the Britons of the southwest cannot be ruled out.

744 *Daniel retired*: The OE verb used here normally has the meaning "resided," and Charles Plummer, ed., *Two of the Saxon Chronicles Parallel* (Oxford, 1892–1899), vol. 2, p. 42, suggests underlying error, with confusion of Latin *resedit* and *recedit.*

748 *Eadberht*: King of West Kent and son of Wihtred. In the A-text,

Eadberht I's accession in 725 is referred to only in an entry in a post-Conquest hand. For his brother, Æthelberht II, king of East Kent (725–762), see AN 760.

750 *the arrogant ealdorman*: The OE adjective *ofermod* (proud, arrogant) refers to an unacceptable excess of *mod* (heart, mind, spirit).

754 *Canterbury*: Romano-British *Durovernum,* a town with triple ditches from the Iron Age and defensive walls added by the Romans. It was both the chief city of the kingdom of Kent and the episcopal seat of the southern archbishop.

Sigeberht: The regnal dates given in AN 754 and AN 755.1 are errors for 756 and 757. On the chronological dislocation between AN 756 and AN 845 that dates the majority of events two (and occasionally three) years early, see the section on "Issues of Chronology" in the Introduction.

755.1 *Cynewulf . . . deprived Sigeberht*: In the first part of this annal, the narrative moves abruptly from brief details of the background of an event at that time thirty-one years in the future to a dramatic account of that event, which echoes the Germanic heroic code of loyalty to the death and the duty of vengeance. The narrative's use of direct speech and other linguistic evidence suggests interpolation at this point of an account composed by another of the contributors to the first compilation, responsible also for a number of entries relating to events in the ninth century. We are told nothing of Cynewulf's claim to the throne, apart from the fact that he is a descendant of Cerdic and that he is said to have the support of the councilors (the *witan,* the body of "wise men" advising the king). Such men included important members of the clergy, members of the royal household, ealdormen, and king's thegns.

the Weald: An area in southern England, once covered with forest, between the North and South Downs, and the site of the Roman fort named in AN 491. The OE reads *on Andred.* See the note for 477.

the stream at Privett: The present-day village of Privett (named after the shrub *Ligusticum vulgare*) is situated on high ground, with no large nearby river, so the term "stream" is the translation normally adopted for *flod.*

thirty-one years: The correct length of his reign was twenty-nine years (757–786).

the company of a woman: The late tenth-century Latin version of this narrative in Æthelweard's *Chronicle,* ed. Alistair Campbell, *The Chronicle of Æthelweard* (London, 1962), 23–24, referring to Cynewulf's visit *cum quadam meretrice* (with a certain loose woman), has supported the general view that the hapax legomenon *wifcyþþe* refers to a dalliance. See Francis Leneghan, "Royal Wisdom and the Alfredian Context of *Cynewulf and Cyneheard,*" *Anglo-Saxon England* 39 (2010): 71–104, esp. 93–97.

chamber: For OE *bur* in the A-text, the B and C versions read *burg* (fortification), in that case presumably a site surrounded by a wall or a stockade.

British hostage: The A-text reports the giving of hostages as sureties of peace, either by the conquered or between opposing forces, on a number of occasions. Here the hostage must be one taken in the course of Cynewulf's many fights with the Britons.

755.2 *the gates*: Whether the gates were locked against them (so Æthelweard's *Chronicle*), or they locked the gates upon themselves, is open to dispute.

755.4 *And that same year*: The insertion completed, the second part of the annal returns to the events of 755 (which in fact occurred in 757), before looking ahead once more.

Æthelbald: Bede, "Continuations" (*EH,* pp. 574–75), under the year 757, reports that he was treacherously killed by his guards.

Offa: The accompanying genealogy, showing Offa, king of the Mercians, to be related to Penda, is presumably provided to demonstrate his credentials.

763 *midwinter*: Christmas Day. The fortieth day after would be February 2, the feast of the Purification of the Blessed Virgin.

773 *sign of the cross*: OE *Cristes mæl.* Not some kind of aurora borealis (so Swanton, *Chronicle,* 50n8), but what Vercelli Homily 12 explains as *Cristes rodetacen* (symbol of Christ's rood).

extraordinary snakes: Only the A-text has the adjective *wunderleca,* where the other texts all use the adverb *wunderlice* (extraordinarily), as though the presence of snakes in southern England was highly unusual. It is of Ireland, however, that Bede wrote that "No reptile is found there nor could a serpent survive; for although serpents have often been brought from Britain, as soon as the ship approaches land they are affected by the scent of the air and quickly perish" (*EH* 1.1, pp. 18–19).

780 *Old Saxons*: In 782 after the continental Saxons had slaughtered Frankish invaders, Charlemagne, in retaliation, carried out a large-scale massacre at Verden (Lower Saxony) on the River Aller.

784 *In this year Cyneheard*: The proper place for the narrative of Cynewulf and Cyneheard inserted into the annal for 755.

785 *a contentious synod*: The context of the events in this annal is a serious falling-out between the archbishop of Canterbury and the king of the Mercians, for which, see Simon Keynes, "Jænberht," in *Wiley Blackwell Encyclopedia,* 262–63. The result was a move by Offa for the creation of an archbishopric of Lichfield and the placing of Hygeberht after Jænberht in the episcopal hierarchy.

787 *Eadburg*: Asser tells at some length several highly uncomplimentary stories about this daughter of Offa, in his *Life of King Alfred,* chapters 13–15, ed. William Henry Stevenson, *Asser's Life of King Alfred: Together with the Annals of Saint Neots Erroneously Ascribed to Asser,* new impression with article by Dorothy Whitelock (Oxford, 1959; originally published, Oxford, 1904), pp. 10–14. As queen, she loathed everyone that Beorhtric favored, poisoning those that she could not dispose of by trickery. The king himself is said to have died as a result of accidentally sharing the poison intended for the favorite who was her current target. As widow, she behaved even more recklessly, and having fallen foul of Charlemagne, ended her life a beggar, dying miserably in Pavia.

three ships: The E-text adds "of Northmen."

792 *Æthelberht's*: Æthelberht II, king of the East Angles, venerated in Hereford as a martyr.

794 *Æthelred, king of the Northumbrians*: In fact, Æthelred came to the throne in 774 and was expelled in 778 or 779 and driven into exile. Restored to the throne in 790, he married a daughter of Offa of the Mercians in 792 and was killed in 796.

departed from the land: It has been suggested that this statement could be a euphemism for "died."

796 *Romney Marsh*: The wetlands of Kent. Present-day Romney Marsh covers approximately 100 square miles (260 km^2) from Rye to Hythe.

Præn: We are told nothing of Eadberht Præn's subsequent fate.

800 *Ecgberht*: Previously driven out by Offa and Beorhtric, Ecgberht became the first of a new line of West Saxon kings, claiming descent, via Ine, from Cerdic.

the Hwicce: The inhabitants of what was originally a kingdom situated in the West Midlands, around Worcester, but by this date had become part of Mercia. Their name is preserved in the place-names Whichford and Wychwood.

men of Wiltshire: The OE is *Wilsætan*. These were ruled by the kings of the West Saxons, hence the rivalry.

805 *Cuthred*: A Mercian, installed as king of the people of Kent by his brother, Coenwulf, king of the Mercians, when the latter regained control of the area.

813 *Cornwall*: The OE reads *Westwalas*. These were Britons living in Cornwall. Compare *Norþwalas*, AN 828.

816 *English Quarter*: The *schola Saxonum*, a hospice in Rome near Saint Peter's used by English ecclesiastics and pilgrims, was established by the pope in the mid-eighth century and supported by donations from England.

823 *Galford*: The first element is *gafol* (tribute, tax, duty). For other references to rent collection and tax, see DOE, under *inlad*, sense 1, "(the right to collect) a tax on goods brought in (to a place)," and *A Thesaurus of Old English*, "15.02.04.01 (n.) Payment for temporary use, rent, hire" and "15.03 (n.) Exaction of tax/tribute," accessed November 7, 2024, http://oldenglishthesaurus.arts.gla.ac.uk.

Ealhstan: Bishop of Sherborne for fifty years. Apart from reporting his death, the only details about Ealhstan's life are those in the entries for 823 and 845, both referring to him as taking an active part in the conflicts with the Danes that occurred in those years. However, in its account of events in 855, Asser, *Life of King Alfred,* chapter 12, tells of an attempt by Æthelbald to overthrow his father, King Æthelwulf—a conspiracy in which Bishop Ealhstan is reported to have played a major part. Upon returning from the continent, Æthelwulf agreed to divide the kingdom, taking for himself Kent and other parts of the southeast annexed by King Ecgberht in 825.

827 *Christmas Eve*: The eclipse is calculated as having taken place at 2:00 a.m. on December 25, 828. When this information was recorded, it seems that the commencement of the year was calculated from September, not Christmas or January. On the dates for beginning the year, see Introduction, "Issues of Chronology."

Bretwalda: The term is here applied to King Ecgberht following his conquest of Mercia and the lands south of the Humber. He is said to be the eighth Bretwalda, thus adding him to the seven kings Bede described as holding *imperium* (rule) over that area (*EH* 2.5, pp. 148–51). Simon Keynes, "Bretwalda," in *Wiley Blackwell Encyclopedia,* 76–77, suggests the term is more "flight of fancy" than description of a real office.

Rædwald: The only Bretwalda named in the A-text without an entry of his own. He was, however, a powerful ruler who having given asylum to Edwin of Deira, and then defeating and killing his rival, Æthelfrith of Bernicia, put the former in charge of both Northumbrian kingdoms. *EH* 2.15, pp. 190–91, however, describes him as "ignoble in his deeds": initially converted in Kent, Rædwald on his return served both Christ and pagan gods.

Dore: In the OE Chronicle texts the name is used exceptionally and specifically of a pass on the ancient boundary between Mercia and Northumbria.

828 *the Welsh*: The *Norþwalas* are the native inhabitants of the Britons' more northerly territorial holding, rather than the Britons of Cornwall.

830 *Abbot Feologild*: There were apparently two candidates to succeed Archbishop Wulfred: Swithred and Feologild. While the F version of the Chronicle records the consecration of Feologild on June 9, 829 (for 832), the A-text firmly records that he died while an abbot. See Nicholas Brooks, *The Early History of the Church of Canterbury* (Leicester, 1984), 143.

833 *Hereferth and Wigthegn*: In a list of bishops of Winchester in a late tenth-century hand, entered in booklet 4 of CCCC 173, Wigthegn is number 13 and Hereferth number 14.

835 *Cornwall*: The OE reads *Westwalas.* See note to AN 813.

837 *army*: This is the first occurrence in the A-text of *here* (army), a word used heavily throughout the accounts of the first and second viking wars, to refer to the invading forces of "heathen men," later identified as *Dene* (Danes) and *þa Deniscan* (the Danish). The earlier two occurrences, both entered by a post-Conquest interpolator, occur at 603 and 606 to refer to Scottish or British fighters. *Here* is used in contradistinction to *fyrde,* the levied troops of the English kings. *Here* can be difficult to translate, since it is used without regard to the size of the force. At AN 892, however, the Chronicle refers to a *great* army, a combined force of perhaps 330 ships. See Richard Abels, *Alfred the Great: War, Kingship, and Culture in Anglo-Saxon England* (New York, 1998), 285–86. Also see the Introduction, "Terms for Warfare, Fighting Forces, Fortifications."

851 *Wicganbeorg*: Benjamin Thorpe, *The Anglo-Saxon Chronicle, According to the Several Original Authorities* (London, 1861), vol. 2, p. 56, suggests Wembury (Devon), while Swanton, *Chronicle,* 64n5, offers Wigborough in Somerset, though observing that "*Wicga* is a common enough name."

Æthelbald: Son of the West Saxon king Æthelwulf, and subsequently ruler of the western part of Wessex, from 855 to 860. After his father's death, he married Judith, his Frankish stepmother.

853 *sent his son Alfred to Rome*: The version given here, describing the young boy as consecrated king by the pope, is that of Asser's *Life of King Alfred,* chapter 8. However, it is clearly in error: see,

for instance, Simon Keynes and Michael Lapidge, eds. and trans., *Alfred the Great: Asser's Life of King Alfred and Other Contemporary Sources,* Penguin Classics (Harmondsworth, Middlesex, 1983), 69 and 232n19. The pope took him as godson, presumably at confirmation. Asser also claims that Alfred went a second time to Rome, this time with his father (*Life of King Alfred,* chapter 11).

855.1 *the tenth part of his land*: There are two different interpretations of Æthelwulf's actions with regard to a tenth of his lands. The Chronicle states that he "booked" these lands—the OE word *gebocian* (literally, "to book") means to give a grant of land by charter; see DOE, under *gebocian,* sense 1. The Chronicle thus suggests that Æthelwulf granted a tenth of his land to religious foundations. Asser's interpretation of the king's action (*Life of King Alfred,* chapter 11) is different: he records that Æthelwulf freed one tenth of his entire kingdom from every royal service and tribute. For a discussion, see Keynes and Lapidge, *Alfred the Great,* 232–34n23.

they were delighted: This statement has to be read in the context of Asser's report of a failed plot against the absent king by Æthelbald, the son who, at that time, controlled Wessex. That on his return Æthelwulf let Æthelbald as sub-king continue to rule the more important western part of the country is clearly seen in Asser, *Life of King Alfred,* chapter 12, as due to the king's appreciation of the very serious consequences of not so doing.

855.3 *Æthelwulf's two sons came to power*: Æthelbald died in 860, at the end of what Asser, *Life of King Alfred,* chapter 17, describes as two and a half "lawless" years as king of the West Saxons. Æthelberht, succeeding him, most unusually receives retrospective compliments from the 860 annalist, writing some considerable time after the event.

860 *a large enemy fleet*: The *Annals of Saint Bertin,* under the year 860 (see Whitelock, *English Historical Documents,* vol. 1, item 23, p. 343), refers to Danes stationed on the Somme.

865 *stayed*: Asser, *Life of King Alfred,* chapter 20, uses the Latin *hiemaverunt* (they overwintered).

stole away: Asser, *Life of King Alfred,* chapter 20, explains that the army did not wait to collect the money, since they knew that they could better profit from booty than from the terms of the peace settlement.

866 *a large army*: Reported by Asser, *Life of King Alfred,* chapter 21, as a great fleet of pagans from the Danube. The A-text modifies its usual term *here* for the invading viking army with *micel* (great).

867 *some inside and some out*: Asser, *Life of King Alfred,* chapter 27, reports that Ælle and Osberht had joined forces to meet the vikings, who retreated into the city. The Northumbrians decided to break into the city. However, once most of their troops were inside, the vikings counterattacked fiercely, virtually annihilating the entire force.

870 *killed the king*: The correct year of King Edmund's death is 869. Edmund was subsequently venerated as a martyr. Accounts of his martyrdom were written by Abbo of Fleury *(Passio sancti Eadmundi)* and Ælfric of Eynsham (*Lives of Saints* 32) in the late tenth century.

871.1 *In this year the army moved*: The annal marks the first of eight years during which Alfred and the West Saxons were fighting for survival. For this annal Asser provides numerous additional details in nine chapters (*Life of King Alfred,* chapters 35–43).

jarls: A Scandinavian term for nobleman. In the early Chronicle (as in this entry), the Danish title *jarl* is often rendered by OE *eorl* (nobleman). In the later Chronicle entries dealing with the second viking wars and following, *jarl* was a title for an underking or governor under Cnut's rule (see DOE, under *eorl,* sense 3), there essentially synonymous with *ealdormann.*

It was in two troops: According to Asser, *Life of King Alfred,* chapter 38, it was Alfred's division that arrived first, King Æthelred having refused to leave his prayers until the Mass was finished.

had control of the battlefield: An idiom of poetic origin (for example, *Beowulf* 2051a), used frequently from AN 831 on and found also, once, in the Old English *Orosius* 3.7, ed. Bately, p. 64, line 25, its equivalent in OE verse was *wælstowe wealdan* (to control the place of slaughter).

a large summer fleet: Texts B, C, D, and E add *to Reading* (at Reading).

871.2 *the West Saxons made peace*: Of the seriousness of the West Saxons' position in 871, Asser, *Life of King Alfred,* chapter 42, observes that the English were virtually destroyed in eight pitched battles that year.

874 *a foolish king's thegn*: Chronicle A omits the name, but it is supplied in the other versions and Asser, *Life of King Alfred,* chapter 46, as Ceolwulf, one of exiled King Burgred's thegns. In the Chronicle's entry under AN 877, Ceolwulf is said to have been given part of a now-divided Mercia by the Danes. Ceolwulf was more than a puppet king, subsequently issuing his own charters and sharing types and moneyers with Alfred in a form of monetary union between Mercia and Wessex. See Abels, *Alfred the Great,* 144–46.

875 *Guthrum*: Leader of a viking force that joined the great army in 871, later becoming king of the East Saxons. A copy of the treaty he subsequently made with King Alfred, in the name Guthrum, still survives; F. L. Attenborough, ed. and trans., *The Laws of the Earliest English Kings* (Cambridge, 1922), 98–101, and Whitelock, *English Historical Documents,* vol. 1, item 34, pp. 416–17.

876 *oaths on the sacred ring*: Versions B, C, and E precede this with a reference to the handing over of hostages by the enemy force. An account of the ring used and of Asser's erroneous version of this passage (*Life of King Alfred,* chapter 56) is given by Keynes and Lapidge, *Alfred the Great,* 245–46. The ring was likely associated with the worship of Thor. Other significant information for this year contained in versions B, C, and E, but not the A-text, include a reference to the seizing of the enemy's raven standard and the alms taken on behalf of the king to Rome and India.

878.1 *Twelfth Night*: The eve of the feast of the Epiphany (January 6).

with difficulty: According to Asser, *Life of King Alfred,* chapter 53, he had no supplies at all apart from what he could seize in repeated forays from either the pagans or those Christians that had surrendered to them.

878.2 *its stronghold*: Presumably Chippenham, on the River Avon, to which, according to Asser, *Life of King Alfred,* chapter 52, the enemy army had moved from Exeter.

crismlysing: The DOE defines *crismlysing* as the "ceremonial removal of the chrism-cloth." At baptism the head was anointed with oil (chrism), and a week later the white cloth bound round it was removed at this special ceremony.

with valuable gifts: The term used in the text, *feoh,* covers both money and property.

879 *a band of vikings*: The term "band" is used here to render OE *hloþ,* which, in the Laws of Ine 13.1, refers to a team of between seven and thirty-five men (Attenborough, *Laws,* 40). However, according to Asser, *Life of Alfred,* chapter 58, the enemy was in fact a large army of pagans that had arrived in Western Mercian territory on the Thames at Fulham.

the sun grew dark for one hour: There was an eclipse of the sun on October 29, 878.

885.1 *built another stronghold*: Asser, *Life of Alfred,* chapter 66, says that this was a *castellum* (fortification) in front of the entrance of the city.

885.2 *Judith*: The daughter of Charles the Bald mentioned but not named in AN 855.1.

the army that had settled in East Anglia: See AN 880.

886 *Æthelred*: Alfred entrusted Mercia to Ealdorman Æthelred, giving him his daughter, Æthelflæd (known as "Lady of the Mercians") in marriage. Æthelred and Æthelflæd continued to hold power in Mercia after Alfred's death. (See below, AN 911 and AN 918.)

887 *Æthelhelm*: Described by Asser as ealdorman of Wiltshire, and so presumably identical with the Æthelhelm of AN 893.6 and 897.

888 *Æthelswith*: Æthelwulf's daughter, unnamed in AN 853. An inscribed gold ring owned by Queen Æthelswith was acquired by

the British Museum in 1897 (London, British Museum AF.458, https://www.britishmuseum.org/collection/object/H_AF-458).

891.2 *Rogationtide*: In this year May 19 to 21. The OE term for Rogation Days is *gangdagas* (walking days), the three days preceding the moveable feast of the Ascension marked by barefoot processions.

892 *the great army that we spoke about earlier*: The part of the enemy force that had gone overseas in 885 (AN 885.1).

the marsh: OE *fenne* (fen), best explained as an error for the word *fæstenne* ("fortification," so texts B and C), with accidental loss of three of its letters.

Appledore: The site of a fortress built by the "great" *(micel)* hostile army of 866.

893.1 *In this year*: To this point in the Chronicle, entries began with the deictic adverb *her* (here), indicating the location on the page of the Chronicle adjacent to the year of the annal. The entries for 893 begin *on þys geare,* and the following three entries demonstrate their interconnection by beginning with related expressions: "immediately after that, in this year," "in the same year." These annals (to the beginning of the annal for 896) were written by the same individual and likely constitute the "First Continuation" of the Common Stock of the Chronicle. See Janet Bately, "The Compilation of the 'Anglo-Saxon Chronicle' Once More," *Leeds Studies in English* 16 (1985): 7–26, at 19, and Keynes and Lapidge, *Alfred the Great,* 278–80.

the king had separated his levies: Alfred's strategic division of his forces into shifts set up a rotation for service for the levies at home and in the field. For a detailed explanation of the various possibilities for their organization, see Keynes and Lapidge, *Alfred the Great,* 285–86n4. Alfred also set up a substantial network of garrisoned fortifications (*burh,* pl. *byrg*) for defense. For an illustration, see "The Burghal Hidage," translated in Keynes and Lapidge, *Alfred the Great,* 193–94.

893.2 *Farnham*: By the River Wey. Æthelweard, *Chronicle,* ed. Campbell, p. 49 (under the year 893), says that Alfred's son Edward led this force.

893.3 *they could not transport him*: Æthelweard, *Chronicle*, ed. Campbell, p. 49, reports that Ealdorman Æthelred (incorrectly identified as *rex*, "king") brought Edward help from London.

893.4 *before Hæsten came to Benfleet*: Alfred had apparently negotiated with Hæsten (much like he had done with Guthrum, AN 878.2), and he and his son-in-law Æthelred stood sponsor to Hæsten's sons in baptism.

893.5 *Shoebury*: Remains of prehistoric ramparts and evidence from Roman times demonstrate that Shoebury (second element *burg*, "fortified place") had been in existence long before 893, while neighboring Prittlewell, now part of Southend, is rich in Anglo-Saxon finds, including the tomb of a king of the East Saxons excavated in 2003/4. See Lyn Blackmore, Ian Blair, Sue Hirst, and Christopher Scull, *The Prittlewell Princely Burial: Excavations at Priory Crescent, Southend-on-Sea, Essex, 2003* (London, 2019). No trace of the Danish fortification in Shoebury has yet been discovered.

893.7 *a deserted city*: Chester, once a Roman legionary city, was called, according to Bede, *Legacæstir* by the English and *Caerlegion* (Chester) by the Britons: *EH* 2.2, pp. 140–41. He reports that it was laid waste in 616. Colgrave and Mynors conclude that it was from that attack that Chester "was desolate right up to Alfred's time" (*EH*, p. 140n2). There were, however, plenty of other occasions for destruction, much closer to AN 893—during the period in the 870s, for instance, which culminated in the partition of Mercia between Danish invaders and Ceolwulf.

894 *And*: The OE *ond* (written *ONd*), which opens the text here (replacing the regular abbreviation "⁊"), is at this point being used as a connective between the three annals, treated as a unit, from 893 to 895—a "historical" rather than an annalistic approach.

Mersea: Today Mersey is a tidal island linked to the mainland by a causeway flooded at high tide. Surviving oak piles used to make the ancestor of the causeway have been dated to the period between 684 and 707.

Chichester: When the Roman walled city of *Noviomagus reginorum* fell into the hands of the Saxons, it is quite possible that the Cissa after whom it was renamed was King Ælle's son.

895.2 *Bridgenorth*: The OE name is *Cwatbrycg*.

896.1 *horse thegn*: Ecgwulf, the king's horse thegn, would have been responsible for the king's horses and transportation. See Keynes and Lapidge, *Alfred the Great,* 289n34.

896.2 *light, swift ships*: The word *æsc* is a loan word from the Old Norse word *askr.* See DOE, under *æsc,* sense 2, "a light, swift ship, especially a Viking ship."

896.3 *obstructed the river mouth*: The precise location of this battle cannot be determined. Candidates include the Exe estuary in Devon or Poole Harbour in Dorset.

geneat: A follower of the king, probably a member of his household. (See Keynes and Lapidge, *Alfred the Great,* 290n39.)

896.4 *the Welsh reeve*: This reference is the single occurrence of *Wealhgerefa.* On its possible range of meanings (indicating responsibility for the Welsh or Cornish borders, for Welshmen at court, or for Welsh horsemen), see Keynes and Lapidge, *Alfred the Great,* 291n42.

900.1 *All Saints' Day*: November 1, in a year calculated as beginning in September, with Alfred thus dying on October 26, 899. His son, Edward the Elder, then succeeded after that date.

900.2 *Æthelwold*: Since Æthelwold was no more than an infant when his father, King Æthelred, died in 871, it was the latter's younger brother Alfred who took over both the ongoing battle with the Danes and the throne. However, after Alfred's death, Æthelwold claimed a superior right to succession.

Tweoxneam: Modern Christchurch, Hampshire.

Wimborne: The burial place of his father Æthelred, Wimborne may have belonged to Æthelwold's family.

Badbury near Wimborne: The place where Edward and his troops will have camped is Badbury Rings, a prominent Iron Age hill fort, in open country on the line of a Roman road to Old Sarum.

joined the army in Northumbria: The OE uses *here.* Versions B and

C report that after Æthelwold joined up with the Northumbrians they received him as king and submitted to him.

consecrated a nun: Abducting a nun from her convent was a serious crime. See the *Laws of Alfred* 8, ed. and trans. Stefan Jurasinski and Lisi Oliver, *The Laws of Alfred: The Domboc and the Making of Anglo-Saxon Law* (Cambridge, 2021), p. 303 (appearing there as no. 9), which specifies a fine of 120 shillings for the offense.

902 *Grimbald*: Grimbald of Saint Bertin (d. 901) was one of the scholars Alfred attracted to Wessex for the translation of the *Regula pastoralis.* He is mentioned in the prose preface to the Old English *Pastoral Care* as "Grimbald, my Mass priest."

903 *the fleet he was with*: Versions B and C are more informative: "with all the boats he could muster."

904.1 *Braydon*: The ancient forest near Cricklade, referred to in a Malmesbury Abbey charter as *silve Bradon* (Braydon Forest).

the dikes: Fleam and Devil's Dykes. Radiocarbon dating suggests that the stretches of parallel ditch and bank between the dikes and the river Ouse were started after around 400 and completed by about 650. Swanton translates *Wusan* as "Wissey." (See Swanton, *Chronicle,* 94 and 94n2.)

904.2 *Hold*: A Norse title applied to nobles in the Danelaw whose wergild was double that of a thegn. See F. M. Stenton, *Anglo-Saxon England,* 3rd ed. (Oxford, 1971), 509. See also DOE, under *hold,* "an aristocratic landowner ranking between *þegn* and *ealdormann/eorl* and corresponding to the English *hēahgerēfa* (cf. ON *höldr*)." See Introduction, "Names of Peoples, Ethnic Groups, or Political Entities."

905 *reeve*: OE *gerefa,* a term for a man who had administrative responsibilities of some kind.

Tiddingford: A. Mawer and F. M. Stenton, *Placenames of Buckinghamshire* (Cambridge, 1925), 81, identify it as Tiddingford Hill.

909 *Asser*: A Welsh cleric from Saint David's and later bishop of Sherborne. Asser first visited King Alfred likely in 885 and subsequently accepted the king's invitation to spend six or more months each year with him as a key contributor to the latter's

program for the revival of learning in England. His *Life of Alfred,* written in about 893, draws heavily on what is assumed to be a now-lost early version of the annals of King Alfred's reign.

911 *Æthelred*: Ealdorman Æthelred was succeeded by his most formidable widow, Æthelflæd (d. 918), sister of King Edward and known as "the Lady of the Mercians" (see note to AN 886). Her achievements are reported in a set of annals known as the Mercian Register, entries in texts B and C for the years 910 to 918.

912 *Martinmas . . . Rogation Days . . . midsummer*: The feast of Saint Martin, celebrated November 11; Rogation Days (moveable), May 17–18; midsummer, June 24. The order of events in this annal (beginning in November) suggests the beginning of the year occurred in September.

913 *Leicester*: OE *Ligeraceaster* (sometimes *Ligoraceaster*), Latin *Ratae Corieltauvorum,* a walled town, near a bridge on the Fosse Way, occupied by a Roman contingent in the fourth century. It is not clear whether it contained a fort. However, its British equivalent was *Cair Lerion,* where *cair* is the word for "fort."

914.2 *fortifications*: Including the manned strongholds (*burg* sg.) that were being set up to protect existing towns.

Flat Holm: Two separate issues are involved in determining the identity of the island, *(æt) Bradan Relice.* There are two small, geographically different, islands at the mouth of the Severn: Flat Holm and Steep Holm. The latter is clearly the *(æt) Steapan Relice* that versions B, C, and D name. The A-text's *(æt) Bradan Relice* (appearing again in text D, AN 1067) likely refers to the other island, Flat Holm. Unless some expected new evidence emerges, it is left to the reader to weigh up which of the two routes to Ireland the survivors might in the circumstances have taken. After this annal, versions B and C incorporate entries from a source known as the Mercian Register, not rejoining the A-text until the latter's annal 937.

915 *Martinmas*: November 11.

916 *midsummer*: June 24.

917.1 *Easter*: April 13, 917.

Towcester: Romano-British *Lactodurum,* a garrison town on Watling Street, protected by a wall, strengthened by stone and brick towers, traces of which survived until modern times. The *burg* referred to is one of the fortifications constructed by King Edward to protect existing settlements: capturing, repairing, or adding fortifications were King Edward's main military strategy.

Rogationtide: May 19–21, 917.

Lammas: August 1.

918 *Rogation Days*: May 11–13, 918.

919 *Manchester*: Romano-British *Mamucium,* a fort whose impressive remains were not finally leveled until the Industrial Revolution of the late eighteenth and early nineteenth centuries.

924 *Æthelstan*: On the death of Edward the Elder, Æthelstan was recognized as king of the Mercians, with his half brother, Ælfweard, king of the West Saxons. The latter, however, survived his father by no more than a month, upon which Æthelstan became king of the Anglo-Saxons, though not finally crowned until September 925.

933 *All Saints' Day*: November 1.

934 *the episcopal see*: Winchester.

937.1 *In this year King Æthelstan*: Known as the *Battle of Brunanburh,* this panegyric is the first of four poems in the A-text (under AN 937, 942, 973, 975) composed in classical OE verse. (Two further poems, entries for 1034 and 1065, are found in texts C and D and are also edited in this volume.) For commentary on the poem, including its versification, see John C. Pope, ed., *Eight Old English Poems,* 3rd ed., prepared by R. D. Fulk (New York, 2001).

937.5 *Brunanburh*: King Æthelstan had raided in Scotland in AN 933. In 937, the Scots (led by King Constantine) combined with the Norsemen (in a fleet led by Olaf [Anlaf], viking king of Dublin) to invade England. The poem records the valor and the victory of the English under Æthelstan and his half brother Edmund. The site of the battle remains unidentified.

937.13 *the field of battle resounded*: The meaning of the OE word *dynede* is vexed. The translation takes the consensus position that the word is *dennian* (to resound). Other suggestions are "to become wet" (from *þanian*), "to darken" (from *dunnian*).

937.35 *viking ship*: The OE word *cnearr* (compare *nægled-cnearrum,* line 53) is an OE reflex of *knǫrr,* an Old Norse word for "large ship."

937.38 *gray-haired warrior*: Referring to Constantine, king of the Scots.

937.54 *Dingesmere*: The second element, *mere,* is used here in its poetic sense, "sea." In this context, the reference is possibly to the area between Merseyside and the mouth of the River Liffey, in Ireland.

937.61 *to enjoy the slaughter*: One of the classic examples of the "beasts of battle" motif in OE heroic poetry. In this motif, an eagle, a raven, and a wolf converge on the battlefield to feast on the slain. See Mark S. Griffith, "Convention and Originality in the Old English 'Beasts of Battle' Typescene," *Anglo-Saxon England* 22 (1993): 179–99. The motif is also used in *The Battle of Maldon,* printed later in this volume, lines 106–7.

942.1 *In this year King Edmund*: The second of the Chronicle poems in the A-text, known as *The Capture of the Five Boroughs.* The boroughs in question were Leicester, Nottingham, Derby, Stamford, and Lincoln. King Edmund's conquest in 942, commemorated in the poem, refers to the reconquest of Danish-held territories in Mercia.

946 *Saint Augustine's Day*: May 26. Edmund was, in fact, murdered, in Pucklechurch, Gloucestershire.

Eadred: In his reign Northumbria finally became an integral part of England once more.

951 *Saint Gregory's Day*: March 12.

955 *Saint Clement's Day*: November 23.

Frome: Place-name transferred from that of the river, which in its turn is of British origin. See P. H. Raney, *The Origin of English Place Names* (London, 1960), 76.

958 *Edgar succeeded to the kingdom*: Edgar acceded as king of the Mercians and the Northumbrians in 957. He became king of the English after October 1, 959, and died in 975. For his much-delayed (possibly second) consecration, see AN 973. Edgar is

remembered for his support of the monastic reform movement in England.

963 *feast of the Holy Innocents*: December 28.

Æthelwold: Previously, abbot of Abingdon. One of the three great monastic reformers associated with the Benedictine revival of the mid-tenth century in England, Æthelwold was a scholar, teacher, writer, and translator. See Barbara Yorke, *Bishop Æthelwold, His Career and Influence* (Woodbridge, 1988), 1–12.

vigil of Saint Andrew: November 29.

964 *drove the priests in the city from the Old Minster*: The priests in question here are secular clergy, who were free to marry and to own property. Appointed bishop of Winchester in 963, in February 964 Æthelwold, with the support of King Edgar, had the secular clergy removed from the Old Minster in Winchester and replaced them with reformed monks from Abingdon. This move was part of an effort to extend the monastic reform further across English ecclesiastical life, in which monks from reformed houses were appointed to episcopal sees.

971 *Romsey*: The town lies in a valley through which the River Test runs. The *ig* in the latter part of the OE *Rumesige* is used in its sense of "raised ground in marshland." See DOE under *īg, īge,* sense b.

973.1 *In this year Edgar*: Along with AN 975, this annal is composed in verse and best described as a routine literary exercise.

973.3 *Acemannesceaster*: The OE name given to the city of Bath in this alliterative-verse annal is unique. However, its first element is also found in the name "Akeman's Street." For its use in the poem, see Jayne Carroll, "*Engla Waldend, Rex Admirabilis:* Poetic Representations of King Edgar," *Review of English Studies,* n.s. 58 (2007): 113–32, at 123–24.

973.7 *Pentecost*: Also known as Whitsunday: May 11, 973.

975.1 *In this year, Edgar, king*: The final poem in the A-text of the Chronicle.

975.9–10 *departed from life on the eighth day*: He died July 8, 975.

975.18 *cast down*: After Edgar's death, there was a movement in Mercia to check the transfer of estates into monastic hands. The most prominent of the antimonastic party was Ealdorman Ælfhere of Mercia, accused (by the monastic party) of destroying monasteries.

978 *Edward was killed*: Edward the Martyr, murdered at Corfe Castle by supporters of his half brother, Æthelred, who disputed the succession. In the following year, his body was removed from Wareham and interred at Shaftesbury, where he was venerated.

984 *Æthelwold*: The description here of Æthelwold as "the benevolent bishop" comes from Wulfstan of Winchester's *Life of Saint Æthelwold.*

day of the two apostles, Simon and Jude: October 28.

993 *Ealdorman Byrhtnoth*: The battle remembered in this annal was also commemorated in *The Battle of Maldon,* an important OE heroic poem edited and translated elsewhere in this volume, whose theme of loyalty unto the death recalls the story of Cynewulf and Cyneheard in AN 755. See Janet Bately, "The Anglo-Saxon Chronicle," in *The Battle of Maldon AD 991,* ed. Donald Scragg (Oxford, 1991), 37–50.

1001 *Æþelingadene*: Possibly connected with one or both of present-day East and West Dene, in Sussex.

The Death of Alfred

Pref. *guiltless ætheling*: Ætheling Alfred was the younger of Æthelred's two sons by Emma. He and his brother, Edward, had lived in Normandy since 1014, when Swein had conquered England and driven Æthelred out. In 1036, with Cnut dead and succession in doubt, Alfred and Edward set out separately for England, perhaps encouraged by their mother (see Introduction, "Background"). Edward returned to Normandy, but Alfred was captured by Godwine and handed over to his half brother Harold. On the politics of murdered royal saints, see D. W. Rollason, "The Cults of Murdered Royal Saints in Anglo-Saxon England," *Anglo-Saxon England* 11 (1983): 1–22, at 16.

Earl Godwine: One of the "new men" of Cnut's reign, when Harthacnut delayed in Denmark after Cnut's death, Godwine backed Harold Harefoot for succession. On Cnut's earls, see Simon Keynes, "Cnut's Earls," in *The Reign of Cnut: King of England, Denmark, and Norway,* ed. A. Rumble (London, 1994), 43–88.

7 *made peace*: After the death of Edmund Ironside, Cnut acceded to the throne in 1016.

14 *blinded*: An act to render him incapable of acceding to the throne. For background, see the discussion in Katherine O'Brien O'Keeffe, "Body and Law in Late Anglo-Saxon England," *Anglo-Saxon England* 27 (1998): 209–32, esp. 213–14. On the connection of blinding to legitimate power among the Carolingians, see Geneviève Bührer-Thierry, "'Just Anger' or 'Vengeful Anger': The Punishment of Blinding in the Early Medieval West," in *Anger's Past: The Social Uses of an Emotion in the Middle Ages,* ed. Barbara H. Rosenwein (Ithaca, 1998), 75–91, at 89–91.

20 *south portic*: The OE word *portic* (loan word from Latin *porticus*) refers to a side chapel for the burial of bishops and kings, rather than a portico. See Frederick M. Biggs, "The Exeter *Exeter Book?* Some Linguistic Evidence," in *The Dictionary of Old English: Retrospects and Prospects,* ed. M. J. Toswell, Old English Newsletter Subsidia 26 (1998): 63–71, at 65. See also R. E. Latham, *Dictionary of Medieval Latin from British Sources* (London, 1975–2013), under *porticus.*

The Death of Edward

1 *In this year*: King Edward the Confessor died on January 5, 1066, although the poem is placed immediately after the prose entry for 1065. In the disputes over succession following the death of Cnut in 1035, Edward had avoided the fate of his younger

brother, Alfred, and returned to Normandy to bide his time. Edward was invited to return to England in 1041 as Harthacnut's heir, and he acceded to the throne in 1042 upon Harthacnut's untimely death.

6–7 *twenty-four and a half*: King Edward acceded to the throne after the death of Harthacnut in June 1042 and was crowned April 3, 1043. He thus ruled twenty-three, not twenty-four years. The C-text does claim, however, he *wæs to cinge gesworen* (was sworn in as king) in 1041 (C-text AN 1041). The C-text of the poem is the earliest surviving version, but there is likely textual corruption underlying the reading "twenty-four."

18 *Cnut conquered Æthelred's people*: In 1015, Cnut invaded England, and he became king in 1016. Cnut then married Emma, Æthelred's widow, in 1017.

30 *Harold*: Harold II was son of Godwine, earl of Wessex, and his Danish wife, Gytha. He inherited the earldom of Wessex when Godwine died in 1053. Despite the poem's assertion of Harold's loyalty, the relations between Edward and the Godwine family were turbulent. The C-, D-, and E-texts of the Chronicle record (with differing details and political inclinations) that Edward despoiled the family of their holdings in 1051, only to be forced to reinstate them in 1052.

The Battle of Maldon

1 . . . *was broken*: The poem in David Casley's transcript (the sole extant source for the text; see the Note on the Texts) begins and ends defective. It is impossible to be certain how much has been lost, but Elliott Van Kirk Dobbie, *The Anglo-Saxon Minor Poems,* vol. 6 of *The Anglo-Saxon Poetic Records* (New York, 1942), xxviii (see also p. 142), contends that the assumption of the loss of a single leaf at beginning and end is sufficient to account for the deficiencies. This does not seem unlikely if Casley's exemplar was cut out of its original manuscript with the aim of preserving the preceding and following texts entire. See further the discussion in the edition of Mark S. Griffith, *The Battle*

of Maldon: A New Critical Edition, Exeter Medieval Texts and Studies (Liverpool, 2024), 6–7, 15–17.

2 *He then ordered*: The subject of the verb must be Byrhtnoth, the nobleman *(se eorl)* of the next sentence. On the significance of *eorl* as an honorific and title, see the note to line 219, below. It seems likely that the command is directed to a particular person. After all, possession of a horse (as well as a hawk) is a sign of high social status, and so reference to one man is likelier than reference to many in this context.

5 *Offa's kinsman*: It cannot be determined for certain whether the kinsman of Offa mentioned here is the same person as the young warrior *(hyssa hwæne)* mentioned earlier or whether, as assumed here, Offa's unnamed kinsman merely witnessed Byrhtnoth's address to the other man and complied with his leader's order. Compare "the kinsman of Gadd" (referring to Offa, line 287).

9–10 *he let his dear hawk fly from his hands . . . battle*: As horse and hawk are marks of higher social status, the gesture of releasing them shows commitment to the fight, as the poet makes explicit in these lines, where the first iteration of the ominous "as long as he could hold a weapon" theme appears.

15–16 *He accomplished his vow*: Eadric's vow *(beot)* is a speech act of promising some future deed and at the same time a speech event or formal occasion; compare Ælfwine's speech in 212–15, below. The vow serves formally to commit the speaker to a course of action, steeling him to the deed. The etymology of *beot* (from **bi-hat*) shows the connection with promising *(hatan)*. Eadric's vow is here interpreted as to fight "in the sight of his lord"; "before" *(ætforan)* could also refer to a heroic advance beyond Byrhtnoth, farther toward the enemy lines. See Stephen J. Harris, "Oaths in *The Battle of Maldon,*" in *The Hero Recovered: Essays on Medieval Heroism in Honor of George Clark,* ed. Robin Waugh and James Weldon (Kalamazoo, MI, 2010), 85–109.

25–41 *At that point . . . you all*: The tone of the messenger's speech is usually regarded as belligerent, but its logic seems reasonable:

The Danes offer peace for a price. Of course the insurance on offer here is protection from the vikings themselves, which accounts for the alternating ingratiating and threatening tone. He speaks *on beot,* which translators usually render as "threateningly," "boastfully," or the like; but *beot* is also a promise (see note to 15–16), usually of a great deed, often in an agonistic framework. Here the viking messenger is making a business proposition: we will insure your peace (under certain conditions). This interpretation gains support from *most* (be allowed) in 30b ("you have the opportunity quickly to send," says the negotiator). Accordingly, it is not necessary to take *stiðlice* (25) to mean "fiercely" or the like. The messenger had to project his voice to communicate across the flood tide; "stridently" or (as here) "loudly" may be preferred. The speaker deftly alternates between "you" singular *(þu)* and plural *(ge)* to isolate Byrhtnoth and load him with responsibility; in a few places "you all" has been used to render *ge* where the reference might not otherwise be plain in translation. The messenger's speech appears to incorporate some Scandinavianisms (whether because of his ethnicity or the use of such in the Danegeld, the area of England settled by Danes, in which parts of Byrhtnoth's jurisdiction were included), making this the earliest use of English literary dialect: see Fred C. Robinson, "Some Aspects of the *Maldon* Poet's Artistry," *Journal of English and Germanic Philology* 75 (1976): 25–40; for an overview of the scholarship see Sara M. Pons-Sanz, "Norse-Derived Terms and Structures in *The Battle of Maldon,*" *Journal of English and Germanic Philology* 107 (2008): 421–44. On other possible uses of dialect forms, see Griffith, *The Battle of Maldon,* 26–27.

33 *that we share such hard battle*: Less likely is the interpretation "that we, so hardy, deal out conflict." A third possibility is "that we deal out conflict so fiercely."

45–61 *Do you hear, seafarer . . . before we give up tribute*: Byrhtnoth's reply is laden with irony, a prominent example being his reference to paying the vikings a tribute of war gear *(here-geatu),* since the word becomes later English *heriot,* in reference to the war gear held in fealty to a man's lord.

47 *ancient swords*: Old weapons are superior because they have been proved in battle.

53 *my lord Æthelred*: Byrhtnoth was the representative of the English king, Æthelred II.

66 *streams of the current flowed together*: The description apparently refers to the way that the waters of the river's main channel and the passage between the island and the shore rise and meet at the island's uppermost end as the incoming tide raises the water level. Doubts about the usual identification of the Northmen's place of encampment with Northey Island are expressed by Daniel Thomas, "*Landes to fela*: Geography, Topography and Place in *The Battle of Maldon*," *English Studies* 98 (2017): 781–801.

69 *shipborne invaders*: This expression renders *æsc-here* on the assumption that *æsc* is a borrowing of Old Norse *askr,* in reference to a type of ship. See William Sayers, "*Æschere* in *The Battle of Maldon*: Fleet, Warships' Crews, Spearmen, or Oarsmen?" *Neuphilologische Mitteilungen* 107 (2006): 199–205. Alternatively, some assume that *æsc-here* means "spear-army," since spears were commonly made of ash (OE *æsc* is sometimes used as a metonym for spear).

80 *Maccus*: The name apparently corresponds to Old Norse *Magnús,* another indicator of the Scandinavian element in the local population, though it has also been argued that the name derives instead from Old Irish or Old Cornish (see Griffith, *The Battle of Maldon,* 163).

86–90 *then the hateful strangers . . . hateful people*: The poet here appears to find fault with Byrhtnoth for his concessions to the invaders, saying that the Northmen *ongunnon lytegian* (began to use a trick) and that Byrhtnoth *ongan for his ofer-mode alyfan landes to fela* (in his hubris, granted too much land). Yet scholars disagree about the extent of Byrhtnoth's culpability in the defeat of the English, citing uncertainty about whether *ofer-mod* (hubris) ever has a positive meaning, and whether Byrhtnoth had any reasonable alternative to granting the vikings' request, and what precisely is guileful about the herald's message. On the last of these points, arguing that the messenger's ruse is to shame Byrhtnoth into giving battle despite his smaller force of men, see Mark S. Griffith, "*The Battle of Maldon*: The Guile of the Vikings Explained," *Notes and Queries* 63 (2016): 180–86. The poet's remark about "too much land" is thus not necessarily a moral judgment passed on Byrhtnoth but an emotional response to the coming tragedy: see Griffith, *The Battle of Maldon,* 117–19.

92 *son of Byrhthelm*: The names of Byrhtnoth and his father show typical agreement of constituent elements (here *byrht,* "bright, shining").

93 *Now*: An alternative meaning for *nu* is "now that," and some editors punctuate accordingly, with a comma after *eow is gerymed* (space is cleared for you).

95–97 *Then the slaughter-wolves . . . carried their shields*: In the corresponding Old English, the maintenance of *w*-alliteration in three successive lines (with nonalliterating *w*-words in the preceding and following lines) is highly unusual.

102 *battle-hedge*: The *wi-hagan* is a defensive phalanx, a line of men, the edges of their shields overlapping.

106–7 *ravens were circling, the eagle eager for carrion*: Ravens and the eagle are among the scavenging animals conventionally said to haunt the battlefield in expectation of their fill of the slain, in a poetic convention known as the beasts of battle motif. The Chronicle poem known as *The Battle of Brunanburh,* printed elsewhere in this volume, incorporates the same motif. See the annal for the year 937 in *The Old English Chronicle, the A-Text to 1001,* lines 60–65, and the note for line 61.

108 *as hard as files*: The form *feol-hearde* has sometimes been interpreted to mean "hardened by the file," by comparison to *fyrheard* (hardened by fire) in *Beowulf.* See Carole Hough, "OE *feolheard* and *irenheard*: Two *Hapax legomena* Reconsidered," *Neophilologus* 84 (2000): 127–36.

109 *grimly sharpened javelins*: The form *grimme* (grimly), not found in Casley, is supplied by most editors for the sake of the poetic meter, assuming that *gegrundene* (sharpened), a late analogical form, stands for earlier *gegrundne,* as would be normal in most Old English poetry. Since *Maldon* is a late composition, how-

ever, it is possible that *gegrundene* should be regarded as comprising four syllables and thus a verse unto itself, rendering the insertion of *grimme* unnecessary.

115 *his sister's son*: A man's *swuster sunu* was reckoned to be his closest kinsman, his most indubitable blood relation, and thus the wounding of Wulfmær would have been particularly grievous to Byrhtnoth.

121 *the chamber attendant*: The OE *bur-þen* was what would later be called a chamberlain, the manager of his lord's household, and thus Edward was certainly one of Byrhtnoth's most trusted supporters.

122 *Thus the strong-minded young fighters fell silent*: The meaning "fell silent" for *stemnetton* is assumed on the basis of Middle English evidence. See Joseph Harris, "*Stemnetton*: *Battle of Maldon,* Line 122a," *Philological Quarterly* 55, no. 1 (1976): 113–17. Given the word's etymology, the meaning could also be "stood firm"; the sense "they contended" is advocated on the basis of comparison to a recurring scene type by Paul Battles, "'Contending Throng' Scenes and the *Comitatus* Ideal in Old English Poetry, with Special Attention to *The Battle of Maldon* 122a," *Studia Neophilologica* 83 (2011): 41–53. Compare also Valentine A. Pakis, proposing the meaning "jeer, insult," in "Insults, Violence, and the Meaning of *Lytegian* in the Old English *Battle of Maldon,*" *Journal of Historical Pragmatics* 12 (2011): 198–229.

126 *of a warrior*: If *wigan* is a noun, as is usually assumed, it may be dative singular (warrior), parallel to *men* (man) in line 125, as assumed here, or nominative plural (warriors), parallel to line 123's *hysas* (young fighters; so the edition of Donald G. Scragg, *The Battle of Maldon* [Manchester, UK, 1981], 106). It could also be a verb meaning "make war," parallel to *gewinnan* (take) in line 125. See Dobbie, *The Anglo-Saxon Minor Poems,* 144, and Griffith, *The Battle of Maldon,* 176.

130 *one hardened in battle*: The *wiges heard* is a Northman who here attacks Byrhtnoth. The latter faces him, is wounded, and exacts vengeance with his assailant's own weapon. In *Njáls saga* the hero Gunnarr turns an arrow shot at him against his at-

tackers, remarking that it will be a humiliation for them if they are harmed by their own missile. See Robert Cook's translation, *Njal's Saga* (London, 2001), chapter 77.

134 *southern*: The spear is *suþerne* because it is of highly valued Frankish manufacture. For alternative interpretations, see the note in Griffith, *The Battle of Maldon,* 177–78.

144 *breast*: The plural *breostum* in singular meaning has sometimes been regarded as a locative singular rather than a dative plural. It seems likelier that for this poet, at least, and the many other Old English authors who use the plural of this word with singular meaning, the plural signifies "chest, breast": see Paul Grimm, *Beiträge zum Pluralgebrauch in der altenglischen Poesie* (Halle, 1912), 15–20.

146 *the deadly point lodged in his heart*: Compare *ætterne* ("deadly"—literally, "poisoned," but with figurative intent) with, in line 47, *ættrynne ord* (poisoned points).

149 *viking warriors*: The word *drenga* is a borrowing from Old Norse, another probable example of literary use of dialect: see the note on 25–41, above.

159–61 *Then a well-armed man came . . . his ornamented sword*: One of the Northmen intends to strip Byrhtnoth's corpse of armor and other valuables. This was commonly a victor's practice, as related at *Beowulf* 2985–89. On the spelling *gefecgan* ("take," becoming Modern English "fetch") beside the more usual *gefetigan* or *gefeccan,* see Scragg, *The Battle of Maldon,* 77.

166 *The yellow-hilted sword*: With gold on the hilt *(fealo-hilte),* though possibly with a suggestion of decay (Scragg, *The Battle of Maldon,* 78).

172 *He looked up to heaven*: One verse is wanting to complement *He to heofenum wlat,* perhaps something like *hleoðrode þa* (cried out then). For alternative treatments, see Dobbie, *The Anglo-Saxon Minor Poems,* 144.

173–80 *I thank you, ruler of peoples . . . may not afflict it*: Inclusion of this dying prayer verges on hagiographical treatment of the hero. For an apt analogue to the prayer, see Scragg, *The Battle of Maldon,* 79, and on hagiographical features of the poem, see Paul

Cavill, "Heroic Saint and Saintly Hero: The *Passio sancti Eadmundi* and *The Battle of Maldon,*" in Waugh and Weldon, *The Hero Recovered,* 110–24.

183 *Ælfnoth and Wulfmær both lay dead*: The OE line lacks alliteration, and *begen* (both), which normally should alliterate, appears to be a mistaken repetition of the same word in the preceding line.

186 *The sons of Odda were the first in flight*: Plural *wurdon* (were) is commonly emended to singular *wearð,* though Scragg, *The Battle of Maldon,* 79, justifies the plural through the eventual naming of all three sons of Odda. Note that *bearn* (sons) may be either singular or plural. On whether the name Odda is English or Scandinavian, and whether, in the latter case, the sons of Odda might be disloyal rather than cowardly, see Carole Hough, "Odda in *The Battle of Maldon,*" *Notes and Queries* 45 (1998): 169–72.

190 *where he had no right to be*: The clause *þe hit riht ne wæs* is perhaps more literally "such that it was not right," though the precise meaning of *þe* is debated: for discussion, see Scragg, *The Battle of Maldon,* 79–80, and Pope, *Eight Old English Poems,* 83.

191 *ran away*: The verb *ærndon* has here an otherwise unattested meaning, usually translated instead as "galloped" or "raced."

212 *Remember now those occasions*: On the reasons for emending to *gemunaþ nu þæra mæla,* and whether *mæla* might mean "speeches," see Scragg, *The Battle of Maldon,* 80–81, and Pope, *Eight Old English Poems,* 84. See also Ad Putter, "The Hero 'Remembers': The Verb *Gemunan* in *Beowulf* and *The Battle of Maldon,*" in *Literature, Emotions, and Pre-Modern War: Conflict in Medieval and Early Modern Europe,* ed. Claire McIlroy and Anne Scott (Leeds, 2021), 83–100. An overview of the many proposed emendations is offered by Carole Hough, "*The Battle of Maldon* Line 212," *Neuphilologische Mitteilungen* 100 (1999): 245–50.

219 *a wise nobleman*: An *ealdormann* was a district official and nobleman of the highest rank. In this poem Byrhtnoth is more commonly referred to as *eorl,* a native word referring in poetry to a warrior that in late Old English, as here, came to be regarded

as equivalent to Old Norse *jarl,* similarly denoting a district leader. For more discussion of *ealdormann,* see Introduction, "Names of Peoples, Ethnic Groups, or Political Entities."

224 *He was both my kinsman and my lord*: No matter how this line is analyzed, the alliteration and stress are unorthodox. The best solution may be to stress *ægðer* (both) and *and* (and): see Pope, *Eight Old English Poems,* 85.

230–43 *Offa made a speech*: Offa, mentioned earlier in line 5, appears here to assume leadership upon the death of Byrhtnoth, as suggested by his use of plural pronouns, by his remaining on the spot (unlike the other speakers) rather than going forth to die, by the next speaker's reply specifically to him, and by the heightened attention to his death (287–94). On Offa's role, see further Mark S. Griffith, "*The Battle of Maldon* and the Vengeance of Offa," in *Tradition and Innovation in Old English Metre,* ed. Rachel A. Burns and Rafael J. Pascual (Leeds, 2022), 79–101.

246–47 *I make this promise . . . I will go forward*: The *beot* (see the note on 15–16, above) could elicit formulaic ideas about not yielding ground, as for example *oferfleon fotes trem* ("[not] flee one footstep," *Beowulf* 2524–25), as well as line 275.

249 *Sturmere Lake*: A small body of water and a village in northern Essex.

261 *the men of the hearth watch*: The *hired-men* belong to the noble's household and are thus trusted supporters.

265 *hostage*: A *gysel* was a person usually of some high social rank who was exchanged between opposing parties to ensure peace, under threat of personal injury. As a person of rank, he would be treated with honors and participate in the affairs of the court hosting him but normally would be under no obligation to fight for those holding him hostage.

270 *sometimes he pierced a man*: The word *tæsde* (pierced) yields Modern English *teased,* and its fundamental meaning is the same in regard to wool or hair. Here it appears to assume a unique sense. It could be an error for *ræsde,* but when used in the sense "attack," that word normally takes an object after the preposition *on.*

275 *he would not give up the measure of one foot of land*: The word *fleogan* (give up) is, literally, "fly," almost certainly a scribal replacement for *fleon* (flee), a substitution found in some other late texts.

277 *He crashed through the shield wall*: Edward breaks the Northmen's *bord-weall,* probably a defensive phalanx like the English *wihagan* (battle-hedge; see the note to 102), though possibly the word refers generically to an individual shield.

282 *the brother of Sibyrht fought earnestly, and very many another*: This line is interpreted as part of the compound subject including *Æþeric,* singular verbs like *dyde* (did) and *feaht* (fought) being normal after a singular first constituent of a compound subject.

283 *They cleft the decorated shield*: The precise meaning of *cellod,* here rendered "decorated," has long been a mystery. Impressive but irreconcilable interpretations are offered by Andrew Breeze, "*Finnsburh* and *Maldon*: *Celæs Bord, Cellod Bord,*" *Notes and Queries* 39 (1992): 267–69, and Donald K. Fry, "*Celæs* and *Cellod*: Decorated in Low Relief," in *Heroic Poetry in the Anglo-Saxon Period: Studies in Honor of Jess B. Bessinger, Jr.,* ed. Helen Damico and John Leyerle (Kalamazoo, MI, 1993), 47–76. See further the note in Griffith, *The Battle of Maldon,* 209–10.

284 *the shield rim burst*: For references to scholarship on the obscure word *lærig,* here rendered "rim," see Andrew Breeze, "Old English *Lærig* 'Shield Rim' in *Exodus* and *Maldon*: Welsh *Lloring* in *Culhwch and Olwen,*" *Zeitschrift für celtische Philologie* 51 (1999): 170–72.

285–88 *Then in the fight Offa struck . . . cut down in the battle*: Given the seeming incompleteness of the account of the attack on Offa and the definite reference to *þone sæ-lidan* (that sea traveler) as if he had already been introduced, it has been argued cogently that a brief passage is wanting here: see John C. Pope, "Offa in *The Battle of Maldon,*" in Damico and Leyerle, *Heroic Poetry,* 1–27. "The kinsman of Gadd" is most likely Offa.

Bibliography

Editions and Translations

The Old English Chronicle, the A-Text

Bately, Janet, ed. *MS. A.* Vol. 3 of *The Anglo-Saxon Chronicle: A Collaborative Edition,* edited by David N. Dumville and Simon Keynes. Cambridge, 1986.

Garmonsway, Norman, ed. and trans. *The Anglo-Saxon Chronicle.* Everyman's Library. London, 1953.

Keynes, Simon, and Michael Lapidge, eds. and trans. *Alfred the Great: Asser's Life of King Alfred and Other Contemporary Sources.* Penguin Classics. Harmondsworth, Middlesex, 1983.

Lutz, Angelika, ed. *Die Version G der angelsächsischen Chronik: Rekonstruktion und Edition.* Munich, 1981.

Plummer, Charles, ed. *Two of the Saxon Chronicles Parallel.* 2 vols. Oxford, 1892–1899.

Swanton, Michael, ed. and trans. *The Anglo-Saxon Chronicle.* London, 1996.

Thorpe, Benjamin, ed. and trans. *The Anglo-Saxon Chronicle, According to the Several Original Authorities.* 2 vols. London, 1861.

Whelocus, Abrahamus [Abraham Wheelock], ed. *Chronologia Saxonica.* In *Historiae ecclesiasticae gentis Anglorum libri v,* by Bede, 503–66. Cambridge, 1643.

Whitelock, Dorothy, ed. and trans. *The Anglo-Saxon Chronicle.* With David C. Douglas and Susie I. Tucker. London, 1961.

The Old English Chronicle, the C-Text

O'Brien O'Keeffe, Katherine, ed. *MS. C.* Vol. 5 of *The Anglo-Saxon Chronicle: A Collaborative Edition,* edited by David N. Dumville and Simon Keynes. Cambridge, 2001.

The Battle of Maldon

Atherton, Mark, ed. and trans. Appendix I to *The Battle of Maldon: War and Peace in Tenth-Century England,* 173–90. London, 2020.

Bradley, S. A. J., trans. *Anglo-Saxon Poetry: An Anthology of Old English Poems in Prose Translation.* London, 1982.

Dobbie, Elliott Van Kirk, ed. *The Anglo-Saxon Minor Poems.* Vol. 6 of *The Anglo-Saxon Poetic Records.* New York, 1942.

Gordon, E. V., ed. *The Battle of Maldon.* 2nd ed. London, 1949.

Griffith, Mark S., ed. *The Battle of Maldon: A New Critical Edition.* Exeter Medieval Texts and Studies. Liverpool, 2024.

Pope, John C., ed. *Eight Old English Poems.* 3rd ed. Prepared by R. D. Fulk. New York, 2001.

Robinson, Fred C., and E. G. Stanley, eds. *Old English Verse Texts from Many Sources: A Comprehensive Collection.* Early English Manuscripts in Facsimile 23. Copenhagen, 1991.

Scragg, Donald G., ed. *The Battle of Maldon.* Manchester, UK, 1981.

———. "The Casley Transcript of *The Battle of Maldon.*" Facsimile of David Casley's transcript, in *The Battle of Maldon AD 991,* edited by Donald G. Scragg, 2–14. Oxford, 1991.

Further Reading

The Old English Chronicle

Abels, Richard. *Alfred the Great: War, Kingship, and Culture in Anglo-Saxon England.* New York, 1998.

Bately, Janet. "The Compilation of the Anglo-Saxon Chronicle, 60 B.C. to A.D. 890: Vocabulary as Evidence." *Proceedings of the British Academy* 64 (1980 for 1978): 93–129. Reprinted in *British Academy Papers on Anglo-*

Saxon England, selected and introduced by E. G. Stanley, 261–97. Oxford, 1990.

———. "Manuscript Layout and the Anglo-Saxon Chronicle." *Bulletin of the John Rylands University Library of Manchester* 70 (1988): 21–44. Reprinted in *Textual and Material Culture in Anglo-Saxon England: Thomas Northcote Toller and the Toller Memorial Lectures,* edited by Donald G. Scragg, 1–21. Cambridge, 2003.

Clark, Cecily. "The Narrative Mode of *the Anglo-Saxon Chronicle* Before the Conquest." In *England Before the Conquest: Studies in Primary Sources Presented to Dorothy Whitelock,* edited by Peter Clemoes and Kathleen Hughes, 215–35. Cambridge, 1971.

Discenza, Nicole Guenther, and Paul E. Szarmach, eds. *A Companion to Alfred the Great.* Leiden, 2014.

Foot, Sarah. "Finding the Meaning of Form: Narrative in Annals and Chronicles." In *Writing Medieval History,* edited by Nancy F. Partner, 88–108. London, 2005.

Keynes, Simon. "Manuscripts of the Anglo-Saxon Chronicle." In *The Cambridge History of the Book in Britain,* vol. 1, *c. 400–1100,* edited by Richard Gameson, 537–52. Cambridge, 2012.

Parker Library on the Web: Manuscripts in the Parker Library at Corpus Christi College, Cambridge. Accessed November 14, 2024. https://parker.stanford.edu/parker.

Pratt, David. *The Political Thought of King Alfred the Great.* Cambridge, 2007.

Reuter, Timothy, ed. *Alfred the Great, Papers from the Eleventh-Centenary Conferences.* Burlington, VT, 2003.

Stafford, Pauline. *After Alfred: Anglo-Saxon Chronicles and Chroniclers, 900–1150.* Oxford, 2020.

Yorke, Barbara. "The Representation of Early West Saxon History in the Anglo-Saxon Chronicle." In *Reading the Anglo-Saxon Chronicle: Language, Literature, History,* edited by Alice Jorgensen, 142–59. Turnhout, 2010.

The Battle of Maldon

Cavill, Paul. "Heroic Saint and Saintly Hero: The *Passio sancti Eadmundi* and *The Battle of Maldon*." In *The Hero Recovered: Essays on Medieval Heroism in Honor of George Clark,* edited by Robin Waugh and James Weldon, 110–24. Kalamazoo, MI, 2010.

Neidorf, Leonard. "*II Æthelred* and the Politics of *The Battle of Maldon*." *Journal of English and Germanic Philology* 111 (2012): 451–73.

Pons-Sanz, Sara M. "Norse-Derived Terms and Structures in *The Battle of Maldon*." *Journal of English and Germanic Philology* 107 (2008): 421–44.

Robinson, Fred C. "Some Aspects of the *Maldon* Poet's Artistry." *Journal of English and Germanic Philology* 75 (1976): 25–40.

Scragg, Donald G., ed. *The Battle of Maldon AD 991*. Oxford, 1991.

Woolf, Rosemary. "The Ideal of Men Dying with Their Lord in the *Germania* and in *The Battle of Maldon*." *Anglo-Saxon England* 5 (1976): 63–81.

Index for *The Old English Chronicle, The Death of Alfred,* and *The Death of Edward*

The Index of Personal Names is keyed to names as they are spelled in the translation, following the conventions of the *Wiley Blackwell Encyclopedia of Anglo-Saxon England,* 2nd ed. Material enclosed in parentheses consists of information from sources other than the A-text (including, in the case of Anglo-Saxon kings, the Appendix in the *Wiley Blackwell Encyclopedia*) to provide an accepted correct dating not used in the A-text. Dates and details other than those in parentheses are those of the A-text, and the dates given to the individual annals are those of the A-text before post-Conquest alterations were made to it. Thus, years listed to the left of the colon indicate accepted dates of reigns, accessions, and the like. Numbers to the right of the colon (whose decimals refer to paragraphs) refer to the annal numbers of the A-text. The symbol * indicates an accidental chronological dislocation inherited from A's exemplar. (For the reader's convenience, this symbol has been confined to entries giving the regnal dates of Anglo-Saxon kings or the equivalent details of an archbishop's appointment.) The letter *g* after a date indicates that the person is named in that entry only in a genealogical list or lists.

The annal entry 1036 refers to *The Death of Alfred,* and 1065 to *The Death of Edward,* each from the Old English Chronicle, the C-text.

Index for *The Battle of Maldon*